Landscaping with Native Plants

# of Southern California

George Oxford Miller

Foreword by Julian Duval, President/CEO of Quail Botanical Gardens

Voyageur Press

First published in 2008 by Voyageur Press, an imprint of MBI Publishing Company, Galtier Plaza, Suite 200, 380 Jackson Street, St. Paul, MN 55101 USA

Voyageur Press titles are also available at discounts in bulk quantity for industrial or sales-promotional use. For details write to Special Sales Manager at MBI Publishing Company, Galtier Plaza, Suite 200, 380 Jackson Street, St. Paul, MN 55101 USA.

Editor: Josh Leventhal
Designer: LeAnn Kuhlmann

Printed in China

Library of Congress Cataloging-in-Publication Data
Miller, George Oxford, 1943-
Landscaping with native plants of Southern California / by George Oxford Miller.
p. cm.
Includes bibliographical references and index.
ISBN-13: 978-0-7603-2967-2 (softbound)
1. Native plant gardening—California, Southern. 2. Landscape gardening—California, Southern.
3. Xeriscaping—California, Southern. I. Title.
SB439.24.C2M55 2008
635.9'517949—dc22
2007029347

On the front cover: California poppies and other natives adorn a colorful wildflower display at La Casita del Arroyo in Pasadena.

On the title page: Desert marigold adds color and softens the prickly profile of teddy bear cholla.

On the back cover: (center, left) Sotol and brittle bush contribute texture and color to the desert landscape at Desert Willow Golf Resort in Palm Desert. *(Center, right)* Native wildflowers provide forage for California's many species of butterflies. *(Bottom)* Author George Miller with bladderpod and yucca, two excellent xeriscape plants, at Joshua Tree National Park. *Photo by Carole Price*

Contents

O Friend!

In the garden of thy heart plant naught but the rose of love.

— Bahá'u'lláh, founder of the Baha'i Faith

Acknowledgments

A book such as this is a composite of many people's knowledge, research, opinions, and experience. Professors, landscapers, gardeners, horticulturists, nursery owners, and native-plant enthusiasts all influenced this book to a great extent. There have been too many people through the years to name individually here, but I do appreciate the cumulative help and encouragement I received.

A special thanks to Martha Latta, past president of the National Xeriscape Council, Inc., and former owner of Garden Villa in San Marcos, Texas, who provided valuable editorial comments and the landscape drawings that illustrate the chapter "The ABCs of Native Plant Landscaping."

Foreword

At a time when urbanization is rampant worldwide and Southern California seems to lead the trend, there are rays of hope. Thinking, acting, or being "green," thankfully, is becoming more and more popular. The obliteration of so much of the native landscape, coupled with the many unsustainable ways in which we impact the environment, has alarmed increasing numbers of people. There is growing interest in fostering a way of life that provides better stewardship of our vital natural resources, such as water, while preserving and celebrating those things that give us our sense of place: our native plants.

San Diego County has the greatest species diversity of any county in the United States, and at the same time it is home to the greatest number of federally listed endangered species of any county outside of Hawaii. Clearly, in many instances the native habitat for so many Southern California plants simply no longer exists and the opportunities to reclaim habitat are few. However, our commercial and residential landscapes provide a wealth of opportunity to provide space for our native species, and given the diversity of the Southern California flora, the plant palette for a garden landscape is particularly rich. Beyond that, these plants generally require less water, are less prone to disease, require fewer chemical amendments, and provide needed habitat for native wildlife.

George Oxford Miller has produced a resource in *Landscaping with Native Plants of Southern California* that illustrates hundreds of native So Cal plants in diagnostic photos and informative text. Just as important, the book helps us to understand how to use and care for these garden treasures. It serves as an important tool for those who already know and appreciate the value of using native plants in landscapes, but also serves to help generate interest and add to the number of people who pursue this worthwhile focus in landscaping.

Julian Duval
President/CEO
Quail Botanical Gardens
Encinitas, California

An Introduction to Landscaping with Native Plants of Southern California

The California state and U.S. flags wave in the breeze at Anza-Borrego Desert State Park in eastern San Diego County.

This book assumes four premises. First, landscaping increases property values and aesthetic appeal and can decrease monthly utility expenses. Second, indigenous plants are superior to most imported species for landscaping because natives are naturally adapted to the region's climate and soil. Third, and to me most important, landscaping with plants indigenous to our area, as opposed to foreign species well adapted to this salubrious climate, helps to repair the environment and restore the biodiversity. Human development can be expected to alter the countryside from its natural state, but it doesn't have to eradicate the biological heritage of our native plants and animals. We can all do our part by replacing some of the plants removed to build our houses, streets, and businesses. Last, by drawing on the rich native plant life of Southern California, we can create stunning garden designs that appeal to all the senses and offer a peaceful retreat in our own backyards.

The botanical diversity of Southern California encompasses plants adapted to the frost-free Mediterranean climate of the South Coast, rich inland valleys, eroded foothills, mountains with fog-drenched slopes that face the Pacific Ocean, arid eastern-facing slopes, snow-capped peaks, and the most extreme deserts in North America. That a plant is native to Southern California certainly does not imply that it can be planted anywhere within the region. Each of the six (or more) major vegetative provinces in Southern California recognized by botanists has a unique community of plants adapted to its specific soil and climatic conditions. For the purposes of landscape applications, this book divides Southern California into six landscape zones based on the temperature variations, frost-free days, moisture, and altitude gradients. This book will help you to analyze your yard and decide which plants best match your specific habitat.

Many of the thousands of native plants growing in our region have characteristics that will enhance your landscape with attractive foliage, flowers, fruit, or bark throughout the year. This book describes more than 250 species of trees, shrubs, vines, wildflowers, groundcovers, and cacti with exceptional landscape merit. I favored plants with a wide landscape range over those with very specific or demanding habitat requirements, though some exceptional specialties are included. The "Native Plant Profiles" describe each species and variety in detail, including each plant's range; specific soil, moisture, and shade requirements; temperature tolerance; size, shape, and suitable landscaping uses; and flower, foliage, and fruit characteristics. Perhaps most important, photographs of the selected species further help homeowners and landscapers decide which plants can best suit their needs.

Before going out and buying new plants, however, every gardener must first come to understand his or her own landscape and the requirements of establishing a garden using native plants. The maps and listings of landscape zones will help you to identify the rainfall and temperature variation within your area. Individual chapters address the issues of landscape maintenance, landscaping to attract wildlife, and xeriscape plantings, with listings of appropriate plants for each situation. The appendices at the back of the book offer suggestions of plants for specific landscape needs. Separate listings itemize evergreen plants and tell you how to colorscape for year-round beauty with flowering trees and shrubs. When used together, this book's chapters, plant descriptions, and appendices answer the majority of questions that a landscaper or gardener will have about landscaping with native plants.

Purple three-awn (*Aristida purpurea*) and other native species align a path at Santa Barbara Botanic Garden.

A Note on Nomenclature

Through the decades and centuries, the native plants that cover our landscape have been known by dozens of common names. The same plants have many names, and different plants have the same name. To avoid confusion, botanists use Latinized names that are applied according to a strict protocol, based on a classification system created by the eighteenth-century botanist Carl Linneaus. Yet, as research expands, some plant species are lumped together while others are split and given new names. Then someone redoes the work with a different methodology (such as DNA analysis), and everything is rearranged again. As a standard for plant names, I used the latest accepted nomenclature for each plant according to the Integrated Taxonomic Information System, referenced at www.itis.usda.gov. Scientific names that are recently discontinued or alternative names that are still used by some agencies are listed in parentheses as synonyms.

In the hierarchy of taxonomic classification, botanists group plants that share a wide range of similar physical characteristics into families. Families are divided into smaller groups called genera, which are further subdivided into species. A species with geographical variation may be split into subspecies and varieties. Taxonomists group plants primarily by flower and seed type. Species with similar flower or seed types are grouped together as a genus; for example, the genus *Arctostaphylos* encompasses more than 100 species, subspecies, and varieties of manzanitas that grow in California. The many related genera from around the world are grouped into the Heath family, Ericaceae, a huge family that includes blueberries, hawthorns, azaleas, and rhododendrons.

Within a species, the basic structure of the flower/seed remains constant, though slight genetic variations can cause differences in flower or foliage color. If a difference is widespread through a population of the same species, it may be classified as a variety or even a subspecies. Horticulturists search for varieties with particular ornamental value and often crossbreed them to produce cultivars (cultivated varieties); the cultivars are then cloned through propagation by cuttings. The new plants may vary from the type species in foliage or flower color, fruit size, growth habit, cold hardiness, drought tolerance, or other qualities.

California poppy (*Eschscholzia californica*) and blue-eyed grass (*Sisyrinchium bellum*) create a colorful native wildflower display at Santa Barbara Botanic Garden.

Why Use Native Plants?

Of the approximately 6,272 species and subspecies of flowering plants that grow within the borders of California, nearly 2,200 call Southern California—defined as the region south of Point Conception—home. The state's rich botanical heritage is a treasure chest for landscapers. Approximately 1,000 of the native trees, shrubs, wildflowers, grasses, and vines exhibit landscaping features that are desirable for formal or wildscape designs.

National interest in landscaping with native plants has mushroomed since the 1980s and 1990s, but the tradition of and interest in gardening with indigenous plants goes back much further in Southern California. In 1915, the native plant pioneer Theodore Payne planted the first public demonstration garden of indigenous plants in Los Angeles' Exposition Park. Payne operated a native plant nursery until 1962, and his work is carried on at the gardens and nursery of the Theodore Payne Foundation in Sun Valley.

During the 1920s, the Santa Barbara Botanic Garden and the Rancho Santa Ana Botanic Garden were founded with the mission of demonstrating and conserving California native plants. In 1940, the East Bay Regional Park District in Northern California established another major garden, the Regional Parks Botanic Garden, with sections devoted to California's natives. Today, many college campuses and municipalities continue the tradition with public gardens that include native plant sections.

Still, the concept of using natives instead of imported species for landscaping grew slowly from a fringe movement to one with broader acceptance. The activities of the California Native Plant Society and similar associations, the pressing needs of water conservation, the enactment of biodiversity conservation laws, and the efforts of devoted and passionate botanists and nursery professionals led to today's fully realized horticultural industry, involving researchers, propagators, wholesale and retail nurseries, and mainstream landscape professionals. From state agriculture departments to local garden clubs, native plants have become top-agenda topics.

Xeriscaping and water-wise landscaping, once only buzzwords, have become part of the standard vocabulary for garden centers, city planners, and home landscapers.

Water-conscious cities have initiated water conservation programs to encourage planting drought-tolerant species, and county extension agents carry the message to local groups and organizations.

Environmental Repair

Most of us are uninformed about and isolated from our natural environment. Instead of placing an inherent value on nature—the source of all life and the root of our material and technological success—today's "cyber society" relates to fast food, expressway commutes, and high-tech gadgets. Even the plants in our neighborhoods reflect our loss of identity with our natural environment. The trees, hedges, and shrubs planted around our homes more often than not come from some distant country via the garden sections of big-box, home-improvement stores.

Agriculture, ranching, and urban sprawl have eliminated or drastically altered natural plant communities throughout Southern California. With the population density along the South Coast topping 22,000 per square mile in urban areas, a growing number of people are concerned about preserving what remains of our natural environment. Community colleges, nature centers, and universities offer classes on ecology and conservation issues. Many people visit state and city parks and greenbelts looking for natural areas representative of the native flora and fauna. In most metropolitan areas, the natural associations of indigenous plants remain only in parklands, public gardens, and preserved sanctuaries.

With some effort and foresight, our neighborhoods could represent the same rich plant diversity that occurs in nature or that existed before our houses were built. A stroll down our own streets could be a lesson in native plant ecology. Our children could grow up familiar with the same plants that provided food and fiber for the Native Americans who inhabited Southern California for thousands of years. We could live among the same plants that mystified the earliest European explorers. Plants are a part of our great natural heritage. The plants that have sunk their roots in our soil since the last Ice Age can help us understand how the health and well-being of our psyches and our society are rooted in the earth.

Native plants attract birds and other wildlife. Here a red-tail hawk rests on an ocotillo (*Fouquieria splendens*) at Anza-Borrego Desert State Park.

Wildlife also benefits from the native plants in our yards. Few of the individual plants, much less the plant associations, that provide forage and shelter for wildlife are left in the wake of urban and agricultural development. As entire plant communities are eradicated by city sprawl and replaced with mass-produced imported species, our songbirds are replaced by starlings and English sparrows, themselves immigrants from Europe. We can encourage the return of our native birds and other wildlife by establishing landscape habitats with plants that provide food and shelter. As the plants mature and begin to flower and fruit, we will once again be rewarded by the sight of butterflies dancing from flower to flower and by the melodies of birds singing in our trees.

Low Maintenance (Not No Maintenance)

Why choose native species over the readily available, inexpensive foreign species? Think low maintenance—and that means dollars saved. By selecting plants native to your area, you create a landscape that is naturally adapted to whatever weather extremes may occur. After tens of thousands of years of climatic vicissitudes, only those species that were able to adapt without supplemental water and fertilizer have survived. When a landscape plant is firmly established, it will require little extra water, even in the driest years. Unusually frigid winters may nip tender twigs, but the plant will survive and fully recover with the next spring growth. Fewer plants will die and require costly replacement. Other than normal landscape maintenance, such as pruning, a native plant requires little attention.

While the low-maintenance feature of our native plants is attractive for homeowners, it is an essential consideration for commercial landscapers. Large businesses allocate sizable budgets for landscaping office buildings and commercial developments. States and municipalities are concerned with plantings for buildings, parks, greenbelts, and thousands of miles of streets and highways. State and local governments spend millions of dollars on landscaping. Plants that minimize water use and labor costs mean sizable savings to you as a homeowner, a businessperson, and a taxpayer.

To illustrate the benefits of native plant and water-wise landscaping, the city of San Diego turned its Ridgehaven Environmental Services office building into a certified "Green Building" landscaped with native and water-wise plantings. Instead of the conventional commercial landscape, the building is surrounded by eight habitat-themed demonstration gardens featuring more than 150 plants that provide year-round beauty and diversity.

Low maintenance is an important factor, but it does not mean "no maintenance." Even the best native plants will require regular care and attention. A great barrier to wider acceptance of native plant landscaping is the negative reaction to struggling, unkempt plants. You, your neighbors, and the neighborhood association want the best appearance possible, so remember, all landscapes—whether comprised of exotic or indigenous species—require regular care.

Variety

Southern California's plants come in all sizes, shapes, and colors. You can landscape your yard to provide visual interest throughout the year with an assortment of natives for spring, summer, and fall flowers and colorful fruit. You can choose evergreen species with green, gray, or whitish foliage, or deciduous plants with spectacular autumn colors.

The plants indigenous to Southern California soil offer so much variety that you can use them in an almost endless combination of landscape designs. And native plants provide a regionally distinct beauty to our neighborhoods, parks, and commercial districts. From Santa Barbara to San Diego, Southern Californians pride themselves on the natural beauty of their region—and they have a lot to boast about.

A chamise plant (*Adenostoma fasciculatum*) provides the overstory to coastal prickly pear (*Opuntia littoralis*) and other native species at Quail Botanical Gardens, Encinitas.

One-third of the plants that are indigenous to the state of California grow nowhere else on earth. The plethora of endemic species that inhabit California's vastly divergent habitats ranks the state first in the nation in number of endemic plants (2,153), mammals (17), reptiles (5), freshwater fishes (20), and amphibians (17), and it is second to Hawaii in number of endemic bird species (2).

With some of the most spectacular plants in North America found within miles of our backyards, it would be a shame not to take advantage of nature's gifts when landscaping our homes, resorts, and businesses. We can make our cities and neighborhoods look like Southern California and not a clone of Miami or Acapulco. As Lady Bird Johnson, former First Lady and founder of the Lady Bird Johnson Wildflower Center, said, "I want places to look like where they are. I want Alabama to look like Alabama, and Texas to look like Texas."

Where to See the Best of the Best

With its long history of enthusiastic native plant pioneers dedicated to preserving the state's unique botanical heritage, Southern California is blessed with numerous public and private demonstration gardens. No matter where you live, you're probably less than an hour's drive from a top-notch botanic garden. These gardens display the best-of-the-best landscape plants in mature settings. Additionally, colleges and cities maintain native and water-wise gardens, and more and more resorts are incorporating indigenous plants into their landscape designs.

Demonstration Gardens

Quail Botanical Gardens in Encinitas is one of the best gardens in the state. It was established in 1956 when Ruth and Charles Larabee deeded their ocean-view house and 30 acres to San Diego County. Now surrounded by developments, the gardens provide an escape into nature for the thousands who visit every year. Fifteen themed gardens showcase plants from around the world, and two areas are dedicated to indigenous plants: the Fire Safety Garden and the California Gardenscape.

"There has been a huge shift in the way people relate to the land since the garden was established," says Julian Duval, the Quail Gardens CEO. "We're a lot more water conscious now when we choose plants for our yards. People want to know about native plants so they can plant water-wise landscapes."

Located on a mostly undisturbed hillside, the Fire Safety Garden displays examples of naturally fire-resistant native plants that are adapted to the natural wildfire regime of the surrounding Coastal Sagebrush Scrub ecosystem. The gardens preserve 10 acres of native vegetation, including the endangered Del Mar manzanita (*Arctostaphylos glandulosa* subsp. *crassifolia*). Chamise and coastal prickly pear, interplanted with bush monkey flower and blue witches, prove how beautiful a wildscape can be.

Paths in the California Gardenscape wind through plantings of popular landscape species and cultivars available at local nurseries. "Our Blue and Gray Garden shows plants with complementary colors," according to Duval. The 'Canyon Prince' rye grass accents groundcovers of 'Canyon Gray' California sage and prostrate coyote brush. Another mixed planting emphasizes the similar shapes of dudleyas, barrel cacti, and agaves. 'Carmel Sur' manzanita and 'Yankee Point' ceanothus demonstrate popular cultivars as specimen plants, borders, and low hedges. Tall sumac hedges show natives used as privacy screens.

Rancho Santa Ana Botanic Garden, dedicated exclusively to native plant horticulture, has been a premier demonstration garden for California plants since 1927. It moved to its current 86-acre location in Claremont in 1951, so you can see numerous examples of mature tree and shrub specimens in landscape designs, as well as the latest selections of cultivars and hybrids developed by the garden's horticulture department.

"The focus now is to develop smaller plants suitable for today's smaller yards," explains Bart O'Brien, research horticulturalist at Rancho Santa Ana. "We're working a lot on sages and small- to midsized manzanitas in the 3- to 4-foot range. Everywhere I go, I look for variations in plants. You never know if the differences are genetic until you grow them out for several generations. There's a lot of hit and miss before we get a plant that is spectacular enough to release commercially."

The garden's extensive collection illustrates that native plant landscapes can be exciting and attractive year-round. Manzanitas bloom November through March, and the blue spikes of ceanothus decorate the garden's paths throughout the spring. Hummingbird sage, California fuchsia, and various cultivars of white, purple, and fragrant sage attract hummingbirds by the dozens. The wildflower garden abounds with color in spring. Arizona ash, maples, and arbors draped with California wild grape provide the vivid fall colors that are so hard to find in this warm climate.

In the desert garden, yuccas, prickly pear, California sunflower, brittle bush, desert thorns, and buckwheats demonstrate water-wise landscaping. Pacific madrone, white alder, California laurel, and oaks shade the paths, and selections of bush poppy, flannel bush, toyon, barberries, and sumacs further illustrate the design versatility of California natives. The garden shop's plant sales in November and April offer thousands of natives potted and ready for the home landscape.

Manzanita (*Arctostaphylos*) with a blooming ceanothus in bloom at Rancho Santa Ana Botanic Garden.

Santa Barbara Botanic Garden has been championing conservation and native plant horticulture since 1925, when the Santa Barbara Museum of Natural History and the Carnegie Institution jointly founded the gardens. Now covering 78 acres, the garden continues to fulfill its original mission to "create a garden that will unite the aesthetic, educational, and scientific."

The garden's horticultural division began working in the 1930s to improve the landscape qualities of outstanding indigenous plants. By careful selection, breeding, and grafting, it has introduced more than forty cultivars to the gardening world. These include ceanothus, salvia, and manzanita cultivars that quickly became standards in California landscape design. Carol Bornstein, director of the facility's Garden Growers Nursery, says the garden has developed a "slew" of irises as well as nine heucheras, or coral bells. "I'm a great proponent of native grasses and sedges," Bornstein says. "*Leymus* 'Canyon Prince' (giant rye grass) is from this garden."

As part of its education mission, the garden offers lectures, seminars, field trips, and classes in gardening, botany, and natural history. Daily guided and self-guided tours focus on native plants for home landscapes, seasonal blooming shrubs and flowers, native trees, and wildflowers. The nursery offers a wide selection of container plants.

Cholla (*Cylindropuntia*) and California brittle bush (*Encelia californica*) create an interesting planting at the Living Desert Zoo and Gardens in Palm Desert.

A median in the road to the Desert Willow Golf Resort in Palm Desert is planted with a colorful combination of penstemon cultivars and brittle bush.

This desert ironwood (*Olneya tesota*) captures the desert sense of place at Desert Willow Golf Resort.

Historically, the demonstration gardens in Southern California were established around the coastal population centers, but one outstanding botanical treasure exists in the Sonoran Desert. The Living Desert Zoo and Gardens in Palm Desert includes an extensive plant collection divided into African and North American desert sections. Facing summer temperatures that top 125 degrees F, desert plants have adapted to the extreme of extremes, so you know they'll thrive in your home xeriscape garden.

"The gardens and our educational classes promote by example the use of native plants for landscaping," says Kirt Anderson, head landscaper in the gardens. "People move here and want buffed-out landscapes year-round, but they have to learn to accept the seasonality of the desert. A lot of native plants go dormant in the summer, and you can't force them to keep blooming. People accept deciduous plants back East, but not here."

The gardens grow about 5,000 plants for their nursery sales. "The uphill battle still is finding native species in wholesale quantities and with enough variety so designers don't keep using the same ten plants over and over," explains Anderson. "We have a 1,000-square-foot greenhouse and one-half acre for seed and plant propagation. The nursery sells the most complete selection of Southwest natives in the area."

Native Cityscapes

When Palm Desert became a developer's dream in the 1960s, sand dunes and sagebrush surrounded the desert community. As growth boomed, the city encouraged the desert oasis image. Water-loving species were planted in medians and parkways, while resorts, condos, timeshares, and dozens of golf courses opened with lush, heavily watered landscapes. Then, in the early 1980s, the city government made a change.

"We decided to quit apologizing for the desert and to push landscaping with desert species," explains Spencer Knight, the City Landscape Manager. "Ten years ago the city passed a water-efficient landscaping ordinance. We replaced median plantings with desert material and required developers to landscape with desert plants. Bare ground and rocks are important in desert ecology. The ordinance requires one foot of open space between plants at mature size and the use of cobble and boulders in the design. The main tendency we have to overcome is that people want to overwater and overplant to get a full look."

With the new water-wise requirements, resorts began to hire designers with xeriscaping skills and to train their landscaping crews in the special requirements of desert plant maintenance. According to Knight, the Desert

Willow Golf Resort was the first full-scale resort to landscape exclusively with desert material. With blooming huisache and desert ironwood trees, brittle bush, chuparosa, penstemons, verbena, creosote bush, sotol, and agaves, the resort demonstrates that a desert landscape design can abound with color and variety.

Many of the older resorts, such as the Marriott Desert Spring built in 1984, still rely on the desert oasis look with lakes, palms, exotic shrubs and hedges, thousands of annuals for seasonal color, and even a flamingo flock. But down the street, the Marriott's newer sister property, Shadow Ridge timeshares, creates an equally attractive landscape with desert plants that create a distinctly western sense of place.

"We've seen a significant shift in people's attitudes and acceptance of desert landscaping," Knight says. "If the design and upkeep is high quality, homeowners don't remove the desert material; but if it's substandard, they tend to replace it with turf."

Native Plants Go Commercial

When the County of San Diego Environmental Services Division purchased an existing forty-year-old office building, the job of redesigning the existing landscape provided both a great challenge and a great opportunity for Pamela Homfelt of pH Exterior Designs. She needed to create a series of gardens that were suited to the vastly different microclimates typically found around homes and buildings.

"The first thing we did was to rip out the turf grass and sprinklers and install a computer-timed system that uses sixty percent less water," Homfelt said. The drought-tolerant landscape, coupled with water-saving plumbing fixtures, saves 316,000 gallons a year compared with the previous landscaping. For a palette of plants, Homfelt selected a mixture of natives and water-wise favorites for seven themed gardens around the building.

A walk around the building is a tour of the ecosystems found across Southern California. The microclimates vary from a blazing exposure on the west side, warm sun on the east side, deep shade on the north entrance, and partial shade on the south-facing courtyard. A sycamore tree shades the entrance, creating a shady forest garden with ferns, barberries, irises, and dry, stream-bed plants. "It only needs watering every week or two in the summer," Homfelt explains.

The drought-tolerant Mediterranean garden on the west side of the building features dwarf juniper, aloes, succulents, and California poppies. Other areas support herb, shade, and cottage gardens. The native plant garden receives morning sun and afternoon shade, perfect for ceanothus, hummingbird bush, Indian mallow, giant rye grass, dudleyas, iris, columbines, and penstemons. The "green" building's landscape shows off more than 150 species of native and drought-tolerant plants suitable for San Diego. In the spring, Homfelt offers tours and classes in native plant landscape design and maintenance.

Recovering a Legacy

In 1932, the federal government moved the Kumeyaay Indians off their reservation to create a reservoir for San Diego's water supply. Members of the tribe pooled their payout and bought the 5,816-acre Barona Ranch in the oak-woodland foothills of Wildcat Canyon near Lakeside. After decades of struggling, the tribe opened the Barona Casino in 1994, and since then they have added a resort and golf course. The extensive landscaping design employs a combination of species native to the surrounding habitat and drought-tolerant ornamental plants.

"We have a tough microclimate here that can drop to 20 degrees in the winter and reach 100 degrees in the summer," explains Kathy Eagle, head of landscaping for the resort. "We use as many native plants as we can work into the landscape. We especially focus on the grasses the tribe traditionally used for making baskets."

Though a majority of the plants are exotics that thrive in the Mediterranean climate, native sycamores and coast live oaks, many salvaged from the resort construction site, line the entrance drive and golf course. Deer grass, wild rye grass, and feather grass border the fairways. Around the resort complex, barberries, honeysuckles, beargrass, and salvias prove their worth with the more far-ranging species. Retention ponds purify all the water from the hotel for landscape use, and most of the plants are grown in two greenhouses.

"We found that the guests have a huge interest in the landscape," says Rick Masura, Assistant Manager of Hospitality. "Guests can see specimen plants in a mature landscape and get ideas about what to plant at home. Guests can visit our greenhouses, take a one-hour tour of the grounds, and attend the monthly classes Kathy offers." Eagle also teaches ornamental horticulture at the nearby Cuyamaca College, which maintains a water conservation garden of drought-tolerant plants.

The property includes an extensive subsistence garden cultivated by tribal members in front of the resort and one of the original houses built in the 1930s. "We're installing a demonstration garden around the house for traditional plants used by the tribe," Eagle says. "Our goal is to use landscaping to educate the public on the use of native and drought-tolerant plants. We're lucky to have tribal support for our horticultural program and conservation projects. We can do more than other commercial properties that don't have the budget."

Bladderpod (*Cleome isomeris*) and Mohave yucca (*Yucca schidigera*) at Joshua Tree National Park.

Landscape Zones of Southern California

Bisected by a conglomerate of mountain ranges uplifted by the shifting tectonic plates, California sits squeezed between the cold Pacific currents and blazing deserts. The wide divergence of climatic, geologic, topographic, and environmental conditions have created a region with one of the greatest biodiversities in North America. This variety of environmental conditions gives California nearly half (about 1,300) of the vegetative associations that occur in the United States. As mentioned previously, some 6,272 species and subspecies of vascular plants call California home; nearly one-third of those (2,153), as well as 17 amphibian, 5 reptile, 17 mammal, 20 freshwater fish, and 2 bird species, occur nowhere else on earth.

With elevations that range from 227 feet below sea level at Sulton Sea in the Sonoran Desert to 11,485 feet above sea level in the San Bernardino Mountains (Mount San Gorgonio), Southern California alone encompasses an extraordinary range of plant communities and vegetation types. This small region includes more than 2,200 species of vascular plants, as well as about 700 naturalized introduced species.

Mountain ranges that run parallel to the coastline block the cool moisture flowing eastward from the Pacific Ocean. The continent's hottest, driest deserts exist on the east side of the ranges, while the rare Mediterranean climate bathes the seaward side. The subtropical Mediterranean climate—with its cool, rainy winters contrasted with either a hot-dry summer (Los Angeles) or cool-dry summer (Santa Barbara)—exists in only five regions in the world outside of the Mediterranean Sea.

With growing conditions that vary within a few miles from the balmy, fog-drenched South Coast that never freezes (Long Beach to San Diego) to blazing deserts that receive less than 5 inches of rain annually, from sun-baked mountain slopes of cacti and yucca to snowy alpine meadows, the plant communities of Southern California contain species derived from both the tropics and the polar tundra.

Botanists have studied, classified, defined, and redefined California plants for more than 200 years. They have described about two dozen naturally occurring associations, or communities, that grow in a continuum from the coastal sand dunes to the alpine slopes at treeline and down the eastern slopes into blazing desert basins. From towering trees to soil fungi, the species within each community have evolved symbiotic relationships that enable a greater survival than when planted in isolation, such as in a yard landscape. This mutual sharing of moisture and nutritional resources enriches the community and usually serves to exclude foreign or exotic species, which must survive on their own without any help from their friends. A landscape comprised of plants from the local community type is better equipped to ward off the unavoidable stresses of nature.

When choosing plants for your landscape, the first essential step is to understand the particular environmental conditions of the site. Many factors can influence a plant's ability to survive and thrive, and conditions can vary dramatically within your property.

As a starting point for determining which plants are candidates for landscaping in your yard, this book divides the region into six landscape zones that correspond to the Southern California plant communities described by Phillip Munz in *A California Flora* (1959). The higher mountain plant communities, where few cities occur, are not included, and the ranges of many of the included plants extend beyond the listed zones into northern California, the western states, Canada, and Mexico.

The biomes, or broad environmental regions (mountains, deserts, coastal), listed with the native distributions for each plant profile correspond to regional descriptions in the 1993 edition of the *Jepson Manual: Higher Plants of California*, by Willis Linn Jepson. By referring to the Native Plant Profiles later in the book, you will be able to determine if a plant is native to your general biome, your specific county, and your local plant community, and whether it will thrive in the specific microhabitat of your yard.

However, selecting plants for your yard involves more than simply determining your landscape zone. A plant has specific habitat requirements and rarely has a continuous geographical distribution throughout its range. Plants have adapted to certain environmental factors—moisture and humidity, sun and wind exposures, soil chemistry, soil temperatures, drainage, seasonal temperature extremes, and number of frost-free days, to name a few. A plant thrives in habitats where it finds these parameters in the optimum combinations and grows in limited numbers in more marginal areas.

Depending on the microhabitat of your yard, a plant may not be suitable for your landscape even if it is listed as belonging to your zone. Conversely, since plant communities often intergrade, with no distinct border, a plant that is native to an adjacent zone may thrive in your yard if it finds the right niche. Each species entry describes in detail what the plant requires to be healthy and attractive. By choosing those plants most suitable for the environmental conditions of your yard, you can have a beautiful landscape for years, even generations, with relatively little maintenance or replacement costs.

Landscape Zones

Coastal Sage Scrub

This semi-arid plant community occurs below 3,000 feet along the coast from Ventura County on the coastal slopes of the Santa Monica Mountains, inland to Riverside in the rain shadow of coastal mountains, south to San Diego, and in areas bordering the Mojave Desert. The characteristic plants—mostly 3- to 4-foot-tall shrubs with soft, aromatic leaves—develop shallow roots in thin, rocky soil and depend on seasonal surface moisture for water. Using a drought-deciduous strategy, they cope with the six-month-long summer drought by shedding their leaves to conserve energy until the rainy winter season. Dominant species include black sage, white sage, California buckwheat, brittle bush, California sagebrush, coyote brush, and ceanothus and manzanitas species. Winter temperatures may drop to freezing, and mild summers occasionally reach 100 degrees F, with fog and overcast days common. The Coastal Sage Scrub Zone receives 12 to 25 inches of precipitation per year. The zone intergrades at higher elevations with the Chaparral Zone.

Mean Annual Precipitation

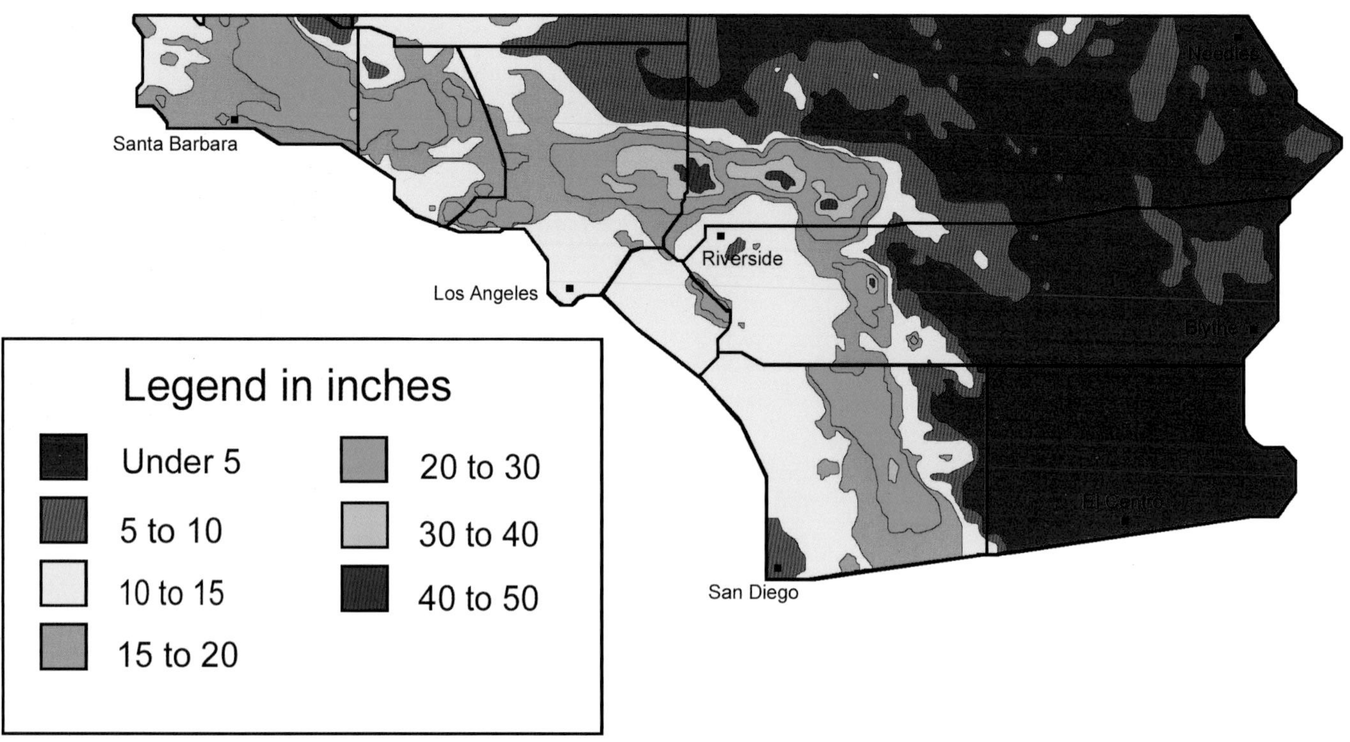

Chaparral

As the most widespread plant community in Southern California, Chaparral occurs on dry, shallow soils in the foothills of the South Coast, Transverse, and Peninsular ranges. Shrubs from 4 to 8 feet high with dense, often thorny branches form impenetrable thickets. When surface moisture is absent, deep taproots reach water trapped in the soil and allow the small, hard evergreen leaves to photosynthesize year-round. Cooler north-facing slopes may have five to ten species, with none dominant; arid, sun-baked south-facing slopes may be dominated by a single species, often chamise (*Adenostoma fasciculatum*). Many of the evergreen shrubs—such as ceanothus and manzanita species, shrub oaks, sumacs, silktassels, and flannel bush—make excellent landscape selections. Winters are moist and usually mild, with occasional hard freezes. Hot, dry summers can reach temperatures of 100 degrees F. This zone receives 12 to 35 inches of precipitation per year. With deeper soil, Chaparral transitions into Foothill Woodland.

Foothill Woodland (including Southern Oak Woodland)

In Southern California, this zone extends through rolling hills and valleys from 300 to 2,000 feet in the Transverse and Peninsular ranges. Dominated by several oak species, the plant community varies from savanna to continuous forest depending on depth of soil. An abundance of perennial and annual wildflowers and grasses fill the open areas. Shrubs occur in drainages and under the forest canopy. Besides oaks, widespread species include California buckeye, California walnut, pinyon pine, toyon, ceanothus species, flannel bush, silktassel, bush mallows, and manzanitas. The habitat has hot, dry summers and low or freezing temperatures in the winter. Average precipitation is 15 to 35 inches per year.

Pinyon-Juniper Woodland

The Pinyon-Juniper belt occurs at elevations of 3,500–7,000 feet in transition areas from desert to mountains. Open groves of pinyon pines and junipers are interspersed with grasses, penstemons, buckwheats, and other wildflowers, and with shrubs such as mountain mahogany, rabbitbrush, sagebrush, ceanothus, winterfat, Apache plume, flannel bush, scrub oaks, and yuccas. Summers are hot and dry, and winter temperatures may drop to 10 degrees F. Typical annual precipitation is 7 to 20 inches. Evapotranspiration, the sum of evaporated water and water loss by plants, may be four times the annual precipitation. This zone is typically found above Chaparral and Joshua Tree Woodland and below the pine/fir montane forests.

Landscape Zones of Southern California

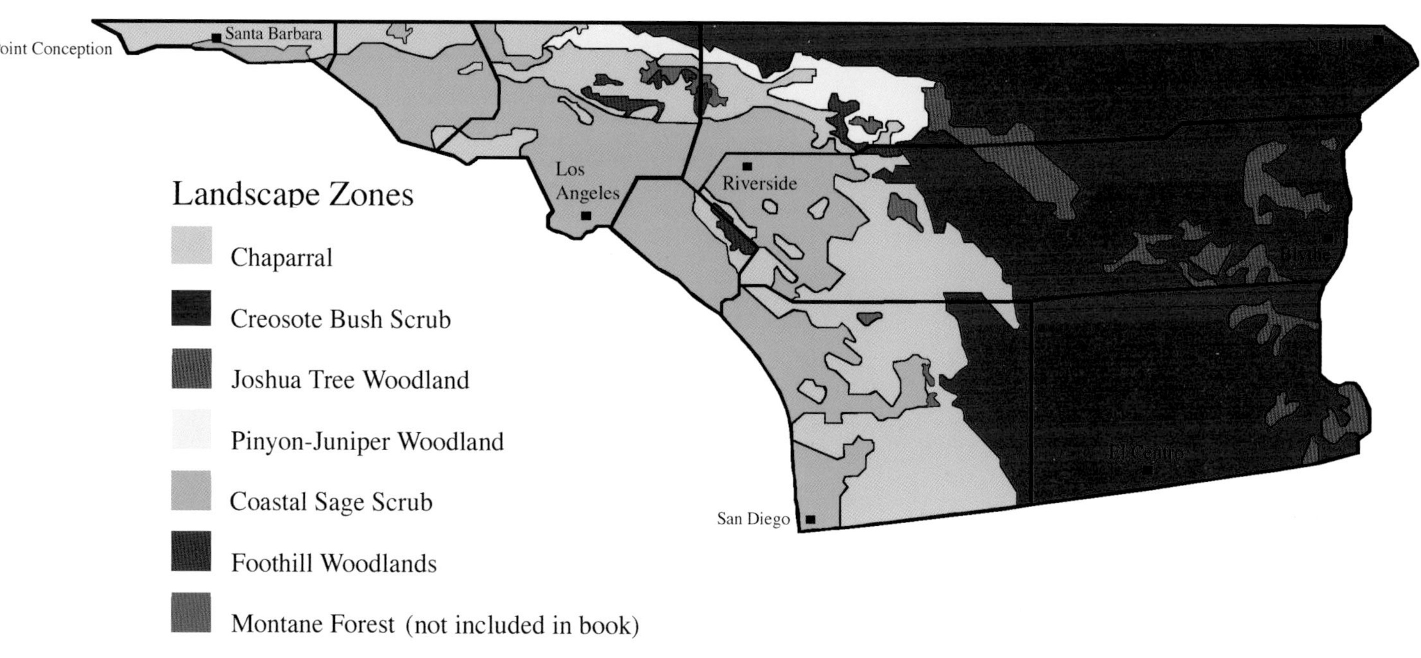

Creosote Bush Scrub

This hot desert plant community occurs below 4,000 feet on sandy, rocky soils that receive moisture mainly by summer thunderstorms. Creosote bush (*Larrea tridentata*) is the dominant species, and other shrubs, cacti, and wildflowers grow in low densities; bare ground is common. Common plants include palo verde, desert ironwood, desert thorn, desert willow, brittle bush, prickly pear, and globemallow. Winter temperatures may briefly drop below freezing, and the zone receives 5 to 10 inches of precipitation per year. Species from this association make excellent xeriscape choices if given full sun and well-draining soil. It intergrades at higher elevations with Joshua Tree Woodland.

Joshua Tree Woodland

Named after its most prominent plant, the Joshua tree (*Yucca brevifolia*), this community occurs at 2,500- to 5,000-foot elevations along the edge of the Mojave Desert and on the eastern slopes of the Sierra Nevada. Temperatures can reach 100 degrees F on summer days but cool significantly at night; winters experience minor snow and temperatures into the teens. The zone receives 5 to 10 inches of precipitation per year. Common plants include Apache plume, desert willow, rabbitbrush, buckwheat species, and juniper species. Plants from this community require well-draining, sandy, loamy soils and full sun. This association typically occurs above Creosote Bush Scrub and below Pinyon-Juniper Woodland.

A layered mix of native trees, shrubs, groundcovers, and cacti create a pleasing year-round display.

The ABCs of Native Plant Landscaping

At least two schools of thought have developed concerning landscaping with indigenous plants. The traditional approach substitutes native plants for the commonly used imported species. Native plants can be used for foundation hedges around buildings, border hedges along walks and drives, and sheared hedges; as accent shrubs planted alone; or as container plants. They can be used in any formal or informal landscape design.

At the other end of the spectrum is the attempt to duplicate the natural plant associations found in the wild, whether chaparral, woodland, or desert. A yard would in effect be a microcosm of nature. The pure wildscape design has no sheared hedges or shaped shrubs, no species or cultivars not from the immediate area.

Of course, landscapers and homeowners modify these extremes considerably. Many intermediate designs lie between the formal and wild landscape designs. One approach that combines the concepts of maintaining natural plant associations and using plants to visually accent open areas is to create landscape islands. Instead of delineating an area by hedges and a few accent shrubs or trees, use a mass planting, or island, of mixed species. A landscape island can be completely contained in an open area or curve out from a building. It can include one side of a drive or accent a corner. Cactus and xeriscape gardens exemplify the landscape island concept.

Mass plantings combine compatible species to make your landscape visually dramatic. Always choose species with the same habitat requirements. Compatible plants have foliage of a similar color, size, and shape. Or they may complement each other with varying shades of foliage and leaf patterns. Species with gray foliage provide a dramatic combination with green-leafed species. A palo verde or desert willow adds a vertical accent for low-growing shrubs such as fairy duster or brittle bush.

A group planting can have a different accent for every season. You can provide year-round color, as well as food and shelter for birds and butterflies. Use deciduous plants to provide shades of bright green with new spring leaves and colorful autumn hues. Use evergreens to add foliage color during the barren winter months. Hedges, borders, and backgrounds do not have to consist of a single evergreen species, but can combine the best nature has to offer. The flexibility of companion planting provides a multitude of design possibilities for an attractive yard throughout each season.

Four Steps for Developing a Master Plan

Step 1: The Dreaming Stage

Landscaping your yard is an investment of money and a commitment to the time a plant takes to mature. You want plants that will be healthy and vigorous and at the same time fulfill your long-term landscaping needs. The first step is to decide what you need and expect from a plant. Do you want a large tree with an expansive canopy or a small tree to shade an entryway? Do you want a deciduous or evergreen tree, a loosely growing shrub or a dense one that can be shaped? If you are just starting to landscape your yard, you will want to develop a master plan for the entire lot, taking into account these and other considerations. Don't worry about selecting particular species at this point. Once you have determined what your goals and needs are for your landscape, you will be able to assess which native plant species are best for you.

The photographs and landscape drawings in this book will give you many ideas for landscaping your yard. Besides the utilitarian benefits (shade, windbreaks, erosion control, and so on), plants provide a visual highlight for an area. Plants add beauty to driveways, sidewalks, patios, pools, porches, corners, and courtyards. Use border plantings to enhance walls, fences, and building foundations. A distinctive plant at the corner of the house or entryway adds special visual appeal. Mass plantings of shrubs or vines beautify slopes, medians, and open areas.

Decide where you want hedges, border plants, large and small shade trees, vines, and groundcovers. Choose evergreens where you want year-round shade, deciduous species for winter sun, and spring- and fall-flowering species for color throughout the year. Use tall evergreen hedges for visual privacy and densely branching or thorny species to provide physical barrier hedges. Keep in mind that you don't need to plant everything at once, but you can add the plants year by year as budget and time allow.

Some shrubs will grow naturally into densely branching, thickly foliated, rounded plants; others seem to flail their limbs at random regardless of how much you prune the errant branches. Decide whether you want a formal or informal look for your design. Patios, courtyards, entryways, and foundation hedges often require a more refined-looking shrub or tree, while border hedges along fences and walls, background shrubs in mass plantings, and xeriscape gardens shine with the wildscape look.

Whether you are a home or professional landscaper, minimizing the time and money spent on yard maintenance may be an important consideration. You can save on

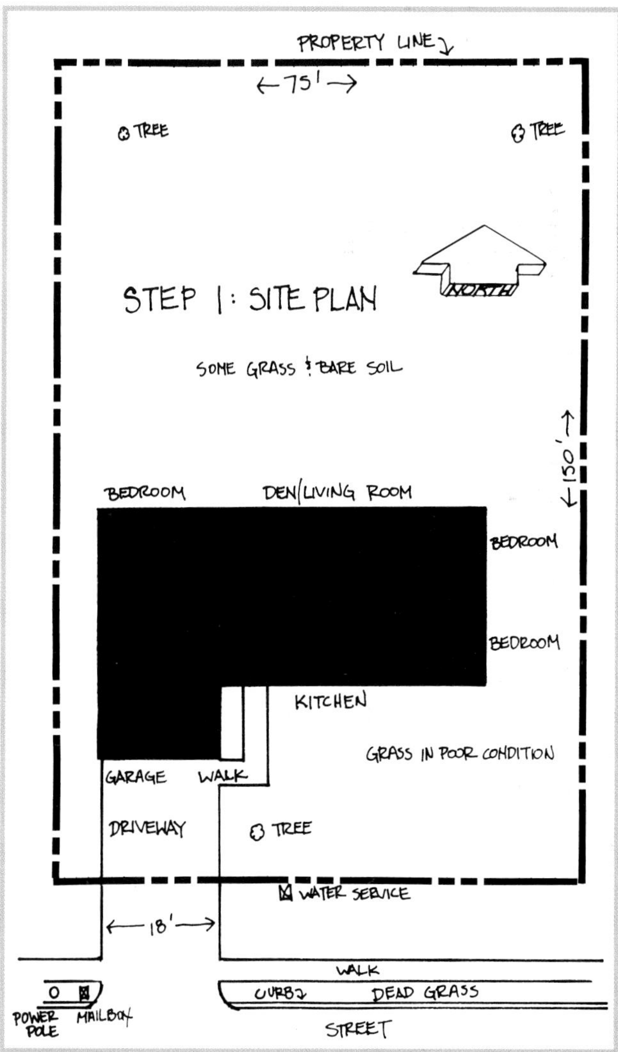

The Dreaming Stage. The first step in developing a master plan for your landscape is making a site plan.

utility costs throughout the year by planting proper combinations of native deciduous and evergreen trees and shrubs and by using drought-tolerant species in arid climates. The chapter on xeriscaping in this book will tell you how to reduce your summer water bill by as much as 44 percent in an arid climate by using drought-tolerant species.

Planting native groundcovers is another way to reduce yard maintenance, prevent erosion, and add an extra touch of beauty. Many shrubs naturally spread by rhizomes or branch rooting and form thick mats; others form dense thickets in nature. Not every low-growing, thicket-forming plant can serve as a groundcover, however, so look for species with densely foliated branching, multiseason attraction, and a growth profile that matches your height requirements. The chapter "Landscaping with Groundcovers" explains alternative uses for many of the plants described in this book.

The chapter "Landscaping with Vines" describes numerous vines that will enhance your landscape. Vines are fast growing, and most tolerate either sun or shade, making them adaptable to almost any landscape design.

Native plants are also useful for attracting birds and other animals to your yard, further enhancing the beauty and enjoyment of the landscape. Many species offer year-round flowers, fruits, and berries for birds, butterflies, squirrels, and other desirable urban wildlife. The chapter "Landscaping to Attract Wildlife" provides a useful overview and planting suggestions.

Step 2: Site Analysis

One of the most important factors determining a landscape plant's success is its location. In the wild, a plant casts its seeds to the wind, trusting that a few will find an optimum habitat and survive. We can't afford this trial-and-error method in our yards. We want our plants not just to survive, but to grow vigorously and be attractive. Before you turn a spade of soil, carefully analyze the environmental conditions of your yard and choose plants that are naturally adapted to the existing growth conditions. This is the most important step for low-maintenance landscaping.

Just because a plant grows in your landscape zone, or even in your immediate area, does not mean that it will grow well in your yard. For optimum performance, the plant must be adapted to four major habitat parameters: the soil type, moisture, drainage, and exposure. Many plants have very exacting requirements. Look at your soil, and not just the fill soil the developer may have spread over your lot. Is it sandy loam, clay, or rocky soil? How fast does it drain after a heavy rain? If your yard stays muddy for a day or so after a rain, don't plant species that require fast-draining soil.

Soil Types and Improvement

The first step in analyzing the landscape potential of your yard or site is to determine the characteristics of the soil. The most important factors are the composition of the soil, which determines drainage, and the soil pH, which influences nutrition. Many soils can be improved with a regular composting and mulching program, which helps balance the pH and improves both fertility and drainage.

Composition

The ageless physical and biological processes that break down rock into soil produce three basic types of soil: sand, silt, and clay. Loam is a mixture of the three and may be classified as sandy, silty, or claylike, depending on the relative percentages of each. A well-balanced loam contains about two-fifths sand, two-fifths silt, and one-fifth clay.

Sand

Soils that are composed of 50 percent or more sand contain large grains that drain quickly, retain little moisture, and dry rapidly after watering. The faster a soil drains, the more nutrients are leached away, so soils classified as sandy or sandy loams tend to be infertile. If your site consists of sandy soil, you should either select plants adapted to sandy habitats or develop a program of improving the soil with organic matter and fertilizers and mulching. Be sure to select species that are adapted to fast-draining, infertile conditions. On the plus side, sandy soils are easy to work and easy to improve, and they warm quickly in the spring, allowing early-germinating species to thrive.

Silt

Silty soils consist of small- to medium-sized particles, smaller than sand and larger than clay, that retain water and nutrients. Silky when wet, this soil type is easy to work. A silty soil may require additional sand to improve drainage if it contains too much clay. Silt is often deposited by floods or otherwise transported by water.

Clay

Clay is the finest-grained soil type, with particles so small that they bind water molecules very tightly, making absorption by roots difficult or impossible.

Soils with more than 40 percent clay retain water, are difficult to work, compact easily, and are slow to warm in the spring. Clay soils should be improved with the addition of organic matter on a yearly basis. Take care when adding sand—too little can turn clay into adobe brick. A good soil mixture will crumble in your hand when dry.

Serpentine

Formed by the intense heat at tectonic induction zones, serpentine soils contain high levels of minerals, such as asbestos, copper, mercury, magnesium, and chromium, but are low in calcium (limestone). Only a few plants, including 20 percent of California's endemic species, have adapted to this soil type. Serpentine soils seldom occur in Southern California, so avoid plants adapted to this soil.

Limestone

Sandy, limestone-derived soils often contain considerable caliche, or small particles of limestone rock. The soil drains rapidly, is alkaline, and is usually shallow. Limestone can be improved with the addition of organic matter. Select species adapted to alkaline, fast-draining soils.

Soil Analysis

To determine the type of soil in your yard or site, you can send a sample to a lab for a full-blown chemical analysis, but usually a few backyard tests will tell you what you need to know to make judicious plant selections.

If you enjoy kitchen chemistry, fill a quart jar one-third full with soil and fill the jar with water. Shake and let it sit for a day, or until all the soil settles to the bottom and the water is clear, with the organic matter floating at the top. You should be able to see the different strata of soil components. Sand, the heaviest, will settle first, followed by silt, and then clay. Measure the thickness of each layer. A layer of sand that equals half or more of the total indicates sandy soil. Similarly, if half is silt, you have silty soil. If the top layer is more than one-quarter of the total, your soil tends toward clay. A well-balanced loam will have nearly equal layers of sand and silt, with less clay.

If you prefer the quick-and-dirty method, squeeze a handful of wet soil through your fingers. Sandy soil is gritty and crumbles, silty soil is firm and silky, and you can make a baseball from clay.

Drainage Test

Soils with either a high clay or sand content may have drainage problems. Conduct a percolation test before you make any soil modifications or plant selections. Dig a round hole in the soil about 6 inches in diameter and 10 inches deep. Fill with water and let it drain completely, then fill it again, and note how long it takes to drain the second time. One hour is an indication of excellent drainage. One to four hours is average to poor, but acceptable. If it takes more than four hours or less than fifteen minutes for the water to drain, you should develop a long-term composting and mulching plan.

Soil pH

Depending on the parent materials, soil varies from acidic to alkaline in its chemical makeup. The pH scale (pH stands for "potential Hydrogen ions") runs from 0 to 14. A rating of 7 is neutral, higher than 7 indicates alkaline soils, and lower than 7 is acidic. Most native plants prefer soil with a pH between 6 and 7.5, though some species require highly acidic or alkaline soil; such preferences are indicated in the "Native Plant Profiles" in this book.

If the pH of your soil is too high or too low, some minerals become insoluble and cannot be absorbed by the plant's root system. The most important minerals—nitrogen, phosphorus, and potassium—are available over a wide range of pH, but iron, manganese, and boron become limited if the pH gets much above 7.5. Plants deprived of these minerals develop chlorotic, or yellow, leaves. An iron deficiency causes the newer leaves to become yellow with green veins, while a magnesium deficiency causes older leaves to develop yellow patches.

To adjust the pH of your soil, add lime to overly acidic soils, those with a pH below 6.5; manure, compost, or, in the extreme, sulfur can be added to soils that are too alkaline (pH above 7.5). The amount of additive depends on both the soil composition and the original pH level. Soil additives can alter the pH by one point or so, but the best option is to select plants that are adapted to your soil. Garden centers sell easy-to-use pH test kits.

Even a small yard has subtle differences in exposure and drainage that can greatly affect the survivability and healthy appearance of a plant. Plants on the north side of the house receive much less sun and heat than those planted on the south. Shade-tolerant species and those more cold-hardy should be used for northern exposures. A southern exposure receives sunlight most of the day, making it hotter and drier in the summer and warmer in the winter. Select sun-loving, drought-tolerant species for these exposures. Plants along a concrete drive, beside a patio, or in a rock garden receive an extra dose of radiated heat that may create a desert habitat. Shaded entryways, on the other hand, might provide the shade and coolness of a riparian forest.

The way you prepare the soil for planting also can create significantly different growth conditions. A layer of mulch several inches thick will protect a forest plant's roots from drying out and overheating, thus simulating the plant's cooler native habitat.

The microhabitats in your yard can change as your landscape matures. In nature, plants modify their environment enough to allow a succession of different plant associations through time. This can also occur in your yard. Years of mulching, or years of hot, dry exposure, can change the soil conditions significantly. As saplings develop into large trees, their shade changes the habitat around them. Sun-loving species may die out and shade-loving ones thrive under the new conditions. When designing your master plan, consider the mature sizes of the species you choose and what they will look like in five or ten years. For instance, you might rather plant one large canopy tree and several small understory trees instead of three large trees that would eventually shade your entire yard. Choose primary plants that will remain compatible as your landscape matures, then fill the gaps with perennials and wildflowers.

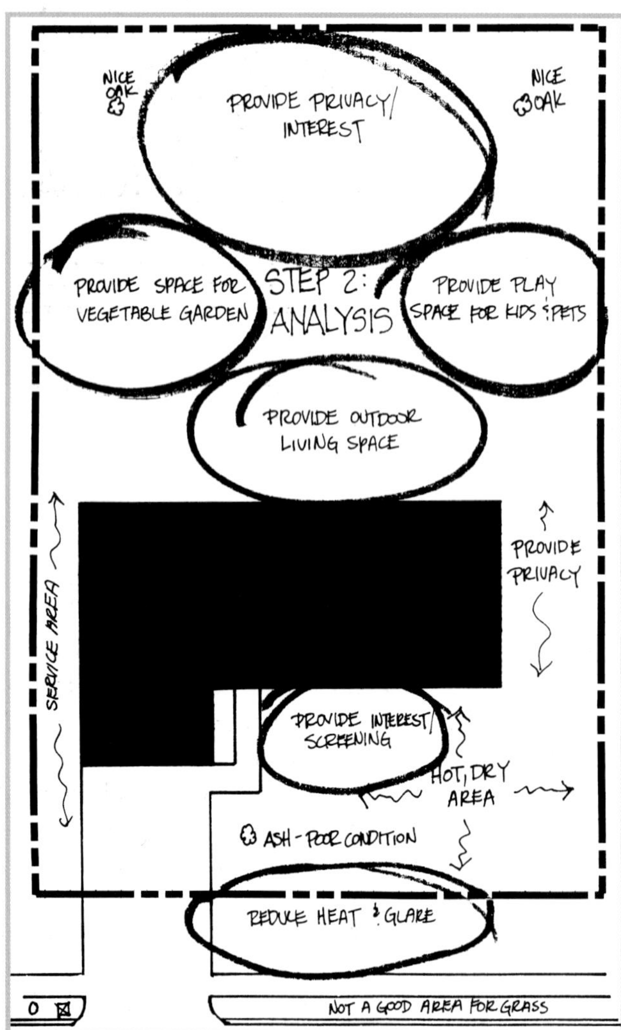

Site Analysis. Determining how you intend to use the different spaces in your landscape requires an understanding of the site's conditions.

Step 3: Choosing the Plants

After you have determined the growth characteristics that match your landscape space, exposure, soil, and drainage, you're ready to compile a list of plant species. The plants most adapted to your local growing conditions are those that grew in your area before it was developed. If you're a native plant purist, stick to plants from your locality. However, many nurseries and landscapers consider all of the South Coast and northern Mexico as the home range for plant selection. Regardless of your perspective, you'll find an abundance of trees and shrubs with striking flowers, fruit, and seeds that make them excellent ornamental landscape plants. After you have selected the trees and shrubs that will be the dominant features in your landscape, you can choose the shorter-lived native wildflowers, groundcovers, vines, and other accent plants to complement your design.

The first step in the plant-selection process is to identify your landscape zone from the map of landscape zones earlier in this book and identify your plant community. The closer that the plants you choose match the local plant association, the better their chances of thriving. Next, refer to the species descriptions of each plant in the "Native Plant Profiles" to determine which are compatible with your particular growing conditions. The species are listed in alphabetical order by scientific name. Also refer to the "Plant Palettes" appendix for species adapted to each landscape zone. Additional information about plants for specific purposes or characteristics can be found in the appendices of evergreen plants and flowering trees and shrubs, as well as in the chapters on xeriscaping and on attracting wildlife. Armed with a list of the trees, shrubs,

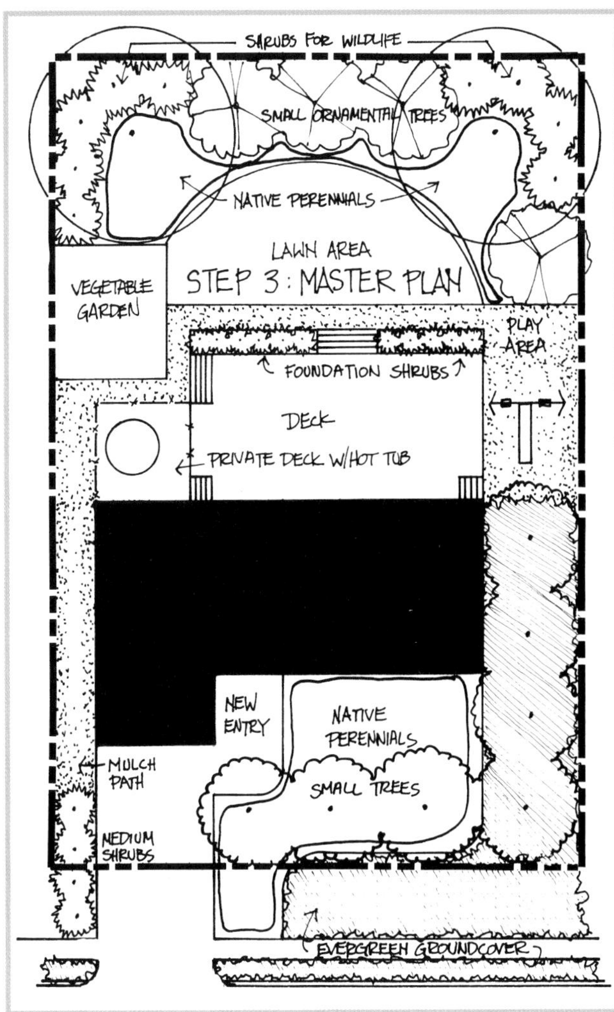

Choosing the Plants. With so many wonderful plants available, identifying those best suited to your landscape involves careful consideration.

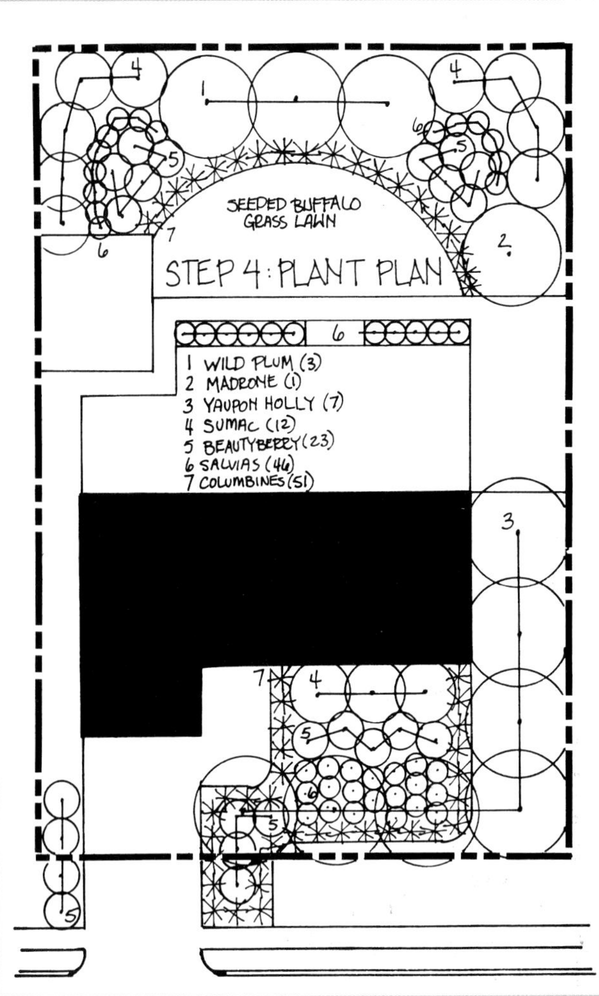

Planting. Placing the plants in their proper spots is the final phase of creating your dream garden.

wildflowers, vines, and groundcovers having the same habitat requirements as your yard, you are ready to begin shopping for plants.

Step 4: Planting

Most plants should be transplanted in the season of least stress—October through February in Southern California—or before the last frost in the spring. A freshly dug plant can survive the shock of having most of its roots removed in the winter because water-stress is reduced at that time. The cooler days stimulate more root growth than stem growth. Container plants planted at this time will also have time to grow an expanded root system before the stress of summer.

You can give your plant a head start with proper site preparation. First, remove all the weeds or grass that compete for moisture. Many plants, especially Chaparral and Creosote Bush Scrub species, grow in a weed-free environment and don't compete well with the invaders. Next, prepare the soil. Preparing the soil helps the plant to begin growing immediately and to establish a healthy root system. Dig a hole about twice as wide as the plant's root ball or container. Large trees should have one foot of clearance around the root ball. This allows for loose, well-prepared soil to surround the root system and stimulate growth. Dig the hole deep enough for 6 inches of loose soil on the bottom. It's very important to make sure the plants are not planted too deeply. Maintain the original juncture of the base of the plant with the soil.

The most important roots of a plant are the surface feeder roots. These tiny rootlets absorb the moisture and nutrients essential for a plant's growth. Soil compaction will physically impede the growth and spread of the rootlets, which directly limits the development of the entire plant, and waterlogged soil will drown the roots. Before you set your plant, loosen the soil 6 to 12 inches deep for several yards around the hole, depending on the size of the plant. Once a plant is established, you should never disturb the surface roots by tilling or by covering with more than an inch of fill dirt.

After placing the plant and filling the hole, form a slight ridge of soil around the circumference of the hole to create a basin to hold in water. Saturate the soil immediately after planting. Weekly watering, particularly of small plants, may be necessary through the first summer, especially if temperatures are extreme. Mulching around the base of the plant reduces water loss and heat buildup in the soil. It also keeps grass from growing around the plant and competing for water. Grasses can reduce the growth of a plant by as much as 50 percent, so keep the area around the plant clear of grass. Some effective materials for mulching include bark or wood chips, leaves, grass clippings, straw or hay, and crushed stone or gravel.

Adding fertilizer granules or time-release fertilizer pellets to the fill around the plant will stimulate plant growth and sometimes double or even triple the growth rate normal in a wild setting. Some nurseries achieve 6 to 8 feet of first-year growth from seedling oaks that receive regular fertilizing and watering. But regular fertilizing of established native plants is unnecessary and often detrimental. Just remember, until a plant grows a network of surface feeder roots, it will need tender loving care and water during dry periods; after that, it needs, or desires, little attention.

For the first year, the plant is vulnerable and should be protected against climatic extremes. Water as frequently as necessary during the first year. Observe the plant, and water when signs of stress appear. A slight leaf wilt or curl, loss of vibrant green color, and browning around the leaf margins are sure signs of insufficient water. If the surface feeder roots die, recovery is slow and growth inhibited.

Always be careful not to overwater. Most natives dislike wet feet. Coastal Sage Scrub species that go dormant in the summer require sufficient water in the spring and fall growing seasons. Weekly sprinklers or drip irrigation in the summer actually harms summer-dormant plants such as ceanothus species. Overwatering quickly kills species that are adapted to summer dormancy and well-draining soil—a lesson hard learned by those of us accustomed to thirsty plants originally from wet climates.

For plants whose main growing season is spring and summer, watering during the first summer after transplanting is important. By the second summer, the plant has gone through two spring growing seasons and should be hardy enough to survive on its own without irrigation, unless the summer is abnormally dry. By not allowing lack of water to inhibit a plant's growth for the first season, you enable the new plant to grow rapidly and become well established.

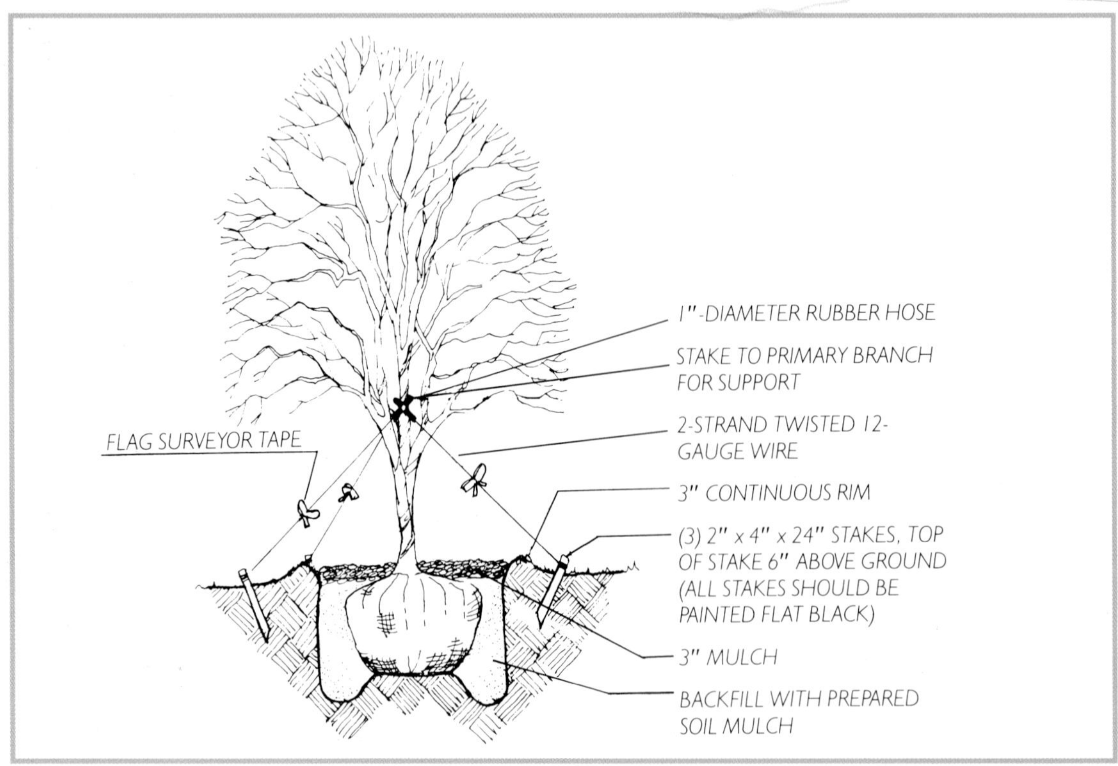

Tree Planting and Staking Detail (not to scale).

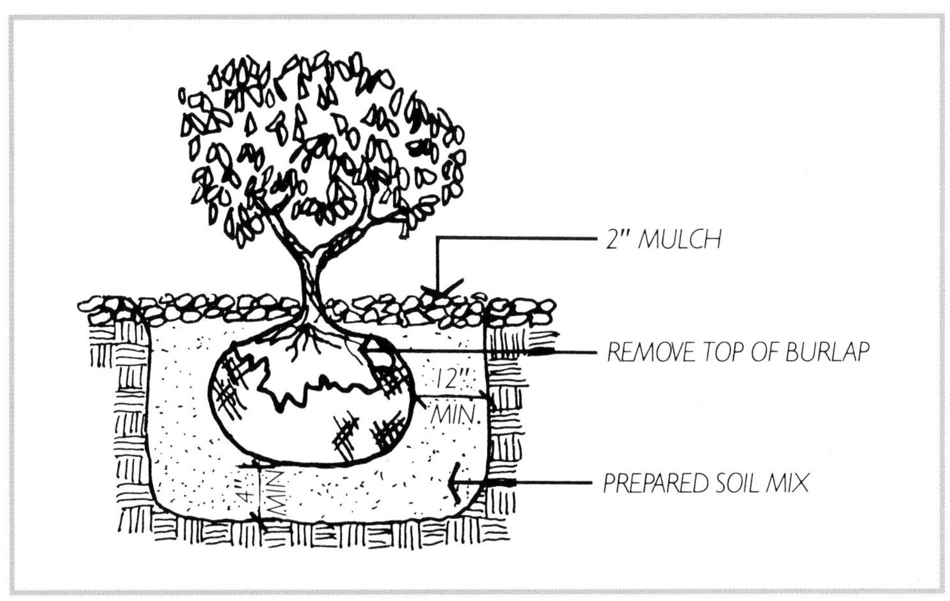

Shrub Planting Detail (not to scale).

So, Where Can I Find Those Wonderful Natives?

A trip to the garden center in Lowe's, Home Depot, or Kmart reveals the same selection of nonnative ornamentals. A few plants native to Southern California have made the mix, but most large-volume retailers carry a combination of alpine meadow flowers, tropical patio plants, Asian flowering shrubs, and naturalized tree hybrids and cultivars.

Fortunately, many locally owned nurseries are well stocked with native trees, shrubs, wildflowers, and seeds, and some sell indigenous plants exclusively. Wholesale growers now propagate natives in large quantities to meet the growing demand for home and commercial landscaping. Arboretums, nature centers, parks, and plant societies often sponsor seasonal native plant sales. Get on their mailing lists, or better yet, join a native plant group or botanical garden near you and visit regularly.

When selecting plants, container or nursery-conditioned stock is much preferred to transplanting plants straight from the fields, because the former have better developed root systems. In the wild, a shrub or tree's roots spread out over a large area to gather water and nutrients. When transplanted, the plant loses many of its roots and is more susceptible to losing important branches or dying. A nursery-propagated and pampered specimen has more roots in its ball or container and is more likely to grow rapidly when planted in your yard. Ask the nursery about the history and age of the trees and shrubs before buying them. If you can find a retailer knowledgeable in natives, he or she will probably be willing and eager to advise you on plants suitable for your landscaping situations.

Digging of trees and shrubs from the wild by home landscapers almost always results in the death of the plant and may be in violation of plant-protection laws. Transplanting is best done by professionals who have the experience, equipment, knowledge, and proper permits. Without expensive mechanized equipment, digging a large root ball is a labor-intensive operation, and no shortcuts make the job easier. Besides the slim chance of success, digging plants from the wild also impoverishes the countryside and in many instances is prohibited by law. Once a plant becomes popular and is deemed economically valuable, it easily can be removed from nature much faster than it can naturally replenish itself. Over 30 percent of the cacti in the United States are endangered or threatened with extinction because of over-collection from the wild. Northern Mexico, where there are fewer restrictions, suffers even more from plant poaching. Stripping plants from nature contradicts the major philosophy of the native plant movement: repairing our damaged environment. Demand nursery-propagated plants. It is more ecologically sound and economically wise.

Maintaining Your Landscape

Every landscape design requires some amount of maintenance, and fertilizing, soil conditioning, spraying, pruning, and replacing dead plants to keep the garden healthy and attractive can represent a continual expense. But while no home or commercial landscape is totally maintenance-free, hardy native plants come as close as we can get to that ideal. Indigenous plants require far less care than many imported exotic species, so a landscape design that incorporates the natural shape and size of natives will require much less periodic attention, expensive irrigation systems, and seasonal expense than one using exotics.

In the wild, a plant often reacts to extremes of drought and temperature by leaf loss, twig damage, dieback, or a generally scrubby appearance. In our landscape, however, we want to avoid these extreme responses and maintain the optimum—or at least average—growing conditions, regardless of how stressful the weather may be. For example, even though the plants might easily survive periods of drought, we may want to provide supplemental watering if the appearance begins to suffer. The exceptions are the summer drought-deciduous plants common to the Costal Sage Scrub community. Just as deciduous trees lose their leaves in response to winter temperature stress, summer drought-deciduous species require a drought-stress-induced dormancy to remain healthy.

A firmly established, vigorously growing plant that has adjusted to its exposure and survived several growing seasons needs little attention. If properly chosen, it will not outgrow its setting and will survive whatever extremes nature has to offer.

Regardless of which plants you use in your landscape, some basic knowledge and skills in plant husbandry will help you keep your plants healthy and attractive. The following information will help you develop the landscape skills required to keep your yard beautiful.

Fertilizing

Fertilizing with a complete fertilizer in the spring stimulates foliage, flower, and fruit production, the primary characteristics we desire in our landscape plants. Fertile soil ensures that a plant will develop its maximum genetic potential, just as it would in an optimum habitat in nature. Once the plant is established and adapted to its new location, fertilizing is usually unnecessary and unwanted. Overfertilizing can harm the plant and the soil microbes that are necessary for a native plant's health.

Complete fertilizers supply the three main nutrients required for a plant's growth: nitrogen, phosphorus, and potassium. In general, nitrogen stimulates foliage growth; phosphorous, root growth; and potassium, flower and fruit production. The three-number rating of a fertilizer expresses the percentage of these compounds. A 10-6-4 fertilizer, for example, contains 10 percent nitrogen, 6 percent phosphorus, and 4 percent potash, or potassium.

When required, fertilizer should be applied early in the year—January or February—before the spring growth begins. Fertilizing can be time consuming and expensive, so don't waste money buying unnecessary fertilizers. Before applying fertilizers, have your soil analyzed to determine if nutrients are lacking. The county agricultural extension agent provides this useful and inexpensive service.

Pruning

Even though you've chosen a plant because its natural growth habit complements your landscape, trees and shrubs often display little regard for our wishes. A shrub may grow scattered branches or a tree produce wayward limbs. Even in the best-designed landscape, some degree of control by pruning is usually required to direct plant growth and maintain tidiness. Just as water and fertilizer maximize growth, intelligent and timely pruning helps the plant to rapidly develop a full size and attractive shape. Almost every tree and shrub in your landscape will at one time or another require pruning.

Perhaps one reason plant growers and landscapers have ignored native plants for so long is their often-unsightly appearance in nature. A wild shrub may have dead limbs, spreading branches, an irregular profile, and other characteristics undesirable for a landscape setting. The unkempt appearance of wild plants results from lack of care. Pruning can transform many native plants into premier landscape specimens. It can make a plant tall or short, open branching or densely foliated, or even convert a shrub into a hedge. Pruning encourages compactness if the shrub is naturally intricately branching. Some species, such as jojoba and buffaloberry, make densely foliated shaped or sheared hedges. Others, such as three-leaf sumac and indigo bush, are open branching and more suitable for informal hedges.

Know the growth habit of your plant before you assault it with pruning shears. The descriptions in the "Native Plant Profiles" section of this book indicate the growth habits and pruning requirements of most species. Following are some general guidelines for pruning that will help ensure a healthy and attractive plant.

Rabbitbrush (*Ericameria nauseosa*) is a striking garden accent, whether pruned or left unsheared.

Jojoba (*Simmondsia chinensis*) can be pruned into an effective hedge or screen.

The Cardinal Rules of Pruning

Swear allegiance to the following principles of pruning before grasping your shears or saw.

1. Know the natural growth habit (shape and size) of the plant. Unless you are developing a shaped hedge, pruning should train the plant toward its natural form. Pruning against the natural growth pattern is fighting the plant instead of training it and will require regular maintenance.

2. Make cuts that will heal rapidly. Every tree branch has a collar of growing cells that reinforces the limb and seals it off from the trunk if it dies. If you trim limbs flush with the trunk, you remove this protective collar and expose the conductive tissues to possible invasion by fungi. Branch collars vary greatly among species; some are prominent, while others are less distinct. Look for a bulge or series of ridges in the bark around the base of the limb. Make your cut flush with the branch collar, and it will heal rapidly.

   Remove large limbs in sections, or at least with three cuts. First, cut into the limb on the underside 6 inches from the collar. Remove the limb with a second cut 4 inches farther out; and finally, cut the stub, leaving the branch collar bulging from the trunk. This procedure prevents a partially severed limb from falling and peeling a strip of bark down the trunk. Always use sharp tools suited for the size of the job.

3. Avoid topping a tree. Removing the terminal growing section of a tree destroys its natural shape and appearance, stunts its growth, and weakens it. You probably will want to remove limbs that compete with the terminal leader, however.

4. Prune in the right season. Evergreens and winter-deciduous trees and shrubs should be pruned in the dormant season, December through February. Wait to prune until after the first freeze to avoid stimulating new growth, which can occur if pruning is done during the growing season. Plants that bloom in the late spring and fall usually produce flowers on the current season's new growth. Pruning in the dormant season allows them to produce new wood in the spring before blooming. Species that flower in early spring, such as redbuds, produce blooms on the previous year's new growth. Prune them immediately after flowering, before new growth starts.

   There are two important exceptions to these seasonal guidelines. Broken or otherwise damaged limbs should be removed immediately, and foliage should be trimmed back on a transplanted tree. The diminished root system of a transplanted specimen cannot supply water to the full canopy of foliage, and the plant may die unless the foliage is reduced in proportion to the root loss. In this situation, trim back the branch tips, or remove most of the leaves.

5. Prune for a reason. Carefully consider the four primary objectives of pruning: improving appearance, directing growth, encouraging fruit or flowers, and maintaining health. Remove a limb only for a very specific purpose; don't vent your frustration from a stalled lawn mower on a nearby shrub.

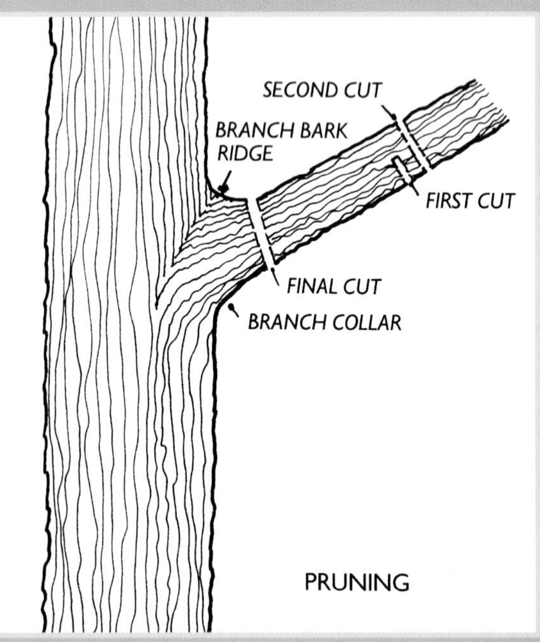

Cuts made in the right places will help your pruned tree heal quickly.

With pruning, Mexican elderberry (*Sambucus nigra* subsp. *canadensis*) can be trained into a tree form to show off its multitrunked base.

Directing Growth by Thinning

Thinning maintains the symmetrical shape and desired size of a tree or shrub by removing excessive or unsightly branches. Removing wayward limbs channels the plant's growth into the desirable limbs. A developing young tree or shrub, especially if it is rapid growing, produces numerous branches, some of which compete with each other for light. The ones that win the race for the sun will shade the others, which then eventually die. Removing these vulnerable branches from the beginning prevents the tree from wasting nutrients and growth on limbs destined to die.

After a hard freeze or severe pruning, a tree often produces water sprouts—straight, rapid-growing, vertical limbs that branch from the trunk or older interior limbs. These shoots can destroy the tree's natural shape and should be removed. Thinning also keeps the lower limbs from obstructing vision or blocking access to the base of the tree.

When thinning small branches, you should make a smooth cut where the branch connects with the main stem. You can change the direction a branch is growing by pruning it one-fourth to one-half inch beyond a twig that is already growing in the desired direction. The twig will assume the primary growth of the branch. Light pruning of the branch tips of many shrub species stimulates new growth and gives the plant a fuller appearance.

Rejuvenation

As some plants, such as desert willow, age, they develop unproductive wood that produces few leaves or flowers. Cutting back the old limbs, or even cutting back the entire plant nearly to the ground, will stimulate growth of vigorous new branches. You may need to remove the old branches over a two- or three-year interval and thin the new branches as they appear.

Encouraging Flowers and Fruit

Many flowering shrubs benefit from light pruning in the dormant season. Pruning the branch tips of salvias, brittle bush, and rabbitbrush produces denser foliage and more flowers. Thinning the interior limbs of a flowering or fruiting plant allows light to penetrate and stimulate more blooms. Some plants, such as desert bird of paradise and desert willow, must be severely pruned every few years to maintain an attractive, full-flowering condition.

Maintaining Health

A plant will not only be more attractive, it will be healthier if damaged, dead, or diseased limbs are removed. Limbs broken by winds, freezes, or careless handling are open doors for invasions of fungi and parasites. Remove them immediately.

Xeriscape planting at Living Desert Zoo and Gardens in Palm Desert.

Landscaping for Water Conservation and Xeriscaping

Southern California may boast the most salubrious climate in North America, but that doesn't mean we still don't have to contend with nature's vicissitudes. The deserts sizzle in the summer, and furnace-like Santa Ana winds sweep down from the mountains in the winter. In the interior, 90-degree days linger far into October, and temperature swings are as unpredictable as a dust devil.

Anyone contemplating landscaping a home or business is concerned with the time and expense of plant maintenance. If you use plants that are not adapted to your yard, fertilizing, soil conditioning, spraying, pruning, and replacing dead plants represent a continual expense. Although native plants don't eliminate the need for regular maintenance, they do go a long way toward avoiding these common problems, and once established, natives require a fraction of the maintenance of many imported species. One of the primary expenses of maintaining a landscape is water; as much as 60 percent of residential water consumption goes to watering yards. The choice of plants can greatly reduce the moisture required to keep your landscape attractive and healthy. Of the thousands of plants native to Southern California, some are water spendthrifts, and some are as frugal as a Depression-era loan officer.

A plant grows by capturing solar energy and converting raw elements, through the process of photosynthesis, into useful nutrients. Plant roots absorb water and dissolved minerals, which are channeled through the plant's vascular system to the food factories in the leaves. The leaves transpire, or lose, a major portion of the water supplied by the roots. Some plants have developed ingenious methods to reduce water loss from the leaves, and many of these species have exceptional landscape value.

Plants combat water loss through the leaf surface, or evapotranspiration, by small leaves or leaves covered with a waxy or woolly coating, as well as by internal cellular and structural adaptations. Many plants native to the Coastal Sage Scrub community adapt to the six-month dry season by losing their leaves in the summer and growing and flowering in the warmer, wetter winter and shoulder seasons. These xerophytic, or drought-tolerant, plants thrive under conditions that would kill or severely stress plants native to more moist areas.

The term *xeriscape*—derived by combining the Greek word for "dry," *xeri*, with "landscape"—became a buzzword in the 1990s among gardeners, landscapers, and urban planners looking for more cost-efficient approaches to planting. Cities, industries, and farmers all recognize water as the state's most precious resource. Most metropolises in Southern California must find ways to conserve water, or their reservoirs and wells will run dry in the near future. In response, many cities, counties, and regional water districts have initiated xeriscape programs to actively encourage property owners to landscape with plants that have a low water consumption. By conscientious landscaping, each of us can help relieve the demand for this critical resource and reduce our personal utility expenses.

Seven Xeriscape Principles

Xeriscaping is not limited to just yuccas and rock gardens. It is a philosophy that incorporates good gardening principles, and it can be practiced anywhere. The National Xeriscape Council, Inc., recommends the following principles:

1. Start with a good design. A master plan incorporates existing and future plants; soil, slope, and exposure; and your house and play areas into a design that meets your needs and conserves water.

2. Improve the soil. A plant needs a healthy root system to thrive and beautify your yard. Compacted, shallow, rocky, or sandy soil may not allow a plant to develop a root system that can sufficiently support luxuriant foliage growth. You can improve your soil by tilling in at least 2 inches of organic material, such as composted leaves, grass clippings, or dried manure. If you have shallow soil, till in 2 to 4 inches of loam topsoil. A proper soil is loose enough for roots to penetrate, has the proper pH for roots to absorb iron, and allows water to percolate slowly into the root zone.

A xeriscape garden can incorporate a variety of foliage colors and shapes, as well as colorful flowers, as shown by this arrangement of prickly pear, agave, and yucca plants at Quail Botanical Gardens.

3. Use mulch. A mulch covers the soil, prevents moisture loss, inhibits weed growth, and modifies extreme soil temperatures. Bark, wood chips, leaves, grass clippings, and colored gravel make good mulching materials. Use 2 to 4 inches of mulch around trees and shrubs, in flower beds, and in landscaped areas. The mulching itself can be an attractive design element in your overall landscape plan.

4. Reduce lawn areas. Turf grass is necessary for outdoor recreation areas, and it dissipates heat and provides a cool space around your house or patio. But in arid locales, lawns guzzle water in the summer and require regular maintenance. To conserve water and save on utility bills, limit your lawn to small recreation and border areas around your house and choose the grass best adapted to your climate and yard. Consider using wildflowers, groundcovers, trees, shrubs, and mulch for the majority of your landscape.

5. Water efficiently. Put the water where and when the plant needs it, and you can cut your water consumption, and water bill, by as much as 30 percent. Learn to tell when a plant needs water. Grass curls and lies flat. Leaves may droop, drop, or lose their shine. Learn to water as often as necessary to avoid drought stress, but without overwatering.

   The way you water influences how much water a plant needs to thrive. Place the water in the root zone and water deeply. Shallow watering encourages a shallow root system, which requires more frequent watering since the upper portion of the soil dries out faster. Drip irrigation, soil basins built around plants, early- or late-day watering, and mulch all help to conserve water. Sprinkler systems used improperly can lose considerable water to evaporation and runoff.

6. Practice good maintenance. Maintenance keeps your plants healthy and attractive. Weeds, injured or dead limbs, and sickly plants detract from your landscape, increase your water bill, and can require costly replacement of plants. (See the chapter "Maintaining Your Landscape.")

7. Choose low-water-use plants adapted to your area. As one might expect, most Southern California plants must be drought tolerant to survive, but some are better adapted to drought than others. Plants that are native to the dry rain shadow on eastern mountain slopes are generally more drought tolerant than species from the coastal exposures. Some species grow only along streams and rivers or in cooler habitats with greater precipitation. They would quickly perish in the hot, arid desert or in an arid landscape setting.

Flowering shrubs are a welcome color addition to a xeriscape garden.

Desert landscaping with brittle bush (*Encelia californica*) and creosote bush (*Larrea tridentata*) at Desert Willow Golf Resort, Palm Desert.

Drought-Tolerant Plants for Xeriscaping

The following list, though not inclusive, delineates many species of trees, shrubs, vines, and groundcovers that will tolerate periods of drought. Refer to the "Native Plant Profiles" for more details.

Trees

Acacia farnesiana, huisache
Arbutus menziesii, Pacific madrone
Celtis laevigata var. *reticulata*, netleaf hackberry
Cercis orbiculata, western redbud
Chilopsis linearis, desert willow
Cupressus arizonica, Arizona cypress
Fraxinus velutina 'Fan-Tex', Fan-Tex ash
Juniperus species, junipers
Olneya tesota, desert ironwood
Parkinsonia 'Desert Museum', Desert Museum palo verde
Parkinsonia florida, blue palo verde
Parkinsonia microphylla, foothills palo verde
Pinus edulis, two-needle pinyon pine
Prosopis glandulosa, honey mesquite
Prunus virginiana var. *demissa*, western chokecherry
Quercus berberidifolia, inland scrub oak
Quercus turbinella, shrub live oak
Robinia neomexicana, desert locust
Sambucus nigra subsp. *canadensis*, Mexican elderberry

Shrubs

Abutilon palmeri, Indian mallow
Adenostoma fasciculatum, chamise
Amelanchier utahensis, serviceberry
Amorpha fruticosa, desert indigo
Arctostaphylos species, manzanitas
Artemisia species, sagebrushes
Baccharis pilularis, coyote brush
Baccharis sarothroides, desert broom
Caesalpinia gilliesii, desert bird of paradise
Calliandra species, fairy dusters
Ceanothus species
Cercocarpus montanus, mountain mahogany
Cleome isomeris, bladderpod
Encelia californica, California brittle bush
Encelia farinosa, white brittle bush
Ephedra species, joint firs
Ericameria laricifolia, larchleaf goldenbush
Ericameria nauseosa, rabbitbrush
Fallugia paradoxa, Apache plume
Forestiera pubescens, desert olive
Fouquieria splendens, ocotillo
Garrya elliptica, coast silktassel
Heteromeles arbutifolia, toyon
Justicia californica, chuparosa
Krascheninnikovia lanata, winterfat
Larrea tridentata, creosote bush
Lycium species, desert thorns
Mahonia species, barberries
Malosma laurina, laurel sumac
Nolina species, beargrass
Purshia stansburiana, Mexican cliffrose
Rhus species, sumacs
Rosa species, wild roses
Salvia species, sages

Vines

Calystegia macrostegia, island morning glory
Clematis ligusticifolia, western virgin's bower
Maurandya antirrhiniflora, snapdragon vine
Parthenocissus vitacea, thicket creeper
Vitis girdiana, desert wild grape

Groundcovers

Artemisia californica, California sagebrush
Artemisia ludoviciana, white sagebrush
Baccharis pilularis, prostrate coyote brush
Dudleya caespitosa, coast dudleya
Leymus condensatus, giant rye grass
Muhlenbergia rigens, deer grass
Nassella species, needlegrass

Cacti and Succulents

Agave species, century plants
Cylindropuntia species, chollas
Echinocereus species, hedgehog cacti
Ferocactus species, barrel cacti
Mammillaria species, fishhook cacti
Opuntia species, prickly pear cacti
Yucca species

Given room to spread, wildflowers such as giant four-o'clock (*Mirabilis multiflora*) serve as an attractive groundcover.

Landscaping with Groundcovers

Almost every landscape, whether small or large, private or commercial, has areas that receive no foot traffic but are also not suitable for trees, shrubs, or even turf grass. A groundcover can turn a visually empty space into an eye-catching attraction. Groundcovers serve two general purposes, one utilitarian, the other aesthetic: They prevent erosion and cover unsightly bare spots, and they add an active or unifying element to a landscape design, a dimension of visual interest beyond what a cover of turf grass or crushed stone can provide.

A grassy lawn is desirable for play and entertaining, but many areas of turf serve no function other than contributing a tailored appearance to the yard. On the other hand, a border filled with sprawling or prostrate plants provides visual relief to a wall, drive, sidewalk, or building front. Decorative groundcovers can also colorfully accent the area beneath open-branching shrubs and trees. A groundcover planting within a large paved area breaks the monotony and imparts a soft, cool feeling to the overall landscape. In cases where a tall plant would block the view in front of a window or store front, a vine or low-growing shrub can enhance the scene without obscuring the view.

Groundcovers also come to the rescue for areas that are difficult to maintain or have marginal growing conditions—such as shady sites or rocky, dry slopes—but where some type of vegetative cover is desirable. When used as an integral feature of a landscape design, groundcovers provide low-maintenance cover, as well as an extra touch of beauty.

Groundcover Qualities

For a plant to be both an effective and attractive groundcover, it must exhibit special growth characteristics. In searching for native groundcovers, landscapers and propagators look for plants that have a low growth habit and dense foliage and can adapt to a wide variety of habitats. The plant must be able to survive and thrive in harsh environmental conditions, such as shade, heat, drought, and infertile soil. In addition, the ideal groundcover grows and spreads rapidly and has evergreen foliage.

Nature has endowed many plants with some of these basic characteristics, but precious few have them all. Unfortunately, plants that are adapted to habitats severely limited in soil nutrients, moisture, or light seldom grow rapidly or develop dense foliage. The task of the propagators is to find those plants and plant varieties that have most of the basic requirements.

Ferns such as the giant chain fern (*Woodwardia fimbriata*) form a groundcover in the cool shade underneath a canopy of trees.

Fortunately, many naturally low-growing shrubs, mat-forming wildflowers, and weakly climbing vines are suitable for use as groundcovers. Some species adapt to almost any situation, while others require a particular habitat. The best have evergreen leaves, attractive flowers, or decorative fruit.

The glossy evergreen foliage of *Mahonia aquifolium* brings an interesting groundcover dimension.

The fine-textured needlegrasses *(Nassella)* replace turf grass at Barona Valley Ranch Resort in San Diego.

Planting and Maintaining Groundcovers

Don't expect to set out a few recommended plants on an arid and rocky or compacted and shady site and get a dense cover of vegetation the next growing season. That a plant has the potential for thick growth doesn't mean it can achieve that growth under marginal conditions. In a landscape setting, you want your plants to thrive, not just survive. A plant can cope with less than the best if it has a robust root system. In many cases, soil preparation is the key to establishing a successful groundcover planting.

If you want a complete cover, you must first remove all the competing vegetation, especially grasses. Do it in the beginning, and you won't have to spend hours removing unsightly weeds later. You also may need to work some organic matter, such as peat, compost, or manure, into the upper 8 to 12 inches of soil to give the roots a healthy growing medium. Third, mulch between the new settings to hold in soil moisture and to reduce weed invasion. In one or two growing seasons, the plants should reach their potential.

Once established, a dense groundcover is not totally maintenance-free. Many plants begin to lose their vigor in two to four years, and bare spots develop. You may need to periodically replace plants to keep the cover complete. Other plants grow so vigorously that they need regular pruning to maintain a tailored appearance. A dense groundcover requires less attention than a lawn, but don't expect it to be totally maintenance-free.

Maybe you're not enamored with a groundcover that requires regular attention. Remember that a groundcover doesn't have to provide complete foliage cover, so if you're willing to excuse some bare spots, other low-maintenance options are available. Many low-growing deciduous shrubs have decorative foliage, flowers, or fruit through most of the year, and perennial wildflowers can provide a seasonal accent. A mixture of ornamental native shrubs and perennial wildflowers can give your landscape seasonal variety and an elegance far exceeding that of a solid planting of turf grass or dwarf junipers.

The succulent coast dudleya (*Dudleya caespitosa*) can fill a garden spot with dramatic effect.

Native Plants Suitable for Groundcovers

Many native plants are suitable for use as groundcovers. The section on groundcovers in the "Native Plant Profiles" includes photos and descriptions of species whose primary landscape function is to provide groundcover, and which offer other attractive attributes for the garden. In addition, many shrubs, wildflowers, and vines can be used as a seasonal-fill groundcover, and these are listed here; for a full description and photos, refer to the "Native Plant Profiles" later in the book.

Low-Growing Shrubs

Agave shawii, Shaw's agave
Arctostaphylos cultivars, manzanitas: 'Arroyo Cascade', 'John Dourly'
Arctostaphylos edmundsonii cultivars, Little Sur manzanitas: 'Bert Johnson', 'Carmel Sur'
Arctostaphylos hookeri 'Wayside', Monterey manzanita
Arctostaphylos uva-ursi cultivars, bearberry manzanitas: 'Radiant', 'Wood's Compact'
Ceanothus cultivars, 'Centennial', 'Joyce Coulter'
Ceanothus gloriosus cultivars, Point Reyes ceanothus: 'Anchor Bay', 'Heart's Desire'
Ceanothus griseus cultivars, Carmel ceanothus: 'Diamond Heights', 'Yankee Point'
Ceanothus maritimus cultivars, maritime ceanothus: 'Frosty Dawn', 'Point Sierra', 'Popcorn'
Eriogonum fasciculatum cultivars, buckwheats: 'Bruce Dickerson', 'Dana Point', 'Theodore Payne', 'Warriner Lytle'
Nolina species, beargrass
Ribes viburnifolium, Catalina Island currant
Rosa woodsii, Wood's rose
Salvia cultivars, sages: 'Dara's Choice', 'Gracias', 'Mrs. Beard'
Salvia leucophylla cultivars, purple sage: 'Bee's Bliss', 'Point Sal'
Salvia mellifera cultivars, black sage: 'Green Carpet', 'Terra Seca'
Salvia munzii 'Emerald Cascade', emerald cascade sage

Perennial Wildflowers

Achillea millefolium, yarrow
Datura wrightii, sacred datura
Epilobium canum cultivars, California fuchsia
Erigeron glaucus, seaside daisy
Mirabilis multiflora, giant four-o'clock
Nama hispidum, rough nama
Oenothera species, evening primroses
Psilostrophe cooperi, paperflower
Solidago species, goldenrods
Thymophylla pentachaeta, dogweed
Viguiera laciniata, California sunflower

Vines

Calystegia macrostegia, island morning glory
Clematis ligusticifolia, western virgin's bower
Lonicera species, honeysuckles
Parthenocissus vitacea, thicket creeper
Vitis species, wild grapes

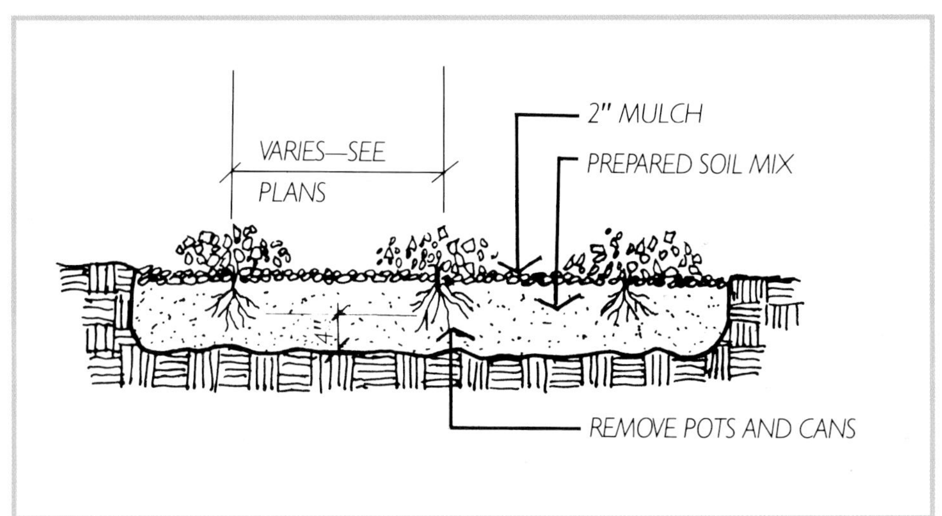

With proper soil preparation and plant spacing, a groundcover will quickly fill in its garden spot.

Thicket creeper (*Parthenocissus vitacea*) will rapidly cover walls and fences for both insulation and ornamental benefits.

Landscaping with Vines

Upright Flower Beds and Hanging Gardens

How would you like to turn that nondescript fence in your yard into an upright flower bed covered with fragrant blossoms? Why not transform your mailbox, gaslight, or porch column into a hanging garden of colorful flowers? Nature has supplied the perfect plants for such a conversion: vines. These versatile plants add natural beauty to your home landscape and require little maintenance.

Nature adapts every plant to a particular habitat and niche. Trees extend their arching limbs toward the sky, shrubs fill the spaces beneath the trees, and grasses and herbs cover the ground. In between, the vines twine in search of the sun. Many vines cling to their support with tendrils; some twist and twine around other objects; others cling with holdfasts.

Vines have other natural features that make them extraordinary landscaping plants. Adapted to growing in the dappled shadows beneath trees, most vines can tolerate both partial shade and full sun. They grow vigorously and are hardy, and many have ornamental foliage, flowers, and fruit. Wherever vines grow, they add natural beauty and visual interest.

Before buying a plant or turning a shovel of soil, you should determine how a vine will best fit into your yard. Do you want a dominant feature, a dense groundcover, or a graceful accent? Low-growing vines with slender stems provide a delicate touch, while high-climbing or thickly branching species rapidly become a major landscape element. Let's see how these special plants can beautify your landscape.

California grape (*Vitis californica*) includes fall color among its multifaceted landscape uses.

Vines As Dominant Features

Wire fences and rock or masonry walls can support vigorously growing, densely foliated vines such as trumpet creeper and grape vines. The thick evergreen foliage turns an ordinary wire fence into an extraordinary privacy barrier covered with flamboyant yellow flowers in the spring. If you want scarlet spring and summer flowers, plant southern honeysuckle. You can enjoy brilliant shades of red and orange foliage in the autumn by planting a thicket creeper along your fence or on an arbor. A slender-stemmed vine with dense foliage can turn a gaslight, a mailbox, or even an unsightly old stump into a prominent landscape feature in your yard. However, most vines will overrun their supports if not pruned periodically.

Vines As Accent Plants

An accent vine should complement but not obscure the object supporting it. Low-climbing vines with thin foliage are good for this. They bring visual interest and gracefully accent a wire fence without obscuring the view. A rock, rail, or lath fence forms the perfect backdrop for slender climbers, such as the unusual snapdragon vine. The small, delicate features complement mailboxes without overpowering them. A gaslight draped with the scarlet fruit of a balsam gourd becomes an eye-catching element of the landscape.

Don't forget that vines can work their magic on porch railings and columns, too. Vines will quickly cover chicken wire or a guide wire wrapped around a post. Some of my earliest memories are of playing on our front porch, shaded by a screen of jasmine growing on chicken wire stretched from the ground to the porch roof.

Customize Your Landscape

The next step after determining whether you need a dominant or accent planting is to choose the type of vine. Do you want a woody or herbaceous species, one with evergreen or deciduous leaves, or one with colorful flowers or fruit? For privacy and screen plantings, you'll want evergreens. In most other applications, deciduous and evergreen vines work equally well. Woody vines will densely cover a fence, porch column, or trellis. Twining vines and those with tendrils quickly climb on fences, trellises, and guide wires around posts, while those with holdfasts climb well on rock and masonry, although they may eventually damage the mortar. Avoid letting vines cover wooden buildings. They hasten decay and must be removed or destroyed when the surface requires painting.

The high-climbing species, such as trumpet creepers, develop thick, heavy branches and should be used only on fences or posts that can provide adequate support. Most low climbers have slender, twining branches that will not damage lath fences or trellises and are easier to contain.

Planting

Like any landscape addition, vines require careful planning and selection. For a dense cover along a fence, plant a high-climbing, thickly foliaged vine every 8 to 12 feet and low-climbing vines with slender stems every 3 to 4 feet. For variety, plant one section of your fence with a spring-blooming species and another with a summer or fall bloomer. Herbaceous perennial vines grow rapidly during the spring and summer and die back to the ground with the first freeze. The rootstock survives the winter and sprouts in the spring.

Nurseries offer a wide selection of woody vines, and you can choose herbaceous varieties from seed stores and catalogs, or you can gather your own seeds. Each vine listed in the "Native Plant Profiles" has flamboyant flowers, ornamental foliage, or colorful fruit and will provide generations of beauty in your yard. So, plant a vine and watch it twine!

Landscaping with Cacti and Succulents

Agave and barrel cactus at Huntington Botanical Gardens, San Marino.

As the first European botanists crisscrossed the Americas, they encountered a bizarre family of plants unknown in the Old World. Unsure of the classification, they applied the Greek word *kaktos*, meaning "thistle." Modern botanists still argue about the proper organization of these puzzling plants. But one thing is constant: From the fifteenth century until the present, plant enthusiasts have found these unique plants irresistible. The demand for cacti was immediate and has increased through the centuries. Today, collectors annually strip tons of cacti from North and South American deserts to sell in souvenir shops and nurseries. With many species now either threatened or endangered, we are loving our native cacti to death. Fortunately, many cacti propagated from seeds and cuttings are available in the nursery trade. As a point of principle, be sure the cactus you buy wasn't collected from the countryside, either in the United States or Mexico. Our native plants belong in nature, too.

Handle with Care

Cacti look tough, feel tough, and grow in a harsh environment, but they need tender care to survive in rock and xeriscape gardens. You see, cacti are specialists. They have adapted to marginal conditions with extremes of heat, light, and drought. Though cacti grow from 14,000-foot mountain peaks to torrid desert basins, most suffer if moved far from home. Many species have become so specialized to local conditions that they exist only in a single desert valley or on a particular geological outcropping. If you want your cacti to thrive, you must understand what makes them different from other landscape plants.

Cacti have drastically modified leaves, stems, and roots to catch, store, and conserve water in a desert environment. A netlike root system spreads out and rapidly soaks up moisture from fickle but usually torrential rains. To combat extended droughts, the thick succulent stems store water for long periods. Instead of normal leaves, which lose considerable water, cactus leaves have evolved into rigid spines. This dense armament both shades and cools the plant and protects the succulent interior from thirsty desert creatures. With no leaves for photosynthesis, the green stems perform the task of food production. A thick, waxy epidermis covers cacti to further reduce water loss. Some cacti are so well adapted to their arid habitat that they transpire 6,000 times less water than ordinary plants. As a result of this reduced transpiration, many cacti grow at an extremely slow rate.

Overwatering: The Kiss of Death

Cactus roots soak up water as fast as possible, and the stems store and hold water as tenaciously as possible. In your garden, you want to find the magic line between watering enough to maximize growth and flowering, and overwatering, which can kill some cacti overnight. A root crown standing in water for twenty-four hours is susceptible to rot and fungus invasion. A well-draining pot or garden is an absolute must. In the winter some cacti lose water to protect against frost and may appear shriveled. Don't water a wilted cactus unless you know the plant is stressed for water. The plant is probably just adapting to the overall environmental conditions. Adopt the saying, "Don't water your cactus until it rains in Blythe," and your cacti will feel right at home.

Planting

Having the right soil mix for potted cacti or in a rock garden is necessary for success. Potted cacti do well in a neutral soil, with an inch or so of granite gravel on the bottom of the pot for good drainage, then several inches of garden potting soil. Fill the remainder of the pot with coarse sand. For gardens, mix sand in with your garden soil if necessary to ensure proper drainage, and plant each cactus on a slightly elevated mound. Be sure your garden doesn't get regular runoff from lawn irrigation. Most of all, pay attention to the natural habitat of the cactus. Some species grow under desert shrubs and may benefit from some added leaf mulch.

Before transplanting a cactus or cutting, let it sit bare-rooted in a shady location for several days until the roots have thoroughly dried and calloused. Fungus easily invades fresh cuts or damaged roots.

Light Is Right

To bloom, cacti need heat and light. Many cacti do not begin photosynthesis until the temperature exceeds 75 degrees F. Your cactus garden should receive more than a half-day of full sunlight to stimulate flowering and growth. The delicate flowers typically burst into bloom during the heat of the day, and many wither by nightfall. Both the spectacular flowers and the short blooming period represent adaptations that help the flower win a race against time. To ensure pollination, the flower must attract insects, thus the showy blossoms. Insects are active when the day is hottest, so the fragile flowers open in the afternoon. A bloom unpollinated during its first day may never get another chance. Many of the unprotected flowers become tidbits for the hungry critters active during the cool of the night.

When your cacti burst into bloom, you can feel a sense of satisfaction for two reasons. First, the ephemeral flowers add a flamboyant, yet delicate, beauty to your yard. Second, you know that your garden duplicates the plant's environmental requirements closely enough for it not just to survive, but to thrive and bloom.

Cacti are a fascinating combination of tough-looking spines and delicate flowers.

Southern California's native wildflowers provide a rich palette of colors and forms, as exhibited by these tidy tips (*Layia platyglossa*).

Landscaping with Wildflowers

Nature seems to defy the logic of every conscientious gardener. Beautiful flowerbeds are the result of laborious hours of fertilizing; of fighting weeds, disease, and vermin; and of carefully mulching and watering the tender seedlings. Yet, without a gardener's care, patches of undisturbed ground across the countryside abound with a luxurious growth of wildflowers from early spring into fall.

The beauty radiating from nature's helter-skelter flower arrangements inspires every flower lover. Like magic, the stony hillsides, open grasslands, deserts, and woodlands burst forth with flower displays that make the most expert gardener envious. What a treat if we could have those unspoiled scenes of nature duplicated in our own yards!

Though you use the same gardening techniques for growing both domestic and native flowers, cultivating wildflowers has one basic goal that is different from formal flower gardening: You are trying to duplicate the conditions in the wild. The standard green-thumb skills and intuition are needed, as well as the ability to recognize the unique growing conditions that enable each species of wildflower to thrive. Traditionally, growers boast of their flower "gardens," but the wildflower enthusiast will want to show you his or her newly created wildflower "habitat."

The first step in cultivating wildflowers is to understand the microhabitat of your plot. Is the area exposed to warm morning, northeast sun or blazing, afternoon southwest sun? Does radiated heat from walkways, drives, walls, or landscape boulders add a few extra degrees of warmth to the plot? Do you need to mulch to keep roots cool and moist or add sand to increase drainage? Carefully scrutinize soil, light, and moisture conditions. What was the natural habitat before houses modified the environment? Don't expect moist woodland species to thrive on a sandy desert lawn.

Each species of wildflower grows within a certain range of environmental conditions. These conditions—the pH, texture, and composition of the soil, the slope, exposure, and moisture—define the flower's optimum habitat. The gardener must replicate the natural conditions as closely as possible if the favored plant is to grow successfully in the home plot.

The wildflower aficionado, before burying a seed or transplanting a seedling, becomes well acquainted with the flower's needs and the garden's microhabitat. A little homework will avoid the oft-repeated mistake, and resulting disappointment, of planting a shade-loving plant in full sunlight, or a plant requiring moisture and humidity in a hot, dry exposure. Choosing the species of wildflowers for your yard should receive as much consideration as planning the most formal landscape.

Perhaps you can create several microhabitats within your yard. An open lawn is ideal for sun-adapted plants, a tree-shaded corner for shade-tolerant species, or a poolside patio for moisture-loving flowers.

The quickest way to stock your garden is by purchasing seeds, seedlings, or bedding plants from a nursery. If this is your preferred course, beware of spectacular offers in almanacs and Sunday supplements. Avoid seed packs with general mixes of wildflower species from across the nation and around the world. They usually contain incompatible shade- and sun-loving plants. Many native seed sources offer mixes specifically designed for the different regions and elevations. You can also buy mixes for hummingbird and butterfly gardens and for seasonal color blends.

Planting Wildflowers from Seed

Whenever possible, you should purchase plants and seeds from a native plant nursery or arboretum in your area. Local garden clubs sometimes offer plant and seed exchanges from surplus plants in the members' yards. Or, you can collect your own seed in permitted areas. Be aware, though, that seed or plant gathering on public land is generally prohibited. Planting seeds and stock from your region ensures that your landscape additions are adapted to your climate and gives you the satisfaction of re-establishing the botanical heritage that existed before urban sprawl engulfed the countryside.

Nearly 100 species and varieties of *Penstemon* are native to Southern California.

Collecting Seed

Many wildflower lovers are not content with buying prepackaged seeds. Obtaining seeds and plants for a carefully prepared garden can be a year-round hobby. Discovering a specimen flower, marking it, and returning to collect the seeds adds to the sense of accomplishment of a successful garden. The timing of seed harvesting is critical, or the collector may find an empty seed pod on the prized flower. Remember, collecting plants or seeds on public property, including roadsides, is illegal.

Many flowers have elaborate methods for dispersing their seeds. Numerous members of the sunflower family (Compositae) send their seeds floating in the breeze, while the dry pods of legumes (Leguminosae) split open, scattering their seeds on the ground. You can either pick the ripe pods and seed heads before they completely dry or place a muslin or paper sack over the flowers after the

The common sunflower (*Helianthus annuus*) offers uncommonly large and profuse blooms.

seeds have formed. After collecting, be sure to dry the seeds completely before storing them so they don't mold. Some seeds have succulent pulp that must be removed by rubbing on a screen. Sometimes you can clean small seeds in a blender at very low speed without damaging them.

Store the cleaned seeds in the refrigerator in jars, or in a cool, dry place safe from insects. Keep the seeds in paper bags (not plastic) to prevent molding, and plant within one year for best results.

Plants adapt to winter freezes by producing seeds that go through a dormant period. This dormancy prevents premature germination on warm fall days. After several months of cold weather, the inherent dormancy is broken, allowing the seeds to germinate as the soil warms up to 40 degrees F. If you obtain seeds in the early spring, you can break the temperature dormancy by storing them in the refrigerator for two to eight weeks before planting.

When to Plant

Wildflowers naturally reseed themselves several weeks after blooming, in the spring for early-blooming species and in summer or fall for late bloomers. Generally, you will want to plant your seeds from late August through November, depending on the onset of winter. This allows the cooler temperatures to break any seed dormancy. Other seeds need the fall rains to germinate, winter moisture to develop a root system, and spring rains to bloom.

Sowing the Seed

The first step in sowing the seed in your garden is to prepare a seedbed. Indiscriminately scattering seed is just setting the table for seed-eating insects and birds. Remove all vegetation just as you would when planting a vegetable garden. Rake the soil to break up the surface no more than an inch deep. Since some wildflower seeds are so small, you might want to mix your seeds with damp sand to give a more even distribution. After evenly scattering the seeds, lightly rake them into the soil, no deeper than two to four times their diameter. Firm up the soil and lightly water.

Watering and Waiting

All seeds need water to germinate, so you should water lightly three to four times a week to ensure optimum germination. If you live in higher elevations with hard winters, water the seedlings and the seedbed weekly until the first freeze if there are no fall rains; at lower elevations, moisten the seedbed weekly through December and January. This will ensure that spring-germinating seeds receive sufficient moisture. If you have a dry spring, supplemental watering will provide for optimum growth and blooming.

You may want to plant your seeds in a protected seedbed, cold frame, or peat pots and wait until the seedlings are well established before transplanting to your garden. You can start many species indoors from January to March, or four to six weeks before they are to be transplanted.

Natural Reseeding

Though annuals live only one growing season, and many perennials only a few, you can have a beautiful wildflower garden year after year by letting the flowers reseed themselves. After the flowers fade and the plants die, be sure to wait until the seeds have fallen before mowing or removing the old plant. Give the plants a good shake to dislodge all the seeds. If you have a naturalized area, leave the mowed stubble to cover and protect the seeds.

If you want a more dependable display of wildflowers, plant perennials along with the annuals. Most perennial wildflowers are herbaceous and die to the ground in the winter, but sprout from the roots with the first warm weather. They add color and beauty and may even spread to form flamboyant blankets of color and mixed bouquets that get prettier as the years pass. As a bonus, many bloom until the first frost.

Paint Your Yard with Perennial Flower Gardens

Imagine a flower garden—bordering your walk, decorating the corner of your yard, or edging your pool—that greets each season with a profusion of different-colored blooms. As the seasons progress, you have an ever-changing combination of flowers, from early-spring bloomers to fall ones that don't fade until the first frost.

Designing a perennial garden takes more forethought than just planting short flowers in the front and tall ones in the back. Half the fun is becoming the artist and arranging the blooming times and colors as though the garden were your canvas. Plant so that you will have a good balance of colors throughout the year. Use masses of each flower to create bold splashes, with adjacent colors complementing each other. Remember, your garden is a three-dimensional canvas. Mix naturally mounding plants with upright, sprawling, and cascading species so that they don't overrun one another. Don't forget foliage color, either. You can combine various shades of grays and greens for a delightful variation of hues.

Place species with attractive foliage—such as desert marigold, dudleya, and dogweed—for a good year-round appearance and to cover the bare spots left when annuals and deciduous species die back. Avoid planting shrubby species, such as brittle bush, sacred datura, giant four-o'clock, and globemallow, which respond to supplemental water by doubling and tripling in size, with penstemons, lupines, larkspurs, violets, and other delicate species that are easily overcome by out-of-control neighbors.

Planting a perennial wildflower isn't the same as planting a tree. Many perennials live only a few seasons, so your flower garden will need periodic maintenance. You'll need to thin and cut back vigorously growing flowers and occasionally replace some plants, but no major replanting will be necessary. As a work-in-progress, your perennial garden will provide season after season of enjoyment as it evolves with your creative touch.

Bringing wildlife into the garden is one of the great attractions of landscaping with native plants. Hummingbirds flock to the blossoms of ocotillo in summer.

Landscaping to Attract Wildlife

There's good news and bad news when you create a well-designed native plant landscape. Chances are, the assortment of food-producing, shelter-providing plants will attract wildlife. A yard that becomes a magnet for wildlife is good if you love birds and butterflies and plant accordingly. It's bad if rabbits and deer consider your tender new plants the best buffet in town. Fortunately, guidelines and programs are available to help you welcome the desirable birds and butterflies and protect your investment from nibbling intruders.

To me, the most compelling reason for landscaping with plants native to my area is to repair some of the environmental damage caused by urban growth. Habitat alteration is inevitable, but we can lessen the impact by preserving as much of the indigenous plant community as possible. If we maintain a diverse association of plants, our neighborhoods will attract and support a variety of birds, butterflies, squirrels, and other enjoyable wildlife.

Wildlife and urban development can be compatible. Many species of animals can coexist with humans if certain requirements are met. Like us, wildlife needs food, shelter, water, and space to carry on daily, or nightly, activities. The animals most successful in cohabiting with humans are ground-feeding birds, butterflies, lizards, and small nocturnal mammals. They share our urban environment without getting in our way too much.

Put Out a Year-Round Welcome Mat

Many people go to extreme measures and great expense to attract birds to their yards. You can easily spend hundreds of dollars on birdhouses for wrens, chickadees, and other hole-nesting species. Maintaining feeders with varieties of seeds and suet can become a daily ritual. For those who love wildlife, having a yard full of birds is worth the trouble and expense. But with the proper selection of landscaping plants, you can let nature furnish most of the room and board, while you relax and enjoy the company.

As you design your landscape, consider the three primary requirements for attracting birds, butterflies, and other wildlife: food, water, and shelter. Select plants that provide a year-round supply of seeds, nuts, flowers, and fruit. Plants with tube-shaped flowers (particularly red) attract hummingbirds; acacias are famous nectar plants for honeybees; flowers in the sunflower and verbena families, milkweeds, and most other showy flowers attract butterflies. Trees and brushy shrubs provide nesting locations for birds that build open nests, such as mockingbirds, cardinals, doves, thrashers, and jays. Providing a constant supply of clean water can be as easy as a dish or birdbath, or as elaborate as a fountain or flowing waterfall. With a diversity of plants in your yard that meet the habitat requirements of a variety of species, you can enjoy a year-round population of resident and migratory birds.

Above: Planting species that provide shelter is a key to attracting wildlife. Here a wren makes its nest in a treelike cholla cactus.

Left: Numerous species of butterflies will alight on daisies and other garden flowers to feed.

Unwelcome Wildlife

A creek, a wooded park, or even a vacant lot can be the home of an opossum, raccoon, or skunk. At night they emerge and unobtrusively forage for food, often dining on rodents and reptiles, as well as gleaning spilled trash and uneaten dog and cat food. For five years, I had an opossum, skunk, and cat living under my house in perfect harmony with each other and us.

Wild mammals are usually considered vermin and reservoirs of disease for our domestic animals and are eradicated when possible. However, in most instances they are as harmless as the squirrels we enjoy in our trees. Snakes suffer a worse reputation. The few poisonous species have instilled such fear in humans that most people consider all snakes public enemies. The harmless snakes eat rodents, lizards, frogs, and toads and should be welcomed neighbors.

As subdivisions spread farther into the countryside and more and more Chaparral and Coastal Sage Scrub become streets and yards, wildlife either dies or adapts to the new environment. A number of small animals often find enough undisturbed habitat to survive and become habituated to urban living. But not all of our wildlife neighbors are welcome guests in your yards. Deer and rabbits often consider our prized landscape plants a tender item for their salad bowl.

You can fence off your garden plot and put wire cages around your saplings, but unless you have an 8-foot-high, deer-proof fence around your home lot, your landscape may become an herbivore buffet. Some plants come with their own defense, either inedible woody, woolly, or prickly foliage, or bitter-tasting, volatile oils. If you have a problem with unwelcome dinner guests, consider some of the deer- and rabbit-resistant plants listed in this chapter. Remember, no plant is deer proof, just resistant. In a hot, dry summer when tender forbs are scarce, deer will feast on plants they normally wouldn't touch.

Wildscapes Program

The National Wildlife Federation sponsors a program with guidelines and specifications for establishing backyard habitats for wildlife (www.nwf.org/backyardwildlifehabitat). The habitat restoration and conservation plan helps rural and urban residents plan landscapes that provide wildlife habitats by planting native vegetation and installing birdbaths, ponds, and feeders. A properly designed backyard landscape provides places for birds, small mammals, and other wildlife to feed and drink, escape from predators, and raise their young.

Deer- and Rabbit-Resistant Plants

Trees and Shrubs

For trees, be sure to cage all saplings and small trees until foliage is above the forage line (about 6 feet high).

Agave species, century plants
Cactus species
Caesalpinia gilliesii, desert bird of paradise
Chilopsis linearis, desert willow
Ericameria nauseosa, rabbitbrush
Fallugia paradoxa, Apache plume
Garrya elliptica, coast silktassel
Juniperus species, junipers
Larrea tridentata, creosote bush
Lycium species, desert thorn
Mahonia species, barberries
Rhus species, sumacs
Salvia species, sages
Yucca species

Wildflowers and Groundcovers

Achillea species, yarrows
Baileya multiradiata, desert marigold
Coreopsis species
Datura wrightii, sacred datura
Delphinium species, larkspurs
Helianthus annuus, common sunflower
Linum species, flax
Lobelia cardinalis, cardinal flower
Lupinus species, lupines
Psilostrophe cooperi, paperflower
Pteridium aquilinum, bracken fern
Salvia species, sages
Solidago species, goldenrods
Thymophylla pentachaeta, dogweed

Flowering Plants That Attract Hummingbirds

Trees, Shrubs, and Vines	Spring	Summer	Fall	Winter
Agave species	X			
Amorpha fruticosa, desert indigo	X			
Arbutus menziesii, Pacific madrone	X	X		
Arctostaphylos species, manzanitas	X			
Calliandra eriophylla, fairy duster	X			
Calystegia macrostegia, island morning glory	X		X	X
Cercis orbiculata, western redbud	X			
Chilopsis linearis, desert willow	X	X		
Comarostaphylis diversifolia, summer holly		X		
Diplacus aurantiacus, bush monkey flower	X	X	X	X
Fouquieria splendens, ocotillo	X	X		
Justicia californica, chuparosa	X	X		
Lonicera species, honeysuckles	X	X	X	
Lycium species, desert thorns	X			
Malacothamnus species, bush mallows		X	X	
Parkinsonia species, palo verdes	X			
Prosopis glandulosa, honey mesquite	X			
Ribes species, currants	X		X	X
Robinia neomexicana, desert locust		X		
Salvia species, sages		X	X	
Sambucus nigra subsp. *canadensis*, Mexican elderberry	X	X	X	X
Trichostema lanatum, woolly blue curls		X		
Yucca species		X		

Wildflowers and Groundcovers	Spring	Summer	Fall	Winter
Aquilegia species, columbine	X	X		
Castilleja species, paintbrushes	X	X		
Delphinium cardinale, scarlet larkspur	X	X		
Dudleya species	X	X		X
Epilobium canum, California fuchsia	X	X		X
Lobelia cardinalis, cardinal flower		X		
Lupinus species, lupines	X			
Mimulus species, monkey flowers		X		
Mirabilis multiflora, giant four-o'clock	X	X	X	
Penstemon species, beardtongues	X	X		
Sphaeralcea species, globemallows	X	X	X	
Symphoricarpos, species, snowberries	X	X		

Cacti and Succulents	Spring	Summer	Fall	Winter
Cylindropuntia species, chollas	X			
Echinocereus triglochidiatus, hedgehog	X			
Ferocactus cylindraceus, California barrel cactus	X			
Opuntia species, prickly pears	X			

Seed and Fruit Plants for Birds

The following plants are particularly suitable for supplying the food and shelter requirements of many bird species. Each plant's primary season for producing seed and fruit is indicated. Refer to the "Native Plant Profiles" for more details on the plants. Select the ones that fit your landscape design and are adapted to your landscape zone.

Trees	**Spring**	**Summer**	**Fall**	**Winter**
Acacia farnesiana, huisache		X	X	X
Acacia greggii, catclaw acacia		X	X	X
Acer macrophyllum, big-leaf maple		X	X	
Alnus species, alders		X		
Arbutus menziesii, Pacific madrone		X	X	
Celtis laevigata, netleaf hackberry			X	X
Cercis orbiculata, western redbud			X	X
Chilopsis linearis, desert willow			X	
Fraxinus velutina, Arizona ash			X	
Juniperus species, junipers			X	X
Pinus species, pines			X	X
Platanus racemosa, sycamore				X
Prosopis glandulosa, honey mesquite			X	X
Prunus virginiana, chokecherry		X		
Quercus species, oaks		X	X	X
Sambucus nigra subsp. *canadensis*, Mexican elderberry	X	X	X	X
Washingtonia filifera, California fan palm			X	X

Shrubs	**Spring**	**Summer**	**Fall**	**Winter**
Adenostoma fasciculatum, chamise		X		
Amelanchier species, serviceberries		X		
Amorpha fruticosa, desert indigo			X	
Arctostaphylos species, manzanitas		X	X	
Artemisia species, sagebrushes	X	X	X	
Baccharis species		X	X	
Ceanothus species and cultivars		X	X	
Cercocarpus montanus, mountain mahogany		X	X	
Comarostaphylis diversifolia, summer holly	X	X	X	
Cornus species, dogwoods	X	X	X	
Encelia species, brittle bushes		X	X	X
Ericameria species, rabbitbrush/goldenbush		X	X	
Eriogonum species, buckwheats			X	
Forestiera pubescens, desert olive		X		
Frangula californica, coffeeberry		X	X	
Heteromeles arbutifolia, toyon				X
Lycium species, desert thorns		X		
Mahonia species, barberries		X	X	
Malacothamnus species, bush mallows		X	X	
Malosma laurina, laurel sumac		X	X	
Myrica californica, wax myrtle			X	
Nolina species, beargrass			X	
Rhamnus species, redberries		X	X	
Rhus species, sumacs		X	X	
Ribes species, gooseberries			X	X
Rosa species, wild roses			X	X
Salvia species, sages		X	X	
Shepherdia argentea, silver buffaloberry				

continued on next page

Seed and Fruit Plants for Birds (continued)

Wildflowers, Vines, and Groundcovers	Spring	Summer	Fall	Winter
Achillea species, yarrows		X		
Eschscholzia californica, California poppy		X		
Helianthus species, sunflowers		X	X	X
Lonicera species, honeysuckles	X	X	X	
Lupinus species, lupines		X		
Mirabilis multiflora, giant four-o'clock	X	X	X	
Parthenocissus vitacea, thicket creeper		X	X	
Solanum species, blue witches			X	
Symphoricarpos species, snowberries			X	X
Viguiera laciniata, California sunflower	X		X	X
Vitis species, wild grape			X	

Cacti and Succulents	Spring	Summer	Fall	Winter
Agave species		X		
Echinocereus triglochidiatus, hedgehog cactus		X		
Ferocactus cylindraceus, California barrel cactus		X		
Mammillaria species, fishhook cacti		X		
Opuntia species, prickly pears		X		
Yucca species		X	X	

A wren carefully rests on the spiny stems of a cholla.

Plants That Attract Butterflies

More than 100 species of butterflies are found in Southern California. A properly designed butterfly garden includes both nectar plants for adults and host plants that provide food for larvae. Butterflies feed on both native and introduced nectar plants, but only lay their eggs on native plants or closely related species. Butterflies need warm, sunny locations for feeding, ideally 4 to 6 hours of sunlight per day. They generally lay eggs on only one or two native species, so a variety of nectar and larval host plants is the key to attracting numerous species. The composite (sunflower, daisy, aster), buckwheat, ceanothus, legume (lupines, acacias), oak, willow, and salvia families attract large numbers of species.

* Plants marked with an asterisk are not featured in this book but attract a large number of butterfly species.

Abutilon species, Indian mallow
larva (laviana skipper)

Achillea species, yarrow
nectar (gray hairstreak, checkerspot species, many species)

Adenostoma species, chamise
larva (gray hairstreak)

Aesculus californica, California buckeye
larva (echo blue, spring azure)

Agave species, agave
larva (giant skipper)

Alnus species, alders
larva (western tiger swallowtail)

Amorpha californica, false indigo
larva (gray hairstreak, common hairstreak, California dogface, southern dogface, silver-spotted skipper, northern cloudy wing)

Arctostaphylos species, manzanitas
nectar (monarch)

Arbutus menziesii, Pacific madrone
larva (western brown elfin, Doudoroff's hairstreak)

**Asclepias* species, milkweed
larva (monarch, queen, acmon blue, striated queen)
nectar (acmon blue, striated queen, west coast lady)

**Aster* species, asters
nectar (many species)

**Astragalis* species, loco weed
larva (many species)

Baccharis pilularis, coyote brush
nectar (monarch, swallowtail species, buckeye, painted lady, acmon blue)

Castilleja species, paintbrush
larva (Wright's checkerspot)

Ceanothus species and cultivars
larva (hairstreak species, pale swallowtail, brown elf, spring azure, echo blue, duskywing species, California tortoiseshell, ceanothus silk moth)

Cercocarpus species, mountain mahogany
larva (hairstreak species)

Celtis reticulata, hackberry
larva (American snout)

Chilopsis linearis, desert willow
larva (western swallowtail)

Coreopsis species
nectar (red admiral)

Cornus glabra, brown dogwood
larva (spring azure, echo blue)

Diplacus aurantiacus, bush monkey flower
larva (common buckeye, variable checkerspot)
nectar ('Chalcedon' variable checkerspot, many species)

Dudleya lanceolata, live forever
larva (Sonora blue)

Encelia californica, California sunflower
larva (fatal metalmark, dusky metalmark)
nectar (many species)

Erigeron species, seaside daisy, fleabane
larva (California dogface)
nectar (many species)

Epilobium species, fuchsia
nectar (giant swallowtail, California dogface, white-lined sphinx moth)

Ericameria species, rabbitbrush, goldenbush
larva (northern checkerspot)
nectar (buckeye, painted lady skippers)

Eriogonum fasciculatum, buckwheat
larva (hairstreak species, blue species, Mormon metal mark, large marble, Gorgon copper, many species)
nectar (acmon blue, square-spotted blue, mournful duskywing, tailed copper, green and gray hairstreaks, American lady, painted lady, Mormon metalmark, many species)

Frangula californica, coffeeberry
larva (pale swallowtail)

Fraxinus species, ash
larva (Melissa blue)

Helianthus species, sunflower
larva (painted lady, bordered patch)

Juniperus species, juniper
larva (hairstreak species)

Linum species, flax
larva (variegated fritillary)

Lobelia species, cardinal flower
nectar (western tiger swallowtail, northern white-skipper)

**Lotus* species, deerweed
larva (many species)

Lupinus species
larva (painted lady, blue species, hairstreak species, many species)
Malacothamnus fasciculatus, bush mallow
larva (northern white-skipper)
Mimulus species, monkey flower
larva (common buckeye, variable checkerspot)
**Monardella* species, coyote mint
nectar (many species)
Olneya tesota, desert ironweed
larva (funereal duskywing)
Penstemon species, beardtongue
larva (long-tailed skipper, 'Chalcedon' variable checkerspot)
Pinus species, pine tree
larva (pine white, elfin species, buckeye)
Platanus racemosa, sycamore
larva (western tiger swallowtail)
Populus species, cottonwood
larva (morning cloak, western tiger swallowtail, viceroy, dreamy duskywing, admiral species)
Prosopus species, mesquites
larva (Palmer's metalmark, long-tailed skipper, hairstreak species, blue, species)
Prunus species
larva (coral hairstreak, pale swallowtail, two-tailed swallowtail, Lorquin's admiral)
Purshia species, cliffrose
larva (painted lady, Behr's hairstreak)
Quercus agrifolia
larva (California sister, propertius duskywing, mournful duskywing)
Quercus chrysolepis, canyon oak
larva (canyon oak, California sister, propertius duskywing)
Quercus douglasii, blue oak
larva (gold-hunter's hairstreak, mournful duskywing, propertius duskywing)
Quercus turbinella, scrub oak
larva (hairstreak species, propertius duskywing)
Quercus lobata, valley oak
larva (mournful duskywing, propertius duskywing)
Rhamnus crocea, redberry
larva (Hermes copper, pale swallowtail)
Rhus trilobata, three-leaf sumac
larva ('Desert' Sheridan's hairstreak)
Ribes species, gooseberry, current
nectar (tailed copper, zephyr angelwing, cloudy copper)
**Salix* species, willow trees
larva (many species)
Salvia species
larva (many species)
nectar (many species)
Sphaeralcea species, globemallow
larva (west coast lady, laviana white-skipper, northern white-skipper, white-checkered skipper)
Stanleya pinnata, prince's plume
larva (Becker's white)
Symphoricarpos species, snowberry
larva (snowberry clearwing moth)
Trichostema lanatum, woolly blue curls
nectar (California dogface, northern white-skipper, western tiger swallowtail, monarch)
**Trifolium* species, clover
larva (many species)
**Viola* species, violets
larva (fritillary species, western meadow, many species)
Yucca species, yucca
larva (giant-skipper species)

Other Butterfly Gardening Resources

Brown, Brian V., and Julian P. Donahue. *Butterfly Gardening in Southern California.* Los Angeles: Natural History Museum of Los Angeles County, 1999.

Stokes, Donald, Lillian Stokes, and Ernest Williams. *Stokes Butterfly Book: The Complete Guide to Butterfly Gardening, Identification, and Behavior.* New York: Little, Brown and Company, 1991.

The Butterfly Site (www.thebutterflysite.com/california-butterflies.shtml)

Las Pilitas Nursery (www.laspilitas.com/butterfl.htm)

Los Angeles Chapter of the North American Butterfly Association (www.naba.org/chapters/nabala)

Wildscaping.com (www.wildscaping.com)

Native Plant Profiles

Trees

Acacia farnesiana

Acacia farnesiana flowers

Acacia farnesiana (*Acacia smallii*)

Huisache or sweet acacia

Native Distribution: dry slopes; naturalized, below 1,000 feet; Southern California: Imperial, Riverside, San Diego County; east to Florida; Mexico.
Landscape Zone: Chaparral.
Size: 15–25 feet tall.
Leaves: deciduous.
Flowers: February–May; round, golden, fragrant.
Fruit: seed pods, round, 2–3 inches long.
Soil: adaptable, well or slow draining.
Exposure: full sun.
Temperature: cold hardy to 20 degrees F.
Water: drought tolerant, 8 inches/year minimum.
Propagation: scarified seeds.
Profile: In the spring, the barren limbs of huisache turn into golden wands and perfume the air with a profusion of flowers. Its fernlike foliage and rounded crown cast dense shade as the tree matures. Lower branches tend to droop and require pruning. The tree's moderate size makes it appropriate for small areas unsuitable for a large tree. It naturally develops multiple trunks and a vaselike shape, and huisache can be trimmed into a densely foliated shrub or sheared hedge. The numerous slender branches have pairs of pinlike thorns, making it an effective physical barrier hedge. In the northern extremes of its range, hard freezes nip flower production, cause limb loss, or freeze the tree to the ground. Huisache, a widespread naturalized plant along the south coast, has been planted ornamentally since the 1600s.

Acacia greggii

Catclaw acacia

Native Distribution: desert washes, flats, grasslands; deserts, below 5,000 feet; Southern California: Imperial, Riverside, San Bernardino, San Diego counties; east to Texas, Nevada, Utah; Mexico.
Landscape Zone: Creosote Bush Scrub, Pinyon-Juniper Woodland.
Size: 15–30 feet, shrubby.
Leaves: deciduous.
Flowers: April–June; creamy yellow spikes.
Fruit: 5-inch, flat pods.
Soil: sandy, alkaline, well draining.
Exposure: full sun to partial shade.
Temperature: cold hardy to 0 degrees F.
Water: drought tolerant, 8 inches/year minimum.
Propagation: scarified seeds.

Profile: This shrubby acacia makes a delightful single- or multitrunked ornamental tree reaching 30 feet, but you'll have to prune it to the desired shape. You'll also have to isolate this bad boy with vicious thorns. In the wild it often forms impenetrable thickets of thorny waist- to head-high shrubs, so don't plant where human contact is probable. On the plus side, blossoms cover the tree in the spring and continue blooming to a lesser extent into fall. Its fragrant flowers and twisted, flat pods accent mixed plantings and make it an appealing specimen plant for a small area. The feathery foliage and irregular crown provide filtered shade.

Acacia greggii flowers

Acacia greggii

Acer macrophyllum

Big-leaf maple

Native Distribution: streambanks, valleys, canyons; South Coast, Transverse Ranges, Peninsular Ranges, below 6,000 feet; Southern California: Los Angeles, Orange, Riverside, San Bernardino, San Diego, Santa Barbara, Ventura counties; north to Alaska.
Landscape Zone: Chaparral, Foothill Woodland, widespread.
Size: 15–50 feet tall.
Leaves: deciduous; 4–10 inches across, orange to yellow fall colors.
Flowers: insignificant.
Fruit: seeds with wings at 90 degrees.
Soil: serpentine and clay tolerant, well or slow draining.
Exposure: full sun to full shade.
Temperature: cold hardy to 0 degrees F.
Water: drought tolerant, 8 inches/year minimum.
Propagation: seeds.
Profile: Everybody loves a maple tree, with its luxuriant summer shade and multihued fall colors. When planted in optimum conditions, this forest stalwart will dazzle you with as much as 10 feet of growth per year—so give it plenty of room to spread. Plant big-leaf maple with shade-tolerant understory shrubs and flowers, such as sumacs, ceanothus and manazanitas species, giant wild rye, fuchsia, ferns, and goldenrod. Look for specimens with multiple trunks if you want an ornate look, or a single trunk for the classic tree profile. The large leaves require considerable lawn maintenance in the autumn after the fall color pageant. Be sure to water transplants generously for the first year.

Top: *Acer microphyllum*

Left: *Acer microphyllum* leaf

Aesculus californica

California buckeye

Native Distribution: streambanks, canyons, slopes, riparian forests; South Coast, Transverse Ranges, Peninsular Ranges, below 4,000 feet; Southern California: Los Angeles, Riverside, Santa Barbara counties; northern California, endemic.
Landscape Zone: Coastal Sage Scrub, Foothill Woodland.
Size: 15–30 feet tall.
Leaves: deciduous.
Flowers: April–September; 4- to 12-inch-tall spikes with white to pink flowers.
Fruit: glossy brown seed, round, 1–2 inches diameter, poisonous.
Soil: adaptable, clay to serpentine.
Exposure: full sun to partial shade.
Temperature: cold hardy to –10 degrees F.
Water: moderately drought tolerant.
Propagation: fall-sown seeds, cuttings.
Profile: In the spring, candles of fragrant, creamy flowers cover the California buckeye, a miniature version of the Ohio buckeye or horse chestnut. The multiple trunks, twisted limbs, silvery bark, dense green foliage, and shrubby profile suit the California buckeye to side yards and restricted spaces. When in flower, the flamboyant spikes make a spectacular landscape accent, but unless the tree receives summer water, it's a one-season show. Without sufficient moisture, this drought-deciduous species loses its leaves, yet the ornate limbs and dangling seed pods continue to add visual interest throughout the winter. 'Canyon Pink', developed by Santa Barbara Botanic Gardens, has abundant, showy flowers in spring. The cultivar offers good tolerance to summer drought, although young plants need regular water until established. Indigenous Americans ground the hard seeds to produce a fish poison. All parts of the plant are toxic, and deer distain the foliage.

Top: *Aesculus californica* branches and trunk

Right: *Aesculus californica*

Alnus rhombifolia
White alder

Native Distribution: streambanks, canyons; South Coast, Western Transverse Ranges, Peninsular Ranges, Sonoran Desert, below 5,000 feet; Southern California: Los Angeles Orange, Riverside, San Bernardino, San Diego, Santa Barbara, Ventura counties; north to Washington, Montana.
Landscape Zone: Chaparral, Foothill Woodland.

Size: 20–50 feet tall.
Leaves: deciduous.
Fruit: 1/2-inch, conelike catkin.
Soil: adaptable, tolerates wet but not compacted soil.
Exposure: full sun to partial shade.
Temperature: cold hardy to –10 degrees F.
Water: requires regular moisture, 40 inches/year minimum.
Propagation: seeds, bare root.

Profile: Plant this fast-growing tree when you have a baby and you can hang a rope swing on it by the time first grade comes around. White alder develops into a handsome shade tree, but it casts a broad shadow that will exclude most shrubs in just a few years. Avoid planting it in areas where you intend to landscape with sun-loving species. White alder naturally occurs along streams and has aggressive roots that seek out water. It's a good choice for sites with poor drainage or for wildlife gardens with flowing water. Plant with other water-loving species such as redosier dogwood, manzanitas, monkey flower, wild rose, or wax myrtle.

Alnus rhombifolia

Alnus rhombifolia bark and trunks

Arbutus menziesii

Pacific madrone

Native Distribution: canyons, slopes; Western Transverse Ranges, Peninsular Ranges, below 5,000 feet; Southern California: Los Angeles, Orange, Riverside, San Diego, Santa Barbara, Ventura counties; Mexico, north to Canada.
Landscape Zone: Foothill Woodland.
Size: 15–30 feet tall.
Leaves: evergreen.
Flowers: February–March; clusters of tiny, creamy blooms.
Fruit: fall; ornate red berries.
Soil: acid, well draining.
Exposure: partial shade.
Temperature: cold hardy to 0 degrees F.
Water: drought tolerant, 30 inches/year minimum.
Propagation: seeds, cuttings.
Profile: With bright, shiny, green leaves, red fruit, and ornate reddish trunks, this tree adds flair to any landscape, but Pacific madrone has specific landscape requirements. If you can emulate its natural habitat of a shady forest with well-draining soil and moderate summer moisture, go for it. Plant saplings in the shade, avoid overwatering, and mulch to protect the roots in the summer. You'll know your madrone is happy by its rapid growth and the accolades it will receive from envious friends. The twisting multiple trunks and ornate bark make this tree a classic landscape choice. The evergreen foliage, abundant flowers, and colorful fruit will enliven small front and side yards, patios, and commercial plantings. Several of the larger manzanita species have similar landscape applications (see *Arctostaphylos* in the shrub profiles). Wildlife love the succulent fruit and butterflies flock to the flowers.

Arbutus menziesii flowers

Arbutus menziesii

Celtis laevigata var. *reticulata* foliage and fruit

Celtis laevigata var. *reticulata* (*Celtis reticulata*)

Netleaf hackberry

Native Distribution: canyons, streams, bottomlands; Peninsular Ranges, 1,500–6,000 feet; Southern California: Riverside, San Bernardino, San Diego counties; east to Texas, north to Washington; Mexico.
Landscape Zone: Creosote Bush Scrub, Joshua Tree Woodland, Pinyon-Juniper Woodland.
Size: 30–40 feet tall.
Leaves: deciduous.
Fruit: fall; round, fleshy, red drupes.
Soil: adaptable, well draining.
Exposure: full sun to partial shade.
Temperature: cold hardy to –20 degrees F.
Water: drought tolerant, 12 inches/year minimum.
Propagation: seeds.
Profile: Many people consider these fast-growing trees a weedy plant, but hackberries definitely have a place in the landscape. They grow almost anywhere, provide abundant shade, and produce tiny fruit that makes excellent forage for birds. The trunk has distinctive, warty growths and the leaves turn yellow in the fall, but don't expect a color pageant. Use this tree for quick-growing deciduous shade for your patio or rooftop in the summer, for confined areas and side yards, as a curb planting, or in naturalized areas. It grows well with agaves, chuparosa, fairy duster, giant wild rye, wild rose, and desert willow.

Celtis laevigata var. *reticulata*

Cercis orbiculata (Cercis occidentalis)

Western or California redbud

Native Distribution: rocky hillsides, mountains, canyons; Peninsular Ranges, below 4,000 feet; Southern California: Los Angeles, Riverside, San Bernardino, San Diego counties; Arizona, Utah, Nevada.
Landscape Zone: Chaparral, Foothill Woodland.
Size: 10–20 feet tall.
Leaves: deciduous.
Flowers: February–April; tiny red flowers before leaves.
Fruit: 2- to 3-inch-long pods.
Soil: adaptable, well draining.
Exposure: full sun to partial shade.
Temperature: cold hardy to 10 degrees F.
Water: moderately drought tolerant, depending on variety, 12–35 inches/year minimum.
Propagation: fall sown, stratified, scarified seeds.
Profile: The redbud greets spring with a blaze of color. Before the leaves emerge, tiny scarlet blossoms cover the bare limbs. The glory lasts for only two weeks, though, then the petals blanket the ground like red snow. Redbuds grow rapidly and have an upright rounded to flat-topped crown that provides moderately dense shade. They are perfect for adding spring color to a limited space, such as a side yard, patio, or isolated corner. Use them as a border along long drives or as a focal plant in a landscape island. Plant with desert ceanothus, Utah serviceberry, or mountain mahogany for complementary white blooms, and with desert willow, bush monkey flower, or wild rose to extend the seasonal color in your yard. Redbuds need a few below-freezing nights to induce spring flowering. In low-desert areas, they may sunburn if planted in southern exposures and will appreciate some summer water.

Cercis orbiculata flowers

Cercis orbiculata

Chilopsis linearis
Desert willow

Native Distribution: sandy soils, desert washes and flats, canyons; Western Transverse Ranges, Peninsular Ranges, Sonoran and Mojave deserts, below 5,000 feet; Southern California: Imperial, Riverside, San Diego, San Bernardino counties; east to Texas, Nevada, Utah; Mexico.
Landscape Zone: Creosote Bush Scrub, Joshua Tree Woodland.
Size: 10–25 feet.
Leaves: deciduous; willowlike.
Flowers: May–September or until frost; clusters of orchidlike, pink to lavender, 1-1/2-inch-long blossoms.
Fruit: 4- to 12-inch seed pods.
Soil: adaptable, well draining.
Exposure: full sun to partial shade.
Temperature: heat tolerant, cold hardy to 0 degrees F.
Water: drought tolerant, 8 inches/year minimum.
Propagation: fresh seeds, semi-hardwood and dormant cuttings.
Profile: This premier, fast-growing plant brings spectacular, trumpet-shaped flowers and bright green, willowlike foliage to your yard. Clusters of up to five blossoms dangle from the branch tips all summer. You'll need to prune desert willow to develop the shape you desire. For background, windbreak, screen, or specimen planting, direct its growth as a large shrub with many branches and thick foliage. Or you can train it into a tree with an upright form and single or multiple trunks. Look for cultivars with flower colors ranging from the natural pinkish purple to deep pink, burgundy, and white. Since flowers grow on new wood, pruning in the dormant season encourages profuse blooming. Desert willow is used in shelter-belt plantings as far north as Kansas. It freezes to the ground, but recovers rapidly and regains its height.

Chilopsis linearis flower

Chilopsis linearis in flower

Chilopsis linearis

Cupressus arizonica

Arizona cypress

Native Distribution: mountain canyons, slopes; Peninsular Ranges, 3,000–8,000 feet; Southern California: Imperial, Los Angeles, Orange, Riverside, San Bernardino, San Diego counties; east to Texas; Mexico.
Landscape Zone: Chaparral, Foothill Woodland, Pinyon-Juniper Woodland.
Size: 20–50 feet tall, 20 feet wide.
Leaves: evergreen.
Fruit: 1-inch cones.
Soil: adaptable, well draining.
Exposure: full sun.
Temperature: cold hardy to –15 degrees F.
Water: drought tolerant, 10–12 inches/year minimum.
Propagation: cuttings.
Profile: The grayish green, juniperlike foliage and classic Christmas-tree shape make Arizona cypress a popular yard tree throughout the West. When planted close together, younger specimens make a striking head-high or taller border hedge or background planting. Use a row planting as a sun screen, to provide visual privacy, or as a windbreak. As the tree matures, it develops a rounded crown, often with spreading branches. You can remove lower limbs to reveal the scaly red bark and shape the plant into a large shade tree. At lower elevations, it benefits from occasional deep watering in the summer. It grows rapidly when young and can live 700 years. Various varieties and forms have been segregated, including silver-, gray-, green-, and blue-foliated varieties and compact, dwarf, and pyramid-shaped forms. A smaller related tree, Sargent cypress, *Cupressus sargentii,* has similar habitat requirements.

Cupressus arizonica

Fraxinus velutina (*Fraxinus pennsylvanica* subsp. *velutina*)

Arizona or velvet ash

Native Distribution: mountain streams, canyons; South Coast, Western Transverse Ranges, Peninsular Ranges, Mojave Desert, 500–5,300 feet; Southern California: Imperial, Los Angeles, Riverside, Orange, San Bernardino, San Diego, Santa Barbara, Ventura counties; east to Texas, Nevada, Utah; Mexico.

Landscape Zone: Chaparral, Foothill Woodland.
Size: 20–30 feet.
Leaves: deciduous; 3 to 5 leaflets per leaf.
Fruit: 1-inch long, winged seeds on female trees.
Soil: adaptable.
Exposure: full sun.
Temperature: heat tolerant, cold hardy to –10 degrees F.
Water: drought tolerant, 8 inches/year minimum.
Propagation: seeds.
Profile: For decades, so many new houses came with a 6-foot-tall Arizona ash sapling in the front yard that overuse spoiled much of the tree's appeal. One aspect of landscaping with native plants is to restore the natural diversity found in nature instead of producing a neighborhood of cloned houses with cloned landscape designs. With the rant out of the way, I have to admit that the 'Fan-Tex' ('Rio Grande') ash, a grafted cultivar of Arizona ash, has a lot to recommend for medium- to large-scale landscapes from Santa Barbara south. The cultivar grows fast, reaching 35 feet, and it has a dense, round canopy and holds a lush appearance longer than the species type. It turns golden in fall. The cultivar is the best form to use for residential yards, parking lots, and street plantings. The smaller flowering ash, *Fraxinus dipetala,* produces a cascade of lilac flowers in the spring, but loses it leaves by midsummer. Its diminutive height is well suited for small-scale yards, patios, and poolsides. For companion plants that provide year-round foliage and color, plant it with coffeeberry, manzanitas, bush poppy, and ceanothus species.

Fraxinus velutina

Juniperus californica

California juniper

Native Distribution: dry slopes, hills; Western Transverse Ranges, below 5,000 feet; Southern California: Imperial, Los Angeles, Orange, Riverside, San Bernardino, San Diego, Santa Barbara, Ventura counties; endemic.
Landscape Zone: Pinyon-Juniper Woodland, Joshua Tree Woodland, Foothill Woodland.
Size: 10–15 feet tall and wide.
Leaves: evergreen; bluish gray, needlelike.
Flowers: insignificant.
Fruit: blue-gray berries on female plants.
Soil: adaptable, well draining, alkaline tolerant.
Exposure: full sun to partial shade.
Temperature: heat tolerant, cold hardy to 10 degrees F.
Water: drought tolerant, 12 inches/year minimum.
Propagation: seeds.
Profile: This shrubby juniper seems tailor made for hedge, background, or accent plantings. Its ornamental evergreen foliage creates year-round cover for privacy hedges, yet it doesn't outgrow its boundaries. The dense branching provides ideal cover for many species of birds, and the berries add to the wildlife attraction. As an anchor plant for a landscape island, California juniper provides a vertical accent and a bluish evergreen foliage color—a great combination with pinyon pine, small oaks, and flowering shrubs such as ceanothus, flannel bush, mountain mahogany, mahonias, and Apache plume. Female trees bear attractive blue-gray berries that remain on the tree for much of the year. The closely related Utah juniper, *Juniperus osteosperma*, has similar landscape applications.

Juniperus californica berries

Below: *Juniperus californica*

Lyonothamnus floribundus

Catalina ironwood

Native Distribution: slopes, hills, canyons; Channel Islands, below 2,000 feet; Southern California: naturalized Los Angeles, Santa Barbara counties; endemic.
Landscape Zone: Chaparral, Foothill Woodland.
Size: 20–50 feet tall.
Leaves: evergreen; lobed, shiny.
Flowers: spring–summer; white, dense, 4- to 8-inch-wide clusters.
Soil: adaptable, well draining.
Exposure: full sun to partial shade.
Temperature: heat tolerant, cold hardy to 20 degrees F.
Water: drought tolerant, 15 inches/year minimum.
Propagation: scarified seeds.
Profile: Catalina ironwood is a handsome immigrant from the Channel Islands that feels right at home in mainland landscapes. And with its glossy, fernlike leaves, shredding bark, and abundant flowers, it's a welcomed guest. Large, flat-topped panicles of flowers cover the tree in spring and make it the center of attention. The tree's ornate qualities make it a handsome single- or multitrunked specimen, while the slender profile suits it to side yards and narrow gardens that have limited space. The bark of this rapid-grower peels away to reveal deep, reddish undertones as a supplemental accent point. The flowers, foliage, and bark complement manzanitas, buckwheats, silktassel, serviceberry, coyote brush, and salvias.

Lyonothamnus floribundus

Lyonothamnus floribundus as a container plant

Olneya tesota

Desert ironwood

Native Distribution: desert washes; Peninsular Ranges, Sonoran Desert, below 5,000 feet; Southern California: Imperial, Riverside, San Bernardino, San Diego counties; Arizona; Mexico.
Landscape Zone: Creosote Bush Scrub.
Size: 15–30 feet.
Leaves: evergreen; bluish, compound, 2 inches long with 3/4-inch leaflets, pair of 1/2-inch thorns at leaf bases.
Flowers: April–May; lavender, pea-like in small clusters.
Fruit: brown pod, 2-1/2 inches long.
Soil: well draining.
Exposure: full sun.
Temperature: cold hardy to 20 degrees F.
Water: drought tolerant.
Propagation: scarified seeds.
Profile: This hardy desert tree adds a gray-green color component to your drought-tolerant landscape. With its smooth gray bark, ornate branching, and airy gray foliage, desert ironwood is an eye-catching, small-scale tree for courtyard, xeriscape, and cactus gardens. As a specimen plant, it accents a garden wall, fence, or courtyard. The prickly thorns on the branches make this a plant you don't want to brush against, so trim it up or keep it in the background. Removing lower limbs also highlights the attractive trunk. Flowers cover the tree with lavender hues in the spring but are short-lasting. For extended color, plant with palo verde, desert willow, brittle bush, wild rose, catclaw acacia, and California sunflower.

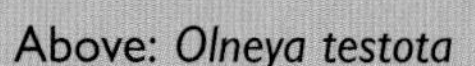

Above: *Olneya testota*

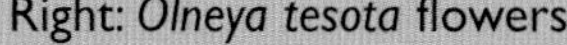

Right: *Olneya tesota* flowers

Parkinsonia florida (Cercidium floridum)
Blue palo verde

Parkinsonia 'Desert Museum'

Native Distribution: desert washes, valleys; Sonoran Desert, below 4,000 feet; Southern California: Imperial, Riverside, San Bernardino, San Diego counties; Arizona, Nevada; Mexico.
Landscape Zone: Creosote Bush Scrub.
Size: 15–25 feet tall and wide.
Leaves: deciduous in cold and drought; 1/2- to 1-inch spines on twigs.
Flowers: March–May; abundant yellow flowers.
Fruit: 2- to 3-inch-long seed pods.
Soil: sandy, well draining.
Exposure: full sun.
Temperature: cold hardy to 10 degrees F.
Water: drought tolerant, 8 inches/year minimum.
Propagation: scarified seeds.
Profile: The fast-growing blue palo verde is one of the most popular landscape trees in low desert cities, and for good reason. Once you see one in full bloom, you'll want a blue palo verde in your xeriscape planting. From March through July (depending on moisture), lemon-yellow flower clusters obscure the branches. The graceful, spreading shape and smooth, bluish green trunk and limbs add to the ornamental effect, though the limbs have 1-inch spines. This truly drought-tolerant plant loses its tiny leaves during dry summers, but the dense array of slender branches still provide filtered shade. The similar foothills, or little-leaf, palo verde, *Parkinsonia microphylla,* has equal landscape value and blooms a few weeks after the blue palo verde. The Desert Museum palo verde, a three-way hybrid between blue and foothills palo verde and Texas palo verde (*P. aculeata*), is thornless and has larger, showier yellow flowers that bloom well into the summer.

Parkinsonia florida

Pinus edulis

Two-needle pinyon pine

Native Distribution: hillsides, mountains; desert mountains, 4,000–7,000-foot elevations; Southern California: Los Angeles, Riverside, San Bernardino counties; northern California, east to Texas, north to Wyoming; Mexico.
Landscape Zone: Pinyon-Juniper Woodland.

Size: 10–25 feet.
Leaves: evergreen; 1- to 2-inch needles.
Fruit: 2-inch-long cone with edible nuts.
Soil: variable, dry, alkaline, well draining.
Exposure: full sun to partial shade.
Temperature: cold hardy to –20 degrees F.

Water: drought tolerant, 16 inches/year minimum.
Propagation: fresh seeds.
Profile: This small-proportioned pine adds a distinctly Western Ranch sense of place to yards and patios throughout the Southern California foothills. Pinyons accent and add year-round greenery to bare walls and corners of buildings, and they can be used as large container plants. They provide an attractive focal plant when mixed with other western species, such as Apache plume, mahonias, cliffrose, and mountain mahogany. Younger specimens have dense foliage and a pyramid shape, resembling a 10- to 15-foot-tall Christmas tree. Pinyons grow slowly, and with age (probably decades) they develop an open, rounded canopy. Two-needle pinyon languishes in desert conditions, so avoid it at low elevations. For a larger pine, choose the four-needle pinyon, *Pinus quadrifolia,* from the Pinyon-Juniper Woodlands, or the drought-tolerant foothills pine, *P. sabiniana,* from the Chaparral and Foothill Woodland landscape zones. Both species develop into erect trees with open foliage.

Above: *Pinus edulis* foliage and cones

Left: *Pinus edulis*

Platanus racemosa

California sycamore

Native Distribution: streambanks, canyons, grasslands; South Coast, Western Transverse Ranges, Peninsular Ranges, Sonoran Desert, below 6,500 feet; Southern California: Imperial, Los Angeles, Orange, Riverside, San Bernardino, San Diego, Santa Barbara, Ventura counties; northern California.
Landscape Zone: Chaparral, Foothill Woodland.
Size: 30–100 feet tall, 20–40 feet wide.
Leaves: deciduous; deeply lobed, 4–9 inches wide.
Fruit: 1-inch sphere.
Soil: adaptable, moist, well draining.
Exposure: full sun to partial shade.
Temperature: cold hardy to –10 degrees F.
Water: requires regular moisture, 45 inches/year minimum.
Propagation: seeds.
Profile: Sycamores grow rapidly and develop into large-scale trees suitable for oversized lots and campus, park, and esplanade plantings. Mature specimens develop a rounded canopy that sheds copious amounts of leaves in the fall. The white, ornate bark flakes away and lower limbs self prune, so ground maintenance is required. That said, the sycamore is one of the most majestic trees in North America. It offers no more challenge in a landscape setting than any other dominant canopy tree, and it should be used more in home, municipal, and corporate landscapes. If you have the room and receive ample rainfall, consider the long-term splendor of this stately sylvan specimen. Understory shrubs must be shade tolerant and able to compete with sycamore's aggressive roots. Plant dogwoods, wild rose, coffeeberry, toyon, laurel sumac, and wild grape.

Platanus racemosa

Populus fremontii subsp. *fremontii*

Western or Fremont cottonwood

Populus fremontii

Native Distribution: streambanks and bottomlands; throughout, below 6,500 feet; Southern California: Imperial, Los Angeles, Orange, Riverside, San Bernardino, San Diego, Santa Barbara, Ventura counties; east to Texas.
Landscape Zone: Chaparral, Creosote Bush Scrub, Foothill Woodland, widespread.
Size: 40–60 feet tall, 30–40 feet wide.
Leaves: deciduous; 1–3 inches long, yellow fall color.
Fruit: copious cottony seeds on female trees.
Soil: adaptable, deep, moist, well draining.
Exposure: full sun.
Temperature: cold hardy to –5 degrees F.
Water: requires regular moisture, 35 inches/year minimum.
Propagation: fresh seeds, semi-hardwood cuttings.
Profile: First the good news: Cottonwoods grow amazingly fast into tall, picturesque trees that bear golden foliage in the fall. Now the bad news: They need regular irrigation, and female trees throw a snowstorm of cottony, wind-blown seeds, so be sure you plant a male. They are also relatively short-lived (30 to 60 years) and have an invasive root system. The water-greedy roots invade sewer pipes, rob water from your lawn, and heave pavement. If you have an average-sized yard, you don't have room for a cottonwood unless it's on your back property line. But if you have acreage or a sizeable yard and want a large shade tree, this makes a good choice. If planted in moist soil, a cottonwood can grow into an attractive shade tree in four to five years, but they eventually outgrow your ability to water them outside their native rainfall range. Several male cultivars exist, so plant the one best suited to your landscape requirements.

Prosopis glandulosa

Honey mesquite

Native Distribution: grasslands, washes, sandy flats; Peninsular Ranges, deserts, below 5,000 feet; Southern California: Imperial, Los Angeles, Orange, Riverside, San Bernardino, San Diego, Santa Barbara counties; east to Texas; Mexico.
Landscape Zone: Creosote Bush Scrub.
Size: 15–30 feet.
Leaves: deciduous.
Flowers: April–August; 2-inch, fragrant yellow spikes.
Fruit: 4- to 8-inch pods.
Soil: adaptable, deep, well draining.
Exposure: full sun.
Temperature: heat tolerant, cold hardy to 0 degrees F.
Water: drought tolerant, 8 inches/year minimum.
Propagation: fresh or scarified seeds, root cuttings.
Profile: Ranchers probably shake their heads in disbelief at the notion of planting thorny mesquites in city yards, let alone importing them from Chile. Although despised on rangeland, mesquite is prized as an arid-climate landscape tree for small- and medium-scale designs. The abundance of yellow spring flowers, the open crown, airy foliage, and twisted, often multiple, trunks add western charm to your yard, patio, or xeriscape garden. The bright green, drooping leaves provide light shade, allowing you to plant sun-loving shrubs and wildflowers beneath them. You can water the tree to speed growth, but once a mesquite sinks its taproot, it can survive the driest summer. The roots may penetrate 60 to 150 feet deep looking for water, so don't plant one near a septic system or pool. A thornless variety exists as well as hybrid crosses between native and South American species. The native screwbean mesquite, *Prosopis pubescens,* has ornate, twisted seed pods and similar landscape uses. It grows in floodplains and needs more water than its super-drought-tolerant relatives.

Prosopus glandulosa

Prosopus glandulosa flowers

Prosopis pubescens seed pods

Prunus virginiana var. *demissa*

Western chokecherry

Native Distribution: rocky slopes, canyons, woodlands, moist areas; Western Transverse Ranges, Peninsular Ranges, below 8,000 feet; Southern California: Los Angeles, Orange, Riverside, San Bernardino, San Diego, Santa Barbara, Ventura counties; east to Texas; north into Canada.
Landscape Zone: Chaparral, Foothill Woodland.
Size: shrubby to 20 feet tall.
Leaves: deciduous.
Flowers: May–June; 3- to 6-inch clusters of white flowers.
Fruit: fall; 1/2-inch dark red to black drupes.
Soil: adaptable, well draining.
Exposure: full sun to partial shade.
Temperature: cold hardy to –20 degrees F.
Water: moderately drought tolerant, 16 inches/year minimum.
Propagation: fall-sown or spring-stratified seeds, cuttings.
Profile: Widely used for ornamental planting and erosion control, chokecherry has dark green, lustrous leaves, abundant spring flowers, and attractive bundles of red to black fruit that ripen in the fall. You can trim this versatile plant into a shrub or let it grow into a small tree. It spreads by root suckers and forms dense thickets in the wild. Use it as an accent for patios or small yards and in mass plantings. You can choose dwarf and full-sized varieties, with broad to narrow leaves and black to amber to yellow fruit. The fruit is eaten by 40 species of birds and numerous small animals. The closely related hollyleaf cherry, *Prunus ilicifolia,* has shiny, ornate leaves and similar landscape uses, but it is slower growing.

Prunus virginiana

Prunus virginiana flowers

Prunus ilicifolia

Native Plant Profiles

Oaks

When Europeans arrived in California in the 1700s, oaks were one of the defining plants of the valleys and foothills. Oak-dominated ecosystems bordered the broad valleys and extended into the foothills of the surrounding mountain peaks and desert ranges. As the dominant tree in forest and woodland ecosystems, oaks influenced the life cycles of the combined flora and fauna of their biotic community. From microbes in the soil to the fifty species of birds and mammals that eat acorns, a complex interrelated web of life cycled around the mighty oak forests and savannas. So, when you plant, or rescue, an oak in your landscape, you're doing more than beautifying your yard: you're helping to preserve the biological diversity and cultural heritage that stretches back in time to the last Ice Age.

Oak ecosystems in California vary from a closed-canopy evergreen forest to an open mixture of deciduous trees, grasses, and shrubs. Different species of oaks and understory plants dominate each type of ecosystem. This habitat diversity accounts for thirty-nine species, varieties, and hybrids of oaks in the state. Oaks vary from tall and stately trees that reach 60 feet high to scrubby species that average 5 to 10 feet tall, and a prostrate species that barely reaches 4 feet. This adaptability and variability is a landscaper's dream, but it's a nightmare for taxonomists trying to organize the genus into a well-defined collection of species, varieties, and subspecies.

If your landscape is suitable in habitat and space for an oak, you should consider the following factors in selecting a species: mature size, evergreen or deciduous, fall color, leaf size and color, and crown shape. Southern California has three canopy evergreen oaks and five deciduous species that mature into large-scale trees that can dominate an area 30 to 50 feet around them. About fifteen species grow as shrubby evergreens.

The system of feeder roots for a large oak extends to the drip line of the canopy and a little beyond. In general, oak ecosystems have evolved to be summer dry. Once established after several summers of TLC, oaks will suffer from summer irrigation, whether directly or from water intended for landscape plants growing near them. For this reason, you should choose companion plants that grow in association with oaks in nature. This summer-dry, no-fertilizer regime also stimulates the natural association of soil fungi and microbes that is essential for the survival of many native plants.

The oak profiles that follow are representative large-evergreen, large-deciduous, and shrubby-evergreen species that thrive in our area, including some typical companion plants for each. Adding an oak to your landscape is a major investment of both dollars and the time required for the tree to mature, so be sure to carefully choose one that is specifically adapted to your area through thousands of years of natural selection.

Quercus agrifolia

Coast live oak

Native Distribution: canyons, woodlands, valleys; South Coast, Western Transverse Ranges, Peninsular Ranges, below 5,000 feet; Southern California: Imperial, Los Angeles, Orange, Riverside, San Bernardino, San Diego, Santa Barbara, Ventura counties; Baja California.
Landscape Zone: Foothill Woodland.
Size: 30–65 feet tall and wide.
Leaves: evergreen; 1–3 inches long.
Fruit: fall; acorn.
Soil: adaptable, well draining.
Exposure: full sun to partial shade.
Temperature: cold hardy to 10 degrees F.
Water: moderately drought tolerant, 20 inches/year minimum.
Propagation: acorns.
Profile: With hollylike leaves and a picturesque profile, the coast live oak is considered the premier of all California's oaks. If you already have one on your lot, plan your entire landscape design around it. If you decide to plant one, make it the focal point and plant only companion species that will accommodate the tree as it develops into a large, dominant specimen. When planting saplings, mulch around the trunk, control weeds, and water weekly during the first two summers. Once the tree becomes well established, turn off the sprinkler. Oaks don't require and survive better without supplemental water. Don't plant thirsty plants near your specimen oak. Think of your landscape as a coast live oak plant community and select only compatible species, such as coyote brush, Mexican elderberry, manzanitas, ceanothus, Pacific madrone, coffeeberry, gooseberry, and snowberry. Other evergreen live oaks with similar habitat needs and landscape uses include the interior live oak, *Quercus wislizenii,* and the canyon live oak, *Q. chrysolepis*.

Above: *Quercus agrifolia* foliage

Left: *Quercus agrifolia*

Quercus berberidifolia (Quercus dumosa)

Inland scrub oak

Quercus turbinella (Quercus dumosa var. turbinella)

Shrub live oak or Sonoran scrub oak

Native Distribution: dry slopes, washes, canyons, desert mountains; Southern California: Los Angeles, Riverside, San Bernardino, San Diego, Santa Barbara, Ventura counties; east to Texas; Mexico.
Landscape Zone: *Quercus berberidifolia:* Chaparral, Coastal Sage Scrub, 1,000–5,000 feet; *Q. turbinella:* Pinyon-Juniper Woodland, Joshua Tree Woodland, 4,000–6,500 feet.
Size: to 15 feet tall, tree or shrub.
Leaves: evergreen; 1 inch long, spiny margins.
Fruit: fall; acorn.
Soil: adaptable, well draining.
Exposure: full sun to partial shade.
Temperature: heat tolerant, cold hardy to 0 degrees F.
Water: drought tolerant, 12–25 inches/year minimum.
Propagation: fresh acorns.
Profile: Oaks come in all sizes, from the stately mammoths to these shrubby species that are barely considered trees at all. Taxonomists can't easily pigeonhole most oak species, especially the hybridizing inland scrub oak complex, which has so much variation that some specimens grow as waist-high bushes and others as bona-fide trees. In your yard, the diminutive size of *Quercus berberidifolia* and *Q. turbinella* is perfect for courtyards, corner gardens, and areas with limited space. A small- to medium-sized landscape matches and really shows off the landscape qualities of these scrub oaks. The hollylike, bluish gray leaves and densely branched crown make both species an excellent background, border, median, or companion foil for larger, more dominant focal plants. For seasonal color in mass plantings, mix with flowering shrubs from the respective landscape zone. Inland scrub oak grows in association with toyon, coyote brush, bush poppy, redberry, silktassel, and snowberry. The shrub live oak community includes Apache plume, hollyleaf cherry, Fremont barberry, silktassel, bladderpod, joint fir, cacti, and yucca. Shrub oaks grow slowly, so you don't have to worry about them outgrowing your landscape plan.

Above: *Quercus turbinella* foliage

Left: *Quercus turbinella*

Quercus lobata

Valley oak or California white oak

Native Distribution: savannas, slopes, valleys; South Coast, Western Transverse Ranges, below 2,000 feet; Southern California: Los Angeles, Riverside, San Diego, Santa Barbara, Ventura counties; northern California, endemic.
Landscape Zone: Foothill Woodland, Pinyon-Juniper Woodland.
Size: 40–80 feet tall and wide.

Leaves: deciduous; 2–5 inches long, 6 to 10 lobes, shiny green.
Fruit: fall; acorn.
Soil: adaptable, well draining.
Exposure: full sun to partial shade.
Temperature: cold hardy to -20 degrees F.
Water: moderately drought tolerant, 24 inches/year minimum.
Propagation: acorns.

Profile: This hardy oak dispels the notion that oaks take generations to mature, probably because valley oak generally grows where it can reach the water table. Like other riparian oaks, it can grow 4 feet a year from acorn and reach 20 feet in five years. Don't make the mistake of misjudging the companion planting and end up with half the plants around the oak struggling or dead in a few years' time, when the tree begins to cast its shadow. Anticipate a large-scale, dominant tree before you turn the first shovel of soil. Valley oak develops a symmetrical, upright, vase-shaped profile, with plenty of room underneath for understory shrubs and perennials. Stay within its plant community and select companion species such as Mexican elderberry, coyote brush, Utah serviceberry, snowberry, manzanitas, redbud, coffeeberry, barberries, and bush monkey flower. Three other deciduous species—blue oak (*Quercus douglasii*), Engelmann oak (*Q. engelmannii*), and black oak (*Q. kelloggii*)—have similar habitat requirements and landscape applications.

Above: *Quercus lobata* foliage

Left: *Quercus lobata*

Robinia neomexicana

Desert locust or New Mexico locust

Above: *Robina neomexicana* flowers
Below: *Robina neomexicana*

Native Distribution: canyons, mountain slopes; Mojave Desert, 5,000–8,500 feet; Southern California: San Bernardino County; east to west Texas, Colorado to Nevada.
Landscape Zone: Pinyon-Juniper Woodland.
Size: 12–20 feet.
Leaves: deciduous; paired, 1/2-inch-long thorns at nodes.
Flowers: April–August; clusters of delicate rose pea-like flowers.
Fruit: fall; 2- to 4-inch-long bean pods.
Soil: adaptable, well draining.
Exposure: full sun to partial shade.
Temperature: cold hardy.
Water: drought tolerant, 12 inches/year minimum.
Propagation: scarified seeds, root cuttings.

Profile: If you see a desert locust when it's covered with showy pink blossoms in the spring and through the summer, you'll know why it's a popular accent plant, even though it's armed with thorns. Its small size adapts it to courtyard, patio, and mixed plantings, but its paired thorns limit use where human contact is expected. In the fall, the flat, thin bean pods dangle from the limbs. In the wild, desert locust spreads aggressively by root suckers and forms thorny, roadside thickets. You can prune it into a single- or multitrunked tree and control suckering by mowing or limiting water. Use this fast-growing tree for erosion control, as a wind break, or as a screen planting. Once established, it is difficult to eradicate.

Sambucus nigra subsp. *canadensis* (*Sambucus mexicana*)

Mexican elderberry

Native Distribution: streambanks, desert washes, and mountain drainages; South Coast, Western Transverse Ranges, Peninsular Ranges, below 10,000 feet; Southern California: Los Angeles, Orange, Riverside, San Bernardino, San Diego, Santa Barbara, Ventura counties; east to Texas; Mexico.
Landscape Zone: Chaparral, Coastal Sage Scrub, Foothill Woodland, Pinyon-Juniper Woodland.
Size: 10–20 feet, single- or multitrunked.
Leaves: evergreen, deciduous in drought conditions.
Flowers: March–September; flat-topped clusters of yellowish white blooms.
Fruit: fall; 1/4-inch diameter, bluish black, in clusters.
Soil: adaptable, deep, moist, poor or well draining.
Exposure: full sun to partial shade.
Temperature: cold hardy to –10 degrees F.
Water: drought tolerant, 16 inches/ year minimum.
Propagation: scarified, stratified seeds, softwood cuttings.
Profile: This delightful little elderberry feels right at home from the hottest desert streambeds to mountain canyons, and especially in yard landscapes where it gets a little extra water. Mexican elderberry grows fast and develops a rounded crown with dense foliage. Prune it into a 10- to 15-foot-tall tree with a twisted single trunk or multiple trunks. Its deep-green foliage, creamy flowers, and bundles of purple fruit will accent the corner of a yard or lot for most of the year. Its small size and long flowering period provide a striking design focal point for a courtyard, poolside garden, or landscape island. For a real show-stopper, underneath it plant a groundcover of hummingbird sage, giant four-o'clock, penstemons, or California fuchsia. If you want to make jelly from the berries, you'll have to race the birds.

Sambucus nigra subsp. *canadensis* flowers

Above: *Sambucus nigra* subsp. *canadensis* in flower

Right: *Sambucus nigra* subsp. *canadensis*

Umbellularia californica

California bay or California laurel

Native Distribution: canyons, valleys, riparian woodlands; Western Transverse Ranges, Peninsular Ranges, below 5,000 feet; Southern California: Los Angeles, Orange, Riverside, San Bernardino, San Diego, Santa Barbara, Ventura counties; Oregon.
Landscape Zone: Chaparral, Foothill Woodland.
Size: 10–40 feet.
Leaves: evergreen; 2–4 inches long, shiny, yellow-green.
Flowers: spring; tiny, yellow-green, clusters of 6 to 10.
Fruit: 1-inch-long green drupe, turns purple-brown.
Soil: adaptable, well draining.
Exposure: full sun to full shade.
Temperature: cold hardy to 10 degrees F.
Water: moderately drought tolerant, 30 inches/year minimum.
Propagation: fresh seeds, cuttings.
Profile: California laurel ranks as a top landscape contender for medium- to small-scale landscapes, offering glossy evergreen leaves and ornate fruit. With deep, rich soils and decades of growth, it will develop into a 40-foot tree with a slender crown. In dry conditions or thin soil, it's perfectly satisfied as a 10- to 15-foot shrub or small tree. You can also prune this versatile plant into a small tree for a handsome specimen or use it to accent a corner or entryway. As a container plant, it provides a foliage accent for a pool or patio. It can be sheared into a hedge or privacy screen. The foliage contains an aromatic menthol-like oil that was used medicinally in the past, and the leaves can be used as a bay-leaf seasoning in cooking. Birds, squirrels, and small mammals relish the olivelike fruit and seeds.

Umbellularia californica flowers

Umbellularia californica

Washingtonia filifera

California fan palm

Native Distribution: oasis, canyons, moist areas in desert scrublands; Sonoran Desert, below 4,000 feet; Southern California: Orange, Riverside, San Bernardino, San Diego counties; Arizona; Baja Mexico.
Landscape Zone: Creosote Bush Scrub, widespread.
Size: 30–60 feet.
Leaves: evergreen; gray-green fronds with stringy tips.
Flowers: May–June; white, 3/8 inch long in 12-inch clusters.
Fruit: fall; 1/2 inch long, oval.
Soil: adaptable, well draining.
Exposure: full sun to partial shade.
Temperature: cold hardy to 15 degrees F.
Water: drought tolerant.
Propagation: seeds.
Profile: In nature, this picturesque palm with a stout trunk grows only in isolated groves around desert oases and in moist, protected canyons. In cultivation, it adorns landscapes from Southern California to Florida. The tree's tall, stately profile topped with fan-shaped fronds is the icon of the sun-drenched, freeze-free climate that makes Southern California cities among the fastest growing in the nation. Planted alone or clustered, California fan palms cast feathery shadows across pools, patios, and courtyards and line streets, entry drives, and commercial properties. They add grace and elegance, but not without maintenance. Every one of the heavy, woody fronds must be removed by hand by someone standing on a tall ladder, or the thatch will surround the trunk like a bushy skirt. California fan palms grow fast from seed (up to 15 feet in 10 years), and they will often sprout in close proximity to the parent tree. They require occasional deep watering. The similar Mexican fan palm, *Washingtonia robusta*, is also widely used in cultivation. It has a slender, 12-inch-diameter trunk and glossy, green fronds, but it suffers leaf damage at 20 degrees F. Another popular palm from the California Floristic Province in Mexico is the Guadalupe Island fan palm, *Brahea edulis*, which reaches 30 feet in height and suffers frost damage.

Washingtonia filifera

Washingtonia filifera, untrimmed

Washingtonia robusta

Shrubs and Small Trees

Abutilon palmeri

Indian mallow

Above: *Abutilon palmeri* flower
Below: *Abutilon palmeri*

Native Distribution: dry, rocky soils, slopes, canyons; Peninsular Ranges, Sonoran Desert, between 1,500 and 2,500 feet; Southern California: Riverside, San Bernardino, San Diego counties; Arizona; Mexico.
Landscape Zone: Creosote Bush Scrub.
Size: 3–5 feet tall and wide, subshrub.
Leaves: evergreen; olive-silver, fuzzy, 1–2 inches long, heart-shaped.
Flowers: April–May and into fall; 2 inches diameter, yellow-orange.
Soil: adaptable.
Exposure: full sun to partial shade.
Temperature: extremely heat tolerant, cold hardy to 25 degrees F.
Water: drought tolerant, 8 inches/year minimum.
Propagation: fall-sown seeds.
Profile: Visualize a small shrub covered with delicate golden flowers nestled among fuzzy, gray-green leaves, then pick out the hottest, driest spot in your yard. Indian mallows love deserts and show their thanks in a yard setting by blooming profusely from spring through fall. Just provide a deep drink whenever it rains in Blythe—as the saying goes. Deadhead the spent flowers and give it a light winter trim to keep it dense. The contrast in color and texture between the flowers and leaves is doubly dramatic when planted with blue flowering sages and ceanothus. Create a landscape island with fairy duster, rabbitbrush, brittle bush, and desert olive, then add some desert marigold, California poppies, and sand verbena for extra color. Besides mixed plantings, this hardy subshrub makes a good border, corner accent, container plant, and background foil for bright green plants. The dwarf Indian mallow, *Abutilon parvulum,* is native between 3,000 and 4,000 feet and has similar landscape uses.

Adenostoma fasciculatum

Chamise

Native Distribution: dry ridges, slopes, flats; South Coast, Western Transverse Ranges, Peninsular Ranges, below 5,500 feet; Southern California: Imperial, Los Angeles, Orange, Riverside, San Bernardino, San Diego, Santa Barbara, Ventura; northern California, Nevada.
Landscape Zone: Chaparral.
Size: 3–10 feet tall.
Leaves: evergreen; 1/2 inch long, needlelike.
Flowers: May–June; white, clusters, 2–5 inches diameter.
Soil: adaptable, well draining.
Exposure: full sun.
Temperature: cold hardy to 0 degrees F.
Water: drought tolerant, 30 inches/year minimum.
Propagation: seeds.
Profile: When this member of the rose family bursts into bloom in the spring, the bush looks like it's been hit by a snowstorm. Clusters of tiny white flowers cover the branches and obscure the minuscule leaves. The rest of the year, this multistemmed, loosely branching shrub is best suited for wildscape and less formal designs. It makes a dramatic backdrop plant or screen along a fence or wall, but be sure it receives full sun.

The closely related red shank, *Adenostoma sparsifolium*, grows in chaparral to 6,500 feet. It has similar habitat requirements but can be trained into a 15-foot, single- or multitrunked tree with shedding, juniperlike bark.

Adenostoma fasciculatum

Amelanchier utahensis

Utah serviceberry

Native Distribution: dry, open slopes, mountainsides, canyons; South Coast, Western Transverse Ranges, Peninsular Ranges, below 11,000 feet; Southern California: Santa Barbara, Ventura, San Bernardino, Los Angeles, San Diego, Riverside; north to Montana, east to Texas; Mexico.
Landscape Zone: Chaparral, Pinyon-Juniper Woodland, Foothill Woodland.
Size: 6–15 feet, shrub.
Leaves: deciduous.
Flowers: April–May; showy, white in 3- to 6-inch clusters.
Fruit: June–July; sweet, blueberry-like, edible.
Soil: adaptable, well draining.
Exposure: full sun; not shade tolerant.
Temperature: moderate heat tolerance, cold hardy to –40 degrees F.
Water: drought tolerant.
Propagation: fall-sown seeds, or stratified in spring to break dormancy.
Profile: Do you have a dry, southwest exposure that needs a boost? Plant a serviceberry and you'll be the first on your block with a blooming tree in the spring. In April, showy clusters of white blossoms cover the bare limbs. For a medley of colors, mix Utah serviceberry with other early boomers such as redbud, ceanothus, and Stansbury cliffrose. The leaves turn shades of yellow and red in fall, and the ornate gray bark and intricate branching give the tree year-round ornamental value. Country churches used to decorate their services with the flowers of *Amelanchier*, hence the common name. At least thirty-five species of birds feast on the summer berries, and deer devour the leaves. The similar Saskatoon, or western, serviceberry, *Amelanchier alnifolia*, grows to 8,000 feet in the Foothill Woodland plant community and higher elevations. Some taxonimists lump the related pallid serviceberry, *A. pallida*, with *A. utahensis*.

Amelanchier utahensis

Amorpha fruticosa

Desert indigo or western false indigo

Amorpha fruticosa

Native Distribution: woodlands, protected slopes, moist canyons, streambanks; South Coast, Peninsular Ranges, below 4,000 feet; Southern California: Los Angeles, Orange, Riverside, San Bernardino, San Diego counties; east to Texas, north to Wyoming; eastern United States.
Landscape Zone: Chaparral, Coastal Sage Scrub.
Size: 4–10 feet.
Leaves: deciduous.
Flowers: May–June; purple flowers on 6-inch spikes.
Soil: adaptable, well draining.
Exposure: full sun to partial shade.
Temperature: cold hardy to –30 degrees F.
Water: drought tolerant.
Propagation: scarified seeds, softwood and hardwood cuttings.
Profile: The distinctive 6-inch spikes of yellow-tipped, deep-purple flowers make desert indigo an attractive addition to an informal wildscape planting. The yellow stamens extend just beyond the purple petals, providing a dramatic contrast of colors. You can prune desert indigo into a multistemmed specimen to add interest to a background planting along a fence, in an entry garden, or in a mixed grouping. The bright green leaves and purple flowers make a striking companion with other small-leafed species, such as serviceberry, desert thorn, salvias, and desert broom. This widespread plant has many varieties, including a white-flowering form, one with crispy-looking leaves, one with variegated leaves, and a dwarf form that is not cold hardy. The related California false indigo, *Amorpha californica,* has 3-inch flower spikes but is not as adaptable to landscape applications. Butterflies love *Amorpha* flowers. The larva to the state butterfly, the California dogface, feed on the leaves, as do those of southern dogface butterfly, common hairstreak butterfly, and silver-spotted skipper.

Arctostaphylos densiflora

Vine Hill manzanita

Native Distribution: open, slopes, ridges, below 300 feet; California: Monterey, Sonoma counties, endemic.
Landscape Zone: Chaparral, widespread.
Size: 1–3 feet tall, rounded.
Leaves: evergreen; shiny, 1 inch long.
Flowers: March–May; white to pink, bell-shaped, 1/4 inch long in clusters.
Fruit: summer; 1/4-inch diameter, applelike pome.
Soil: adaptable, coarse, well draining.
Exposure: full sun to partial shade.
Temperature: cold hardy to –10 degrees F.
Water: drought tolerant, 25 inches/year minimum.
Propagation: cuttings, sprouting, layering.
Profile: With 114 recognized species, varieties, and cultivars of manzanitas, California is ground zero for this versatile family of plants. These landscape gems have ornate, sinuous, red stems; evergreen leaves; and blueberry-type flowers. Though limited in distribution in the wild and classified as endangered, Vine Hill manzanita is one of the most common species in residential and commercial landscapes. It includes half a dozen cultivars that vary from shrubs to specimen trees, which are widely available in the trade. The rounded shape, dense foliage, evergreen leaves, and abundant bell-shaped flowers make these cultivars a favorite for borders, hedges, and mixed plantings. The 'Howard McMinn' cultivar is probably the most commonly available large-scale manzanita and the most garden adaptable. The 'Harmony' and 'Andy Griffiths' cultivars are similar. They can be trained into a sheared hedge or pruned into a striking specimen tree. Hummingbirds feast on the flowers and wildlife on the fruit of these manzanitas.

Arctostaphylos accenting a fence

Arctostaphylos fruit and foliage

Arctostaphylos densiflora 'Howard McMinn'

Arctostaphylos edmundsii

Little Sur manzanita

Arctostaphylos edmundsii

Arctostaphylos edmundsii 'Greenspear'

Native Distribution: coastal bluffs, hills; California: rare and endemic to Monterey County.
Landscape Zone: Chaparral, Coastal Sage Scrub, widespread.
Size: 6-inch groundcover to 3- to 5-foot-tall shrub.
Leaves: evergreen; leathery, 1 to 1-1/2 inches.
Flowers: March–May; white to pink, bell-shaped, 1/4 inch long in clusters.
Fruit: summer; 1/4-inch diameter, applelike pome.
Soil: adaptable, coarse, well draining.
Exposure: full sun to partial shade.
Temperature: cold hardy to 15 degrees F.
Water: drought tolerant, 20 inches/year minimum.
Propagation: cuttings, sprouting, layering.
Profile: The versatile Little Sur manzanita—with half a dozen cultivars, all highly tolerant of garden settings—can fill landscape niches from groundcovers to mounding shrubs. The dense foliage of 'Bert Johnson' forms a rounded shrub that naturally maintains a manicured appearance. The 3- to 5-foot 'Greenspear', introduced by Rancho Santa Ana Botanic Garden, is considered one of the easiest manzanitas to grow. Use it either as a border hedge or foreground planting. The cultivar 'Carmel Sur' spreads rapidly to form a carpet of prostrate branches covered with bright green leaves. Other *Arctostaphylos edmundsii* cultivars have gray-green or reddish leaves, which add foliage variation to your yard, and white to pink flowers. These cultivars provide year-round color and texture to mixed plantings of ceanothus, salvias, fuchsias, and wildflower plots of poppies, goldenrod, and lupines. With so many cultivars available, be sure to choose one adapted to your application and habitat. Wildlife relish manzanita fruit.

Arctostaphylos glauca

Big-berry manzanita

Native Distribution: open, dry hillsides, ridges; Western Transverse Ranges, Peninsular Ranges, below 4,500 feet; Southern California: Imperial, Orange, Los Angeles, Riverside, San Diego, San Bernardino, Santa Barbara, Ventura counties; central California, east to Texas, north to Utah.
Landscape Zone: Chaparral, Joshua Tree Woodland, widespread.
Size: 6–20 feet tall.
Leaves: evergreen; leathery, 1 to 1-1/2 inches.
Flowers: December–March; white to pink, bell-shaped, 1/4 inch long in clusters.
Fruit: summer; 1/2-inch diameter, applelike pome.
Soil: adaptable, coarse, well draining.
Exposure: full sun to partial shade.
Temperature: cold hardy to –10 degrees F.
Water: drought tolerant, 12 inches/year minimum.
Propagation: cuttings, sprouting, layering.
Profile: In the varied world of manzanitas, some grow knee high; others develop into attractive shrub-trees. Big-berry manzanita grows into a 7- to 10-foot-tall specimen with a vaselike shape and multiple stems. You can prune the lower limbs to show off the spectacular red bark of the gnarled trunks. The gray-green, evergreen leaves, ornate bark, and blueberry-type flowers make it a dramatic accent plant for patios, poolsides, or landscape islands. This adaptable species grows from desert to mountains, and it is best suited for landscapes at lower elevations that experience hot summers. Another widespread tree-sized species, pointleaf manzanita (*Arctostaphylos pungens*), grows in Chaparral at 3,000 to 7,000 feet and has similar habitat requirements and landscape uses.

Right: *Arctostaphylos* ornate branching

Below: *Arctostaphylos* fruit

Artemisia californica

California sagebrush

Native Distribution: coastal, dry foothills; South Coast, Western Transverse Ranges, Peninsular Ranges, below 2,600 feet; Southern California: Los Angeles, Orange, Riverside, San Bernardino, San Diego, Santa Barbara, Ventura counties; north to Mendocino County.
Landscape Zone: Chaparral, Coastal Sage Scrub.
Size: 3–5 feet tall, shrub or sprawling groundcover.
Leaves: gray, finely textured, thread-like.
Flowers: fall; minute on spikes, allergenic pollen.
Soil: adaptable, clay or sandy, well draining.
Exposure: full sun.
Temperature: cold hardy to 0 degrees F.
Water: drought tolerant, 12 inches/year minimum.
Propagation: winter-collected seeds.
Profile: Not many plants can match the endurance of California sagebrush in hot, dry locations, especially along the coast. Its feathery, sliver-gray foliage makes an eye-catching accent in a xeriscape garden or landscape island of mixed plants. It also works well as a backdrop against fences or walls. It enjoys the company and pleasantly contrasts the green foliage of manzanitas, coyote brush, and California encelia. Unlike many artimesias, *Artemisia californica* is well mannered and doesn't spread by root shoots. Several varieties and cultivars of this versatile sagebrush exist, so choose one that suits the size and composition of your design. The 'Canyon Gray' and 'Montara' cultivars form sprawling groundcovers 2 to 3 feet high and 4 to 10 feet across. Prune them back to keep the plants flat. Seed-eating birds enjoy *Artemisia* seeds.

Artemisia californica 'Montara'

Artemisia californica 'Canyon Gray'

Artemisia tridentata

Artemisia tridentata

Great Basin sagebrush

Native Distribution: deserts to timberline in arid soils; South Coast, Western Transverse Ranges, Mojave Desert, below 10,000 feet; Southern California: Imperial, Los Angeles, Orange, Riverside, San Bernardino, San Diego, Santa Barbara, Ventura counties; western half of the U.S.; Canada, Mexico.
Landscape Zone: Coastal Sage Scrub, Pinyon-Juniper Woodland, Joshua Tree Woodland.
Size: 3–8 feet tall, 4 feet wide.
Leaves: evergreen; 1/2 to 1-3/4 inches long, silvery, hairy, wedge-shaped with 3 lobes.
Flowers: fall; minute on spikes, allergenic pollen.
Soil: adaptable, well draining.
Exposure: full sun.
Temperature: cold hardy to –30 degrees F.
Water: drought tolerant, 10 inches/year minimum.
Propagation: seeds.
Profile: Though Great Basin sagebrush is probably the most common range plant in the western United States, it deserves a place in our wildscape landscape designs. Besides being a premier foliage plant, its aromatic leaves produce the refreshing desert aroma that fills the air after a thunderstorm. In your yard, the small, three-lobed, grayish green leaves will contrast well with pinyon pines, manzanitas, and junipers. The gray foliage also complements rabbitbrush, winterfat, and barberries. Great Basin sagebrush grows rapidly if water is available. You may occasionally have to cut it back to maintain dense branching and foliage. As with all *Artemisia* species, the wind-blown pollen of *Artemisia tridentata* may cause allergic reactions in sensitive people.

Baccharis sarothroides

Desert broom

Native Distribution: sandy hillsides, washes, roadsides; Peninsular Ranges, Mojave Desert, Sonoran Desert, below 3,000 feet; Southern California: Imperial, Riverside, San Diego counties; east to New Mexico; Mexico.
Landscape Zone: Creosote Bush Scrub, Coastal Sage Scrub.
Size: 3–9 feet tall.
Leaves: evergreen; 1/4 to 1-1/2 inch long, stems green.
Flowers: June–October; heads of small yellow flowers on female plants.
Fruit: fall–winter; showy, white seed heads.
Soil: sandy, rocky, clay, well draining.
Exposure: full sun to partial shade.
Temperature: cold hardy to 10 degrees F.
Water: drought tolerant, 12 inches/year minimum.
Propagation: seeds.
Profile: Plant this large, bushy evergreen with brilliant green stems to screen a fence or for a privacy hedge, background, or windbreak. The dense array of slender branches creates a thick, rounded profile, although desert broom is a little wild-looking for a formal design. For mass coverage, plant on 4- to 5-foot centers. In the summer, white flower heads cover the branch tips of the female plants as though they had been dusted with snow; they also produce copious amounts of seeds that sprout vigorously. You may be better off choosing a male plant to avoid the seed litter. If the shrub becomes woody, prune in the winter. Limiting water after the plant is established encourages dense growth. Several hybrids are available that are smaller and more rounded. For complementary green foliage, consider planting with mesquite, ironwood, fairy duster, desert willow, and chuparosa. The similar coyote brush, *Baccharis pilularis*, grows at elevations below 2,000 feet and has browner stems; it also has a popular dwarf form (see profile under Groundcovers). *Baccharis* flowers are an excellent nectar source for butterflies. Deer tend to ignore the genus.

Above: *Caesalpinia mexicana*
Left: *Caesalpinia gilliesii*

Caesalpinia gilliesii

Desert bird of paradise

Caesalpinia gilliesii flowers

Caesalpinia pulcherrima flowers

Native Distribution: roadsides, vacant lots, dry hills, washes; naturalized, below 1,000 feet; Southern California: Riverside, San Bernardino, San Diego, Santa Barbara counties; native to Argentina, Uruguay; naturalized throughout desert Southwest; west to Texas, Florida; Mexico.
Landscape Zone: widespread.
Size: 5–10 feet high, 4–6 feet wide.
Leaves: deciduous, evergreen when frost free; fernlike leaflets.
Flowers: spring and early summer, sporadically thereafter; yellow, 4–5 inches long, showy with long, red stamens.
Fruit: curly, fuzzy pod persistent on branches unless removed.
Soil: adaptable, well draining.
Exposure: full sun.
Temperature: extremely heat tolerant, root hardy to 5 degrees F, twig damage and leaf loss at 25 degrees F.
Water: extremely drought tolerant.
Propagation: seeds.
Profile: Originally introduced from South America, *Caesalpinia gilliesii* was too tough to die in the western deserts of North America and became naturalized from California to west Texas. Flamboyant spikes of airy yellow flowers burst into bloom with long, red stamens that add summer color to a xeriscape garden or patio planting. The tropical, fernlike leaves and multiple, slender trunks complement mesquite, nolina, yuccas, and ocotillo. This large, irregular shrub can be trained to 15-foot tree, but it looks best as an informal shrub. An occasional deep watering encourages blooming. The seeds and green seed pods are toxic.

The closely related Mexican bird of paradise, *Caesalpinia mexicana,* has yellow flowers, broader leaflets, and freezes back as a herbaceous perennial at 18 degrees F. It can be shaped into a 10-foot tree. The widely used *C. pulcherrima* has red flowers and spines and is severely damaged by freezing. Prune it to 12 inches in the winter, and by summer it will grow into a 6-foot, airy bush covered with flowers.

Calliandra eriophylla

Fairy duster

Native Distribution: sandy washes, hills, dry plains; Sonoran Desert, below 4,500 feet; Southern California: San Diego, Riverside, Imperial counties; west to Texas; Mexico.
Landscape Zone: Creosote Bush Scrub.
Size: 1–3 feet.
Leaves: deciduous; compound with fernlike leaflets.
Flowers: March–April; clusters of reddish heads with 1-inch tassel-like stamens.
Fruit: flat, 2-inch pod.
Soil: adaptable, coarse, well draining.
Exposure: full sun to partial shade.
Temperature: heat tolerant, root hardy to 5 degrees F.
Water: very drought tolerant, 10 inches/year minimum.
Propagation: seeds.
Profile: When rose to purple tassels cover the slender limbs of this loosely branching shrub, you'll know how it got its name. In the early spring, fairy duster turns a mass planting into a colorful pompom rally. With extra water, it can carry its unusual flowers into the summer with another burst of blooms in the fall. Use fairy duster as a low border or foreground planting, landscape island accent, container plant, or to draw attention to a patio or courtyard garden. The puffball blooms and lacy leaflets match well with mesquite, catclaw acacia, ironwood, desert thorns, yuccas, and agaves. Baja fairy duster, *Calliandra californica,* has a similar growth habit and 2-inch, red flowers. Native to Baja California, it suffers twig damage at 25 degrees F. If you enjoy hummingbirds, plant a fairy duster in your yard.

Calliandra californica flower

Calliandra californica

Calliandra californica flower

California Lilacs

With bundles of colorful and fragrant flowers, evergreen leaves, and a variety of growth forms, California lilacs of the genus *Ceanothus* rate near the top of any list of California landscaping plants. Best of all, regardless of where you live, you can find a *Ceanothus* suitable for your yard. By some reports, all but two of the *Ceanothus* species in the world, which grow from Canada to Guatemala, occur within the borders of California. The California Native Plant Exchange lists eighty-one taxa (species, subspecies, varieties) of *Ceanothus* on its website (www.cnplx.info). In addition, plant propagators in the nursery trade have developed dozens of hybrids and cultivars offering a variety of landscape qualities.

The eight counties of Southern California harbor about sixteen native species of *Ceanothus* that produce showy blossoms in colors that range from white to vibrant blues. Most likely, you will be buying one of the numerous hybrids and cultivars offered by nurseries. Some are suited to hot, dry exposures, others to cooler, coastal habitats. Size varies, often within a single species, from prostrate groundcovers to shrubs 20 feet tall and wide, so take care to pick one that is appropriate for the scale and conditions of your site. Consult a knowledgeable native plant nursery for *Ceanothus* species and varieties known to thrive in your area. The main characteristics you will want to consider are the plant's mature size, the limb structure (erect, spreading, or arching), the leaf texture (shiny to fuzzy), and flower color, shape, and bloom time.

Shrubby *Ceanothus* plants respond well to an annual trim immediately after flowering. A light pruning keeps the branching tight and helps maintain vigor. Tall species can be trained into medium-sized trees by removing lower branches as they develop.

Listed here are representative species, varieties, hybrids, and cultivars that grow well in Southern California habitats.

Above: *Ceanothus* used as a groundcover
Upper left: *Ceanothus* in flower
Middle left: The 'Far Horizon' cultivar is a colorful shrub form of *Ceanothus*
Lower left: *Ceanothus* 'Far Horizon' flowers

Ceanothus arboreus
Island ceanothus

Native Distribution: wooded slopes, canyons; Channel Islands, below 1,000 feet; Southern California: naturalized Los Angeles, Santa Barbara counties.
Landscape Zone: Chaparral, widespread.
Size: 20 feet tall, 10 feet wide.
Leaves: evergreen; 2–3 inches long, fuzzy undersides.
Flowers: February–May; spikes of blue flowers in dense clusters.
Soil: adaptable, sandy, clay, well draining.
Exposure: full sun.
Temperature: heat tolerant, root hardy to 10 degrees F.
Water: drought tolerant, 12 inches/year minimum.
Propagation: spring-sown seeds, softwood cuttings.
Profile: Take a clue from the Latin name of this fast-growing California lilac, *arboreus*, which means tree: it's the largest member of the vast *Ceanothus* genus. Island ceanothus is a longtime standard in the nursery industry. You can prune it as a specimen plant or shape it into a screen or hedge. The downy leaves give the plant an ornate appearance. The hybrid 'Owlswood Blue', discovered in Oakland in 1947, grows 3 to 9 feet tall and has vibrant blue flowers on 6- to 8-inch spikes that bloom in February to March. Another hybrid, 'Ray Hartman', discovered in 1951, grows as a large shrub or small tree, 10 to 15 feet high, and bears shiny leaves; the 3- to 5-inch-long spikes of blue flowers show in March to May. The drought-tolerant 'Tassajara Blue' has dark green leaves and grows to 8 feet tall. These vigorous growers are well suited to the coastal cities of Southern California.

Ceanothus arboreus flowers and foliage

Ceanothus cyaneus
San Diego mountain lilac or lakeside ceanothus

Native Distribution: dry ridges, mountain slopes; South Coast Ranges, Transverse Ranges, Peninsular Ranges, below 1,200 feet; Southern California: Riverside, San Diego counties; Baja California.
Landscape Zone: Chaparral, widespread.
Size: 10–15 feet tall and wide.
Leaves: evergreen; 1 to 1-1/2 inches long.
Flowers: March–June; spikes of blue flowers in dense clusters.
Soil: adaptable, clay, well draining.
Exposure: full sun.
Temperature: heat tolerant, root hardy to 10 degrees F.
Water: moderately drought tolerant, 20 inches/year minimum.
Propagation: spring-sown seeds, softwood cuttings.
Profile: If you live in a coastal, freeze-free zone, this fast-growing beauty will stop the traffic on your street when it bursts into bloom. Showy clusters of fragrant blue flowers cover the shrub and steal the show from any other plant in your or your neighbors' yards. A number of cultivars have been developed from this versatile species, so select one that best suits your design scale and growing conditions. The flamboyant 'Sierra Blue' grows to 15 feet and is more cold hardy but less drought tolerant than the straight species.

Ceanothus greggii

Desert ceanothus or cup-leaf ceanothus

Ceanothus greggii

Ceanothus greggii flowers

Native Distribution: dry hills, rocky slopes; Transverse Ranges, Peninsular Ranges, White Mountains, desert mountains, below 7,500 feet; Southern California: Imperial, Los Angles, Orange, Riverside, San Bernardino, San Diego, Santa Barbara, Ventura counties; west to Texas, Nevada, Utah; Mexico.
Landscape Zone: Chaparral, Pinyon-Juniper Woodland, Joshua Tree Woodland.
Size: 1–5 feet.
Leaves: evergreen; leathery, 1/4 to 1 inch long.
Flowers: March–June; white to bluish, 3/8-inch-long petals in dense clusters.
Soil: adaptable, well draining.
Exposure: full sun.
Temperature: heat tolerant, cold hardy to –20 degrees F.
Water: drought tolerant, 15 inches/year minimum.
Propagation: spring-sown seeds, softwood cuttings.
Profile: If your yard has a hot, dry exposure, *Ceanothus greggii* may be the ceanothus for you. Desert ceanothus' dense clusters of fragrant, creamy, lilac-like flowers bring spring color to a xeriscape garden, landscape island, or mixed planting. The intricately branching, grayish white shrub forms a rounded profile. Use it as an informal hedge along a fence or rock wall or in border plantings where it receives full sun and reflected heat. Deep watering in the spring encourages profuse blooming. The shrub's small leaf structure matches well with scrub oak, desert ironwood, mesquite, catclaw acacia, desert indigo, and fairy duster. Hoary-leaved ceanothus, *Ceanothus crassifolius*, grows in similar conditions. It has hollylike leaves with bristles and fuzzy white undersides.

Ceanothus griseus

Carmel ceanothus

Native Distribution: dry hills, rocky slopes; coastal, below 700 feet; Southern California: Santa Barbara, Ventura counties; central coast.
Landscape Zone: Coastal Sage Scrub, widespread.
Size: 1–12 feet, groundcover to shrub.
Leaves: evergreen; glossy, 1–2 inches long.
Flowers: spring–fall; blue, 2- to 3-inch-long clusters.
Soil: adaptable, well draining.
Exposure: full sun to full shade.
Temperature: heat tolerant, cold hardy to 10 degrees F.
Water: drought tolerant, 25 inches/year minimum.
Propagation: spring-sown seeds, softwood cuttings.
Profile: Though originally from the central and northern coastal regions of the state, *Ceanothus griseus* has a large number of hybrids and cultivars that make it one of the most widespread species in the nursery trade. The flowers vary from light to dark blue and develop on 2- to 3-inch clusters from spring through December. The 'Louis Edmonds' cultivar grows into a shrub 6 feet high and twice as wide. Plant it as a border or sheared hedge, let it sprawl over a masonry wall, or let it dominate a corner with its showy flowers and foliage. Among the many groundcover selections, 'Yankee Point' grows to 3 feet tall and 'Diamond Heights' to 1 foot tall.

Ceanothus griseus 'Yankee Point' flowers

Ceanothus griseus 'Yankee Point'

Ceanothus thyrsiflorus

Blue blossom

Ceanothus 'Far Horizons'

Ceanothus 'Snow Flurry' flowers

Native Distribution: wooded slopes, canyons; central, north coast ranges, below 2,000 feet; Southern California: Los Angles, Riverside, San Bernardino, San Diego, Santa Barbara, counties; central coast north into Oregon.
Landscape Zone: Chaparral, widespread.
Size: 5–25 feet tall and wide.
Leaves: evergreen; 1–2 inches long, deep green.
Flowers: May–June; spikes of blue flowers in dense clusters.
Soil: adaptable, well draining.
Exposure: full sun.
Temperature: heat tolerant, root hardy to 10 degrees F.
Water: not drought tolerant, 32 inches/year minimum.
Propagation: spring-sown seeds, softwood cuttings.
Profile: The showy blue blossom ceanothus thrives along the Pacific coast from Oregon to Santa Barbara and in scattered locations south to San Diego County where favorable habitats exist. For this plant to shine, it needs the right conditions and a little TLC. It prefers locales without hard freezes or prolonged drought, so if you're very far from the coast, protect it and give it a monthly deep drink in the summer. Several crosses and cultivars exhibit improved landscape qualities. The natural hybrid *Ceanothus* X *regius* occurs in Los Angeles, Orange, Riverside, Santa Barbara, and Ventura counties. The shade-tolerant 'Skylark' matures into a rounded shrub 3 to 5 feet high and wide. 'Snow Flurry', which has glossy leaves and white flowers, reaches 18 feet tall and wide. Adding to the complexity of the species, the 'Taylor's Blue' variety grows as a 3-foot-high groundcover.

Cercocarpus montanus (Cercocarpus betuloides)

Mountain mahogany

Native Distribution: rocky canyons, dry mountain slopes; Transverse Ranges, Peninsula Ranges, below 8,000 feet; Southern California: Imperial, Los Angeles, Orange, Riverside, San Bernardino, San Diego, Santa Barbara, Ventura counties; east to Texas, north to Montana; Mexico.
Landscape Zone: Chaparral.
Size: 5–15 feet.
Leaves: almost evergreen; wedge-shaped, 1 inch long.
Fruit: summer–fall; 1- to 3-inch, feathery, spiral tail on seeds.
Soil: adaptable, well draining.
Exposure: full sun.
Temperature: heat tolerant, cold hardy to 0 degrees F.
Water: drought tolerant, 12 inches/year minimum.
Propagation: scarified, stratified seeds, softwood cuttings.

Profile: If you want a densely foliated, almost evergreen shrub with an interesting fall display, plant a mountain mahogany. Just when many plants are fading, this shrub comes into its most beautiful season. As the seeds begin to mature, they develop a twisted feathery tail, and by September they almost obscure the leaves. You can shape the plant into a compact shrub or hedge suitable for screen, border, or foundation plantings. When planted alone, mountain mahogany accents open areas or landscape islands. Given time and proper pruning, this slow-growing plant will become a small, multitrunked tree with ornate shaggy, reddish bark. Botanists recognize seven varieties in this confusing species, each with a slightly different form and distribution, but all have excellent landscape applications. Another species with exceptional landscape value is the curl-leaf mountain mahogany, *Cercocarpus ledifolius*. A native of Pinyon-Juniper Woodland, it has evergreen leaves with white undersides.

Cercocarpus montanus seed heads

Cercocarpus montanus

Cleome isomeris (Isomeris arborea)

Bladderpod

Native Distribution: desert washes, flats, coastal hills, slopes; South Coast, deserts, Channel Islands, below 4,200 feet; Southern California: Imperial, Los Angeles, Orange, Riverside, San Bernardino, San Diego, Santa Barbara, Ventura counties; Arizona, Baja California.
Landscape Zone: Coastal Sage Scrub, Creosote Bush Scrub, Joshua Tree Woodland.
Size: 3–5 feet tall and wide.
Leaves: evergreen; 1/2 to 1-1/2 inches long.
Flowers: winter–spring, throughout year; 1–2 inches long, yellow with extended stamens, in dense clusters on branch tips.
Fruit: fall–winter; 2-inch pod.
Soil: adaptable, alkaline, sandy, clay, well draining.
Exposure: full sun.
Temperature: heat tolerant, cold hardy to 0 degrees F.
Water: drought tolerant, 8 inches/year minimum.
Propagation: fall-sown seeds.
Profile: The hardy bladderpod will bring four-season color and a foliage accent to your landscape. Clusters of bright yellow flowers decorate the branch tips in winter and spring, and throughout the year when moisture is sufficient. The stamens extend beyond the petals to produce a spidery effect, and the pods, about the size of snow peas, dangle from the limbs and add texture. The compact branching and rounded shape makes bladderpod a good companion with desert indigo, fairy duster, Indian mallow, bush monkey flower, and desert bird of paradise. For landscape layering, use it as a foreground to larger shrubs such as manzanitas, sumacs, junipers, and acacias. This plant ranges from the coast to the deserts, so for best results, obtain one that was grown from local seeds. The 'Dorado' cultivar is adapted to desert conditions. Be warned: this member of the caper family produces an unpleasant odor when brushed against.

Cleome isomeris

Cleome isomeris flower

Comarostaphylis diversifolia

Summer holly

Native Distribution: coastal, hillsides; South Coast, Western Transverse Ranges, Peninsular Ranges, below 2,000 feet; Southern California: Imperial, Los Angeles, Orange, Riverside, San Diego, Santa Barbara, Ventura counties; Baja California.
Landscape Zone: Chaparral.
Size: 20 feet tall and wide.
Leaves: evergreen; 2–6 inches long, serrated edges.
Flowers: spring; white, blueberry-type.
Fruit: fall; red, 1/4-inch, round drupe.
Soil: adaptable, sandy, clay, well draining.
Exposure: full sun.
Temperature: heat tolerant, cold hardy to 0 degrees F.
Water: drought tolerant, 12 inches/ year minimum.
Propagation: seeds.
Profile: With tassels of bell-shaped flowers in the spring, showy red berries in the fall, and evergreen leaves, this member of the blueberry (not holly) family decorates your landscape throughout the year. Summer holly grows relatively slowly, but in five years or so it will become large enough for an effective screen, hedge, or background along a fence. With its ornate flowers and fruit, it makes a dramatic two- or three-season accent for a courtyard or landscape island. For year-round colorscaping, compatible companion plants include copper leaf, manzanitas, ceanothus, hollyleaf cherry, and woolly blue curls.

Comarostaphylis diversifolia

Coreopsis gigantea

Giant coreopsis

Native Distribution: hillsides, dune fields; South Coast, Channel islands, below 200 feet; Southern California: Los Angles, Orange, Riverside, San Diego, Santa Barbara, Ventura counties; central coast.
Landscape Zone: Coastal Sage Scrub.
Size: 2–6 feet tall.
Flowers: February–March; 3-inch yellow head with yellow center.
Soil: adaptable, well draining.
Exposure: full sun.
Temperature: cold hardy to 25 degrees F.
Water: drought tolerant, 12 inches/year minimum.
Propagation: seeds, cuttings of young basal shoots.
Profile: Imagine a 2-foot-tall perennial shrub with a limbless trunk, shaggy leaves, and a crown covered with buttery, yellow flowers. Step back in time before rabbits and goats were introduced to the Channel Islands, and this bizarre shrub could have been a 10-foot-tall "tree." In your yard, giant coreopsis shines as an eyecatching accent with its dark green, feathery leaves and contrasting brilliant flowers that cover the plant in the spiring. For a multiseason colorscape, paint the landscape around this focal plant with the blues and reds of seaside daisy, lupines, penstemons, bush monkey flower, and California poppy. Mix with blue and gray grasses, sages, and dudleyas for complementary foliage and texture.

Coreopsis gigantea

Cornus sericea fall color

Cornus sericea fruit and foliage

Cornus sericea (Cornus stolonifera)

Redosier dogwood

Native Distribution: moist areas, streambanks; South Coast, Western Transverse Ranges, Peninsular Ranges, below 9,000 feet; Southern California: Los Angeles, Orange, Riverside, San Bernardino, San Diego, Santa Barbara; north to Alaska, east to Maine; Canada, Mexico.
Landscape Zone: Chaparral, Foothill Woodland.
Size: 4–12 feet tall.
Leaves: deciduous; showy red branches.
Flowers: May–July; clusters of white blossoms, 2–4 inches across.
Fruit: fall; white drupe, 1/3-inch diameter.
Soil: adaptable, clay, serpentine.
Exposure: full sun to full shade.
Temperature: cold hardy to –20 degrees F.
Water: requires regular moisture, 38 inches/year minimum.
Propagation: scarified and cold-stratified seeds.
Profile: If you live in a high-rainfall area or have naturally moist soil, this open-branching shrub will provide year-round color for your yard. Creamy flowers cover the branches in the spring followed by white fruit in the summer and reddish leaves in the fall. But the show's not over when the leaves drop. The red branches provide a dramatic accent all winter. For its spreading limbs to have the natural, airy, irregular appearance, dogwoods must be planted in dappled shade. Dogwoods have a sensitive network of surface feeding roots easily damaged by drought, tilling, or adding a thick layer of soil, so mulch lightly to preserve moisture. They make an ideal accent for small yards or patios. Plant as a medium-sized specimen in a shady corner or entryway or a multistemmed background for a landscape island. For a colorful combination, mix with redbud, flowering ash, or Mexican elderberry with an understory of snowberry, flannel bush, or matilija poppy. A related species with brownish purple stems and similar landscape uses is brown dogwood, *Cornus glabrata*. In the fall, numerous birds feed on the fruit of dogwoods.

Cornus sericea

Dendromecon harfordii

Island bush poppy

Native Distribution: dry slopes, below 2,000 feet; endemic to Channel Islands.
Landscape Zone: Chaparral, Coastal Sage Scrub, Foothill Woodland.
Size: 3–12 feet tall.
Leaves: evergreen; 2–3 inches long.
Flowers: spring–fall; yellow, 2 inches diameter.
Soil: adaptable, well draining.
Exposure: full sun to partial shade.
Temperature: cold hardy to 5 degrees F.
Water: drought tolerant, 10 inches/year minimum.
Propagation: seeds, cuttings.
Profile: Like an actor donning a costume and assuming a flamboyant persona, island bush poppy transforms itself every spring with a wardrobe of showy butter-yellow flowers that last into December. Use this fast-growing shrub from the Channel Islands as a container plant for poolsides or porches or as a color component in a landscape island. For colorscaping schemes, bush poppy adds a dramatic flowering companion to midsized shrubs such as brittle bush, salvias, ceanothus, and bush monkey flower. It adds a vertical element to a perennial flower garden of California poppies, buckwheat, California fuchsia, and evening primrose. The less ornamental mainland species, *Dendromecon rigida,* has narrow leaves and a spring blooming season.

Dendromecon rigida

Dendromecon harfordii flower

Dendromecon harfordii

Diplacus aurantiacus

Diplacus aurantiacus flowers

Diplacus aurantiacus (Mimulus aurantiacus)

Bush monkey flower

Native Distribution: coastal, hillsides, canyons, disturbed areas; South Coast, Western Transverse Ranges, Peninsular Ranges, Sonoran Desert, below 7,500 feet; Southern California: Imperial, Los Angeles, Riverside, San Bernardino, San Diego, Santa Barbara, Ventura counties; Oregon.
Landscape Zone: Chaparral, Coastal Sage Scrub, Joshua Tree Woodland, Foothill Woodland.
Size: 3–5 feet tall.
Flowers: spring, fall; 1–2 inches long, orange, red, or yellow.
Exposure: full sun to partial shade.
Temperature: cold hardy to 0 degrees F.
Water: drought tolerant, 18 inches/year minimum.
Propagation: seeds.
Profile: Bush monkey flowers are right at home in a state known for its botanical diversity. What's a taxonomist to do with a closely related group of plants with flower colors ranging from yellow to red? Some split them into thirteen species within the genus *Mimulus*; others lump them into one species in the genus *Diplacus*. This gets confusing when you ask for plants at the local nursery, where they are probably still listed as *Mimulus*. Regardless of the name you choose, bush monkey flower rates tops in landscape applications. The abundant flowers delight hummingbirds, so you know this shrub's a garden hit. Combine with honeysuckles, lupines, salvias, currants, and fuchsias for an island of complementary flower types. Bush monkey flower comes in numerous colors and varieties and dozens of cultivars, so pick one adapted to your habitat conditions.

Encelia californica

Encelia farinosa

Encelia californica

California sunflower or California brittle bush

Encelia californica flower

Native Distribution: scrubby, sandy, or gravel hills; South Coast, Peninsular Ranges, below 2,000 feet; Southern California: Los Angeles, Orange, Riverside, San Bernardino, San Diego, Santa Barbara, Ventura counties; Arizona, Utah, Nevada.
Landscape Zone: Chaparral, Coastal Sage Scrub.
Size: 2–4 feet tall and wide, mounding.
Leaves: evergreen, deciduous in drought conditions; 2–4 inches long.
Flowers: spring, fall after rain; yellow rays, brown center, 2 inches wide on long stems that extend beyond foliage.
Soil: sandy, rocky, well draining.
Exposure: full sun.
Temperature: heat tolerant, cold hardy to 20 degrees F.
Water: drought tolerant, 12 inches/year minimum.
Propagation: seeds.
Profile: In a wet springtime, California sunflower floods the roadsides and hills with waves of brilliant yellow. Plant this durable subshrub in the hottest, driest spot in your yard and watch it burst into bloom after winter and spring rains. Bright yellow, daisylike flowers borne on 6-inch stems obscure the leaves. When not in bloom, the bright green foliage adds variety to a xeriscape garden or mass planting. Mix it with palo verde, acacias, mesquite, or ironwood for understory interest, or use it as a texture contrast with agaves, chollas, yuccas, jojobas, and salvias. The plant goes dormant and loses it leaves in extreme drought, but irrigate sparingly. It takes over your garden if given excess water, so keep your shears handy. Plant *Encelia californica* on the South Coast and the closely related brittle bush, *E. farinosa,* inland.

Ephedra species

Joint fir or Mormon tea

Native Distribution: sandy, rocky plains, hills; South Coast, Coastal and Peninsular ranges, deserts, below 7,500 feet; Southern California: Imperial, Los Angeles, Riverside, San Diego, San Bernardino, Santa Barbara, Ventura counties; east to Texas; Mexico.
Landscape Zone: Creosote Bush Scrub, Chaparral, Joshua Tree Woodland, Pinyon-Juniper Woodland.
Size: 1–4 feet.
Leaves: minuscule, scalelike.
Flowers: spring; tiny, in stem nodes, red to yellow according to species.
Fruit: summer; tiny cones on female plants.
Soil: sandy, rocky, well draining.
Exposure: full sun.
Temperature: heat tolerant, cold hardy to –10 degrees F.
Water: drought tolerant, 8 inches/year minimum.
Propagation: fresh or stratified seeds.

Profile: The smooth, green to yellowish, pencil-like stems of the densely branching joint fir provide an eye-catching focal point in your cactus or xeriscape garden or patio, pool, or container plantings. In the absence of leaves, the broomlike stems carry on photosynthesis and give the plant its green color. Male and female plants are separate and have slightly different flower colors, but the blooms are too small to make much difference. Ephedras complement beargrass, sotol, prickly pear, ocotillo, and yuccas, and add year-round green to a mixed planting with deciduous shrubs. Nine species and varieties, all with similar landscape applications, grow in California. Some are adapted to Death Valley conditions, others to high, cool deserts, so pick one that is native to your area. The most widespread species, California joint fir, *Ephedra californica,* occurs throughout Southern California, except Orange County.

Ephedra

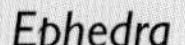

Ephedra

Ericameria laricifolia

Larchleaf goldenbush or turpentine bush

Native Distribution: desert slopes, canyons; desert mountains, Mojave Desert, 3,000–6,500 feet; Southern California: San Bernardino, Riverside counties; to Texas, Utah, Nevada; Mexico.
Landscape Zone: Creosote Bush Scrub, Pinyon-Juniper Woodland.
Size: 2–4 feet tall.
Leaves: evergreen; needlelike, 1/16 inch wide, 3/4 inch long.
Flowers: September–October; heads of 1/2-inch golden flowers.
Soil: limestone, well draining.
Exposure: full sun.
Temperature: extremely heat tolerant, cold hardy to –20 degrees F.
Water: drought tolerant, 8 inches/year minimum.
Propagation: seeds.

Profile: The compact shape, dense branching, and attractive fall flowers make this close relative to rabbitbrush an ideal colorscape choice. An array of bright yellow flowers crowns the stiff, erect branches throughout much of the fall. The lemon flowers and dark green leaves make an attractive border for your walk or drive or a foreground accent in a mixed planting. To add year-round color to a wildscape design, plant it with spring-blooming sages, coyote brush, ceanothus, and Indian mallow. The 'Aguirre' clone has especially showy flowers and rich green foliage. The aromatic leaves give *Ericameria laricifolia* its other common name, turpentine bush. A trim after blooming keeps the foliage dense. The closely related golden fleece, *Ericameria arborescens,* in Chaparral and Foothill Woodland, and the narrowleaf goldenbush, *E. linearfolia,* widespread below 6,000 feet, have similar landscape applications.

Ericameria laricifolia

Ericameria nauseosa pruned to show off trunk

Ericameria nauseosa (Chrysothamnus nauseosus)

Rabbitbrush

Native Distribution: dry soils; Transverse Ranges, Peninsular Ranges, Mojave Desert, below 10,000 feet; Southern California: Imperial, Los Angeles, Orange, Riverside, San Bernardino, San Diego, Santa Barbara, Ventura counties; east to Texas, north to Canada; Mexico.
Landscape Zone: Chaparral, Pinyon-Juniper Woodland, Joshua Tree Woodland, Pinyon-Juniper Woodland, Foothill Woodland.
Size: 2–5 feet.
Leaves: partially evergreen; needlelike, 2-1/2 inches long.
Flowers: July–October; clusters of showy, rayless, yellow flowers.
Soil: adaptable, alkaline, well draining.
Exposure: full sun to partial shade.
Temperature: cold hardy to –10 degrees F.
Water: drought tolerant, 8 inches/year minimum.
Propagation: fresh seeds, hardwood cuttings.
Profile: With bluish green leaves, woolly white stems, and yellow flowers in fall, rabbitbrush accents your landscape throughout the year. The slender, erect stems grow from a woody base and are densely covered with the narrow, ashen leaves. You can plant rabbitbrush in mass and grow as an unsheared hedge along fences or walls, or shear it into a well-mannered border plant. In a mixed-species planting, it provides a striking contrast with evergreens such as barbarries, silktassel, joint fir, manzanitas, and pinyon pine. For a bouquet of fall colors, plant it with Mexican elderberry, chuparosa, snowberry, and goldenrod. You may have to prune this fast-growing plant back in the winter to keep it full and to encourage blooming. Butterflies are attracted to the shrub's copious blooms.

Left: *Ericameria nauseosa*
Below, left: *Ericameria nauseosa* flower
Below, right: *Ericameria nauseosa* in bloom

Eriogonum fasciculatum

California buckwheat

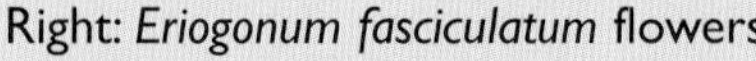

Right: *Eriogonum fasciculatum* flowers

Below: *Eriogonum fasciculatum*

Native Distribution: desert flats, slopes, washes; widespread, below 7,500 feet; Southern California: Imperial, Los Angeles, Orange, Riverside, San Bernardino, San Diego, Santa Barbara, Ventura counties; Arizona, California, Nevada, Utah.
Landscape Zone: Coastal Sage Scrub, Creosote Bush Scrub, Pinyon-Juniper Woodland, Foothill Woodland.
Size: 1–4 feet high, spreads to 4 feet, subshrub.
Leaves: evergreen.
Flowers: March–November; white to pink, 1/8 inch wide in dense terminal clusters.
Soil: adaptable, well draining.
Exposure: full sun to partial shade.
Temperature: heat tolerant, hardy to 15 degrees F.
Water: drought tolerant.
Propagation: seeds, cuttings.
Profile: Looking for a long-blooming addition for your butterfly or xeriscape garden? This low-mounding subshrub won't crowd its neighbors in a mixed planting or landscape garden. Heads of dense white to pink flowers cover the plant from early spring through fall. The tiny, dark green leaves have a woolly covering underneath, which adds year-round visual interest. To maintain its ornamental appearance, trim the plant in midwinter to encourage new, dense growth. A summertime drink encourages prolonged blooming. California buckwheat makes a good colorscape mix for mounding shrubs such as manzanitas, ceanothus, and bush monkey flower. Four varieties of *Eriogonum fasciculatum* grow across Southern California, and numerous cultivars that vary in size and flower color are available at nurseries. 'Dana Point' forms a shrub 3 feet high and wide; 'Bruce Dickerson' and 'Theodore Payne' grow as 1-foot-high groundcovers. Two other popular shrubby buckwheats, island buckwheat (*E. arborescens*) and ashyleaf buckwheat (*E. cinereum*), have similar landscape applications.

Eriogonum fasciculatum in bloom

Eriogonum crocatum foliage and flowers

Eriogonum giganteum

Eriogonum giganteum

Saint Catherine's lace

Native Distribution: dry, rocky slopes, below 1,500 feet; Southern California: endemic to Channel Islands.
Landscape Zone: Chaparral, Coastal Sage Scrub.
Size: 4–8 feet high and wide, rounded shrub.
Leaves: evergreen; 2–3 inches long, gray, woolly.
Flowers: May–December; white to pink, 1/8 inch wide in dense terminal clusters.
Soil: adaptable, well draining.
Exposure: full sun to partial shade.
Temperature: heat tolerant, hardy to 15 degrees F.
Water: drought tolerant, 12 inches/year minimum.
Propagation: seeds.
Profile: With its dense, silvery foliage and commanding size, this giant buckwheat will be the star attraction for much of the year. A profusion of 12-inch-wide flower clusters turn Saint Catherine's lace into a summertime spectacle, and the show continues as the flowers fade to a bright rusty-red in the fall. Use the plant as a focal point in a landscape island, as a corner accent, or as a backdrop for smaller shrubs, such as fuchsias, bush lupines, coyote brush, bush monkey flower, goldenrod, and fuchsia-flowered gooseberry. This extremely drought-tolerant buckwheat adapts well to garden and xeriscape settings and readily produces seedlings. The long flower stalks can be trimmed for dry flower arrangements. Butterflies love the flowers, and birds flock to the seed heads. The related conejo buckwheat, *Eriogonum crocatum,* has similar applications.

Fallugia paradoxa

Fallugia paradoxa flowers

Fallugia paradoxa

Apache plume

Native Distribution: dry, rocky slopes, flats; desert mountains, 3,000–7,000 feet; Southern California: Riverside, San Bernardino, counties; east to central Texas; Mexico.
Landscape Zone: Joshua Tree Woodland, Pinyon-Juniper Woodland.
Size: 3–8 feet.
Leaves: evergreen; lobed, 3/4 inch long.
Flowers: April–October; 1 inch diameter, white.
Fruit: summer–winter; showy, tassel-like seed head.
Soil: adaptable, well draining.
Exposure: full sun.
Temperature: heat tolerant, cold hardy to –10 degrees F.
Water: drought tolerant, 8 inches/year minimum.
Propagation: fresh seeds, layering, root suckers.
Profile: Apache plume contributes year-round to high-desert landscapes. Its fragrant, snow-white flowers bloom continually until October, and the pinkish feathery plumes almost obscure the shrub for much of the year, making it a great component of a colorscape design. The seed heads resemble miniature feather dusters and reminded early settlers of the feather headdress worn by the Apaches. Plant this ornamental shrub as a specimen, a backdrop along a fence, or in a mass planting. It has evergreen foliage, a well-rounded shape, and forms dense clumps, making it suitable for hedges and screens. Apache plume grows rapidly and flowers the first or second year from seed. Prune in the winter, since it flowers on new spring growth. You may need to cut it back severely every few years. An occasional deep watering in the summer encourages flowering.

Forestiera pubescens (Forestiera neomexicana)

Desert olive

Native Distribution: stream sides, hillsides, valleys; Transverse Ranges, Peninsular Ranges, Mojave Desert, below 7,000 feet; Southern California: Los Angeles, Riverside, San Bernardino, San Diego, Santa Barbara, Ventura counties; east to Texas, Nevada to Oklahoma.
Landscape Zone: Creosote Bush Scrub, Chaparral, Coastal Sage Scrub, Foothill Woodland.
Size: 6–10 feet tall, 6 feet wide.
Leaves: deciduous; 1 inch long, yellow fall color.
Flowers: March–May; insignificant.
Fruit: summer; 1/4 inch, oval, bluish, on female plants.
Soil: adaptable, well draining.
Exposure: full sun.
Temperature: cold hardy to –30 degrees F.
Water: drought tolerant, 24 inches/year minimum.
Propagation: seeds, cuttings, layers.
Profile: This ornate shrub goes by many names, and it fits many landscape applications. Desert olive is most beautiful when pruned into a 10- to 20-foot-tall tree for a patio, courtyard, or specimen planting, where it can show off its ornate gray bark, multiple twisting trunks, and airy branching. You can also let it grow into an informal screen or background plant, or shear it into a hedge. In group plantings, the small, glossy leaves direct attention to accent plants such as fairy duster, bush monkey flower, and bird of paradise. In the fall, desert olive demands its own attention with a colorful display of dense, yellow foliage. Birds and small wildlife enjoy the fruit, but you need plants of both sexes to produce fruit, so plant several at a time.

Above: *Forestiera pubescens* fruit
Below: *Forestiera pubescens* grown as a shrub
Lower left: *Forestiera pubescens*

Fouquieria splendens

Fouquieria splendens

Ocotillo

Fouquieria splendens flower

Native Distribution: desert slopes, flats; Sonoran Desert, below 2,300 feet; Southern California: Imperial, Riverside, San Bernardino, San Diego counties; east to Texas, Nevada; Mexico.
Landscape Zone: Creosote Bush Scrub.
Size: 6–15 feet.
Leaves: tiny, emerge briefly after rain.
Flowers: March–June; clusters of red flowers.
Soil: rocky, calcareous or igneous, well draining.
Exposure: full sun.
Temperature: cold hardy to 20 degrees F.
Water: drought tolerant, 8 inches/year minimum.
Propagation: fresh seeds, cuttings.
Profile: Ocotillo is one of the strangest plants of the arid West, and one that was used in Southwest landscapes for centuries before Europeans arrived. Numerous thorn-covered, wandlike branches sprout from a short stem or root crown. The branches are barren during most of the year, but after a rain, tiny green leaves sprout and cover the plant. In the spring, clusters of scarlet, bell-shaped flowers crown each waving branch tip. The intense contrast between the spiny branches and the brilliant flowers adds flair to any landscape design. The airy structure of the plant accents without dominating a group planting, and it provides a vertical element for a xeriscape garden. In humid climates, ocotillo is prone to rot and will seldom flower. Most mature plants for sale come from the wild, so be sure yours has been rescued from a bulldozer, not stripped from natural areas. Nurseries sometimes carry the shrubby Mexican species, palo adan, *Fouquieria diquetii.* Its wands branch more than those of ocotillo, and it is more frost sensitive.

Frangula californica (Rhamnus californica)

Coffeeberry

Native Distribution: coastal foothills, shaded canyons, scrublands, forests; South Coast, Western Transverse Ranges, Peninsular Ranges, desert mountains, below 7,500 feet; Southern California: Imperial, Los Angeles, Orange, Riverside, San Bernardino, San Diego, Santa Barbara, Ventura counties; north to Oregon, Arizona; Mexico.
Landscape Zone: Coastal Sage Scrub, Chaparral, Creosote Bush Scrub, Pinyon-Juniper Woodland, Joshua Tree Woodland, Foothill Woodland.
Size: 6–15 feet tall and wide.
Leaves: evergreen; oval, 1–3 inches long.
Fruit: July–November; red maturing black, 1/4- to 1/2-inch diameter.
Soil: adaptable, sandy, clay, well draining.
Exposure: full sun to partial shade.
Temperature: cold hardy to –20 degrees F.
Water: drought tolerant, 24 inches/year minimum.
Propagation: cuttings, fresh seeds in fall, stratified seeds in spring.
Profile: Adapted to a wide range of natural habitats, light exposures, and soil conditions, coffeeberry feels at home in most landscape settings. In a few years' time, this fast-growing species develops into a 6- to 12-foot mounding shrub with dense, evergreen leaves. The flowers don't count for much, but from summer through fall the ornate fruit punctuates the foliage with drupes that mature from bright red to glossy black. Coffeeberry makes an attractive foundation, privacy, or border hedge or a background screen along a fence. Plant it to accent the corner of your yard or patio, or as a wildlife-friendly forage and nesting plant in a wildscape design. In mixed plantings, its dark green to grayish leaves and red fruit complement toyon, sages, ceanothus, and silktassel. A number of available cultivars, such as 'Mound San Bruno', 'Eve Case', and 'Leatherleaf', will mature to between 3 and 6 feet tall, so be sure to buy one that won't outgrow your landscape. See the groundcovers section of the Plant Profiles for low-growing cultivars of *Frangula californica*. Once a coffeeberry is established, pruning, watering, and maintenance are minimal; all you have to do is enjoy. Birds love the fruit and hummingbirds and butterflies the nectar.

Fremontodendron californicum

California flannel bush

Fremontodendron californicum 'Ken Taylor' flower

Native Distribution: dry, rocky ridges, slopes; South Coast, Western Transverse Ranges, Peninsular Ranges, 1,000–6,500 feet; Southern California: Imperial, Los Angeles, Orange, Riverside, San Bernardino, San Diego, Santa Barbara, Ventura counties; Arizona, Baja California.
Landscape Zone: Chaparral, Pinyon-Juniper Woodland, Foothill Woodland.
Size: 5–20 feet tall, up to twice as wide.
Leaves: evergreen; 2 inches, lobed.
Flowers: spring; 3 inches across, yellow.
Soil: adaptable, well draining.
Exposure: full sun to partial shade.
Temperature: cold hardy to –10 degrees F.
Water: drought tolerant, 25 inches/year minimum.
Propagation: seeds.

Profile: Flannel bush is one of California's premier native landscape plants. It grows rapidly into a large-scale shrub, is covered with buttery yellow flowers in the spring, and has ornately lobed, evergreen leaves. Cultivars usually develop a spreading or cascading profile up to twice as wide as tall. These outstanding qualities make the plant ideal as a mixed garden background, an accent in a courtyard or patio, or a focal shrub in a side yard. Use it in a colorscape design with toyon, ceanothus, barbarries, matilija poppy, salvias, and California fuchsia. Avoid summer water, which may cause root rot. Bristle hairs cover the stems and leaves of the species and some cultivars—hence its common name—which can irritate sensitive skin. Numerous cultivars exist that vary in size, profile, and leaf color and texture. The smaller 'Ken Taylor' and 'El Dorado Gold' grow 4 to 8 feet high and 4 to 6 feet wide, and 'Dara's Gold' grows into a low mound with bright green leaves. 'San Gabriel' reaches 18 feet high and 12 feet wide, while 'Pacific Sunset' and 'California Glory' reach 20 feet high and wide.

Fremontodendron californicum 'Ken Taylor'

Garrya elliptica

Coast silktassel

Native Distribution: dry slopes, canyons, dunes, below 2,600 feet; Southern California: Santa Barbara, Ventura counties; north into Oregon.
Landscape Zone: Chaparral, Coastal Sage Scrub, Foothill Woodland.
Size: 8–25 feet tall, erect.
Leaves: evergreen; gray-green, 2–4 inches long.
Flowers: January–February; 4- to 12-inch tassel on male plants, 2–4 inches long on female plants.
Fruit: summer; 1/4-inch purple drupes on female plants.
Soil: adaptable, well draining.
Exposure: full sun to partial shade.
Temperature: heat tolerant, cold hardy to 10 degrees F.
Water: moderately drought tolerant, 27 inches/year minimum.
Propagation: scarified, stratified seeds, semi-hardwood cuttings.

Profile: Coast silktassel is evergreen, fast growing, densely foliated, and tolerant of drought and heat. The winter flower tassels decorate the tree like silvery Christmas tinsels. When planted alone as a specimen, this foliage-accent plant develops a full, symmetrical shape, growing in time to 15 to 25 feet. The gray-green leaves contribute year-round texture to a mixed planting with deciduous species. Use as a visual or privacy screen, or prune into a medium-sized background or boundary hedge. In hot interior or sunny, dry exposures, supplemental water will enhance growth and appearance. In a companion planting, it complements snowberry, blue blossom ceanothus, Pacific madrone, coyote brush, and bush monkey flower. Nurseries tend to carry the 'James Roof' and 'Evie' cultivars, both of which offer dramatic catkins. The related Fremont silktassel, *Garrya fremontii*, grows in the Chaparral and Foothill Woodland and has similar landscape qualities.

Garrya elliptica

Garrya elliptica fruit

Heteromeles arbutifolia

Toyon or Christmas berry

Native Distribution: South Coast, Western Transverse Ranges, Peninsular Ranges, below 4,000 feet; Southern California: Los Angeles, Orange, San Bernardino, San Diego, Santa Barbara, Ventura, Riverside counties.
Landscape Zone: Chaparral, Foothill Woodland.
Size: 6–15 feet tall, 4–5 feet wide.
Leaves: evergreen; leathery, 2–4 inches long.
Flowers: June–July; white clusters.
Fruit: October–January; 1/4-inch red pome.
Soil: adaptable, sandy, clay, serpentine, well draining.
Exposure: full sun to full shade.
Temperature: cold hardy to 0 degrees F.
Water: drought tolerant, 12 inches/year minimum.
Propagation: seeds planted in flats.
Profile: Few plants offer top-notch ornamental features for every season of the year. With its showy bundles of white flowers, clusters of red berries, evergreen leaves, and adaptability to a wide range of habitats, toyon is one of Mother Nature's grand gifts to California landscapers—and to wildlife, too. Butterflies and bees feed on the flowers, and birds and small mammals depend on the fruit as a primary source of winter food. If you can find a place for a toyon in your yard, treat yourself and the wildlife to a delight for years to come. You can use toyon as a large-scale background screen, shear it into a foundation hedge or formal shrub, or show off its natural beauty by pruning off the lowers limbs to develop it into a multitrunked shrub or small tree. The colorscaping possibilities are prodigious. For companion plants, toyon is compatible with coast live oak, big-leaf maple, serviceberry, coyote brush, coffeeberry, bush monkey flower, and sumacs. Several yellow-berry cultivars are available.

Heteromeles arbutifolia foliage and fruit

Heteromeles arbutifolia

Justicia californica (Beloperone californica)

Chuparosa or hummingbird bush

Native Distribution: dry soils of deserts, washes, rocky foothills; Peninsular Ranges, Sonoran Desert, below 2,600 feet; Southern California: Imperial, Riverside, San Bernardino, San Diego counties; Arizona; Mexico.
Landscape Zone: Creosote Bush Scrub.
Size: 3–4 feet tall.
Leaves: drought-deciduous; oval, 1 inch long.
Flowers: spring, summer, or after rain; 1-1/2 inches long, tube shaped, red.
Soil: adaptable, alkaline, well draining.
Exposure: full sun.
Temperature: heat tolerant, twig damage at 25 degrees F, root hardy to 20 degrees F.
Water: drought tolerant, 10 inches/year minimum
Propagation: seeds.
Profile: Chuparosa is a must for desert hummingbird gardens. The flamboyant red, tubular flowers bloom for much of the year and cover the rounded shrub, especially if given occasional deep watering. The long bloom period complements a colorscape design and adds to the palette in a landscape island or xeriscape garden. For a colorful hummingbird buffet, combine chuparosa with California fuchsia, fairy duster, lupines, salvias, and penstemons. Prune any freeze-damaged limbs in the spring after the last frost. Numerous cultivars exist, including yellow-flowered forms such as 'Tecate Gold'. The widely used Mexican honeysuckle, *Justicia spicigera,* is shade tolerant and has orange flowers.

Clockwise, from left:

Justicia californica

Justicia spicigera

Justicia californica flowers

Krascheninnikovia lanata (Ceratoides lanata, Eurotia lanata)

Winterfat

Native Distribution: dry soils of deserts, flats, slopes; Western Transverse Ranges, desert mountains, Mojave Desert, below 9,000 feet; Southern California: Los Angeles, Riverside, San Bernardino, Santa Barbara counties; east to Texas; north to Canada.

Krascheninnikovia lanata

Landscape Zone: Creosote Bush Scrub, Pinyon-Juniper Woodland.
Size: 1–3 feet tall.
Leaves: evergreen.
Fruit: fall–winter; showy, cottony seed heads along stems of female plants.
Soil: adaptable, alkaline, sandy, clay, well draining.
Exposure: full sun; not shade tolerant.
Temperature: heat tolerant, cold hardy to –30 degrees F.
Water: drought tolerant, 5 inches/year minimum.
Propagation: stratified seeds, softwood cuttings.
Profile: Numerous erect, slender branches grow from a woody base of winterfat, an ornate addition to your desert garden. Woolly hairs densely cover the narrow, bluish green leaves that crowd the stems. From September through December, plumes of fluffy white seeds cover the female plants. The seed plumes remind me of miniature sticks of cotton candy, especially when they glow in the afternoon sun. The dried plumes make an attractive addition to flower arrangements. Use this fast-growing shrub as a color accent with evergreen plants such as desert broom, coyote brush, ephedra, pinyon pine, and California juniper. The spreading root system and low profile make winterfat a good choice for groundcover in hot, arid locations. You'll probably need to trim it back before it begins its spring growth, to keep it thick. Winterfat requires climates with cold nights to thrive. Across its native range from Southwest deserts to Canada, it serves as an important winter forage for mule and white-tailed deer, Rocky Mountain elk, bighorn sheep, pronghorn, rabbits, and ground squirrels.

Larrea tridentata

Larrea tridentata flowers and foliage

Larrea tridentata

Creosote bush

Native Distribution: sandy scrublands; South Coast, Mojave and Sonoran deserts, below 3,500 feet; Southern California: Imperial, Los Angeles, Riverside, San Bernardino, San Diego counties; east to Texas, Utah; Mexico.
Landscape Zone: Creosote Bush Scrub.
Size: 3–6 feet.
Leaves: evergreen; resinous, 3/8 inch long.
Flowers: spring–winter; yellow, 1/2 inch.
Fruit: fuzzy capsules.
Soil: adaptable, alkaline, well draining.
Exposure: full sun.
Temperature: extremely heat tolerant, cold hardy to –10 degrees F.
Water: drought tolerant, 4 inches/year minimum.
Propagation: scarified seeds soaked in water; results are erratic.
Profile: Creosote bush grows in the hottest, driest deserts in the West. When given the advantages of a landscape setting, this normally open-branching shrub develops into a densely foliated specimen plant with a rounded profile. Lemon-yellow flowers or fuzzy seeds accent the plant throughout most of the year. Use as a border hedge or an accent in a cactus garden. In xeriscapes or mixed plantings, the green foliage complements salvias, brittle bush, sagebrush, rabbitbrush, and Apache plume. When mass planted, creosote bushes add more than looks to your yard. After a rain, they perfume the air with that invigorating desert aroma. Extra water in the summer speeds growth, but overwatering kills. Creosote bush clones itself with root suckers, so it survives long after the main plant dies. The clones may be the earth's oldest living organisms. One specimen in the Mojave Desert, known as "King Clone," is estimated to be 11,700 years old.

Lavatera assurgentiflora

Island mallow, malva rosa

Native Distribution: coastal slopes, valleys, below 1,000 feet; Southern California: Channel Islands, endemic; naturalized along coast from San Diego north to Marin County.
Landscape Zone: Coastal Sage Scrub.
Size: 3–12 feet tall and wide.
Leaves: evergreen; 2–6 inches long, 5 to 7 lobes.
Flowers: spring–fall; violet-lavender, 2–3 inches long.
Soil: adaptable, alkaline, well draining.
Exposure: full sun to partial shade.
Temperature: cold hardy to 20 degrees F.
Water: drought tolerant, 9 inches/year minimum.
Propagation: seeds.
Profile: Island mallow is a large, robust plant that grows fast, has maplelike leaves, and offers vibrant, hibiscuslike flowers. Best suited for informal designs, it provides eyecatching interest in a landscape island, as a garden backdrop, or as a focal point in a corner of the yard. It adds a tropical atmosphere to a patio or poolside setting. But keep the shears handy; island mallow needs periodic pruning to maintain a neat appearance. If you live on the coast and get salt spray, this island endemic will feel right at home. For companion plants, choose bush monkey flower, coyote brush, blue witches, bracken fern, California fuchsia, California sage, and salvias. Nurseries likely have cultivars available, including the spreading 'Purisima'. Hummingbirds and butterflies feed on the flowers and birds the seeds. This plant is rare and endangered in the wild.

Lavatera 'Purisima' flower

Lavatera 'Purisima' (*L. assurgentiflora* X *L. venosa*)

Lepechinia calycina

California pitcher sage or woodbalm

Native Distribution: rocky slopes; South Coast, Western Transverse Range, below 3,000 feet; Southern California: Los Angeles, Santa Barbara, Ventura counties; northern California, endemic.
Landscape Zone: Chaparral, Foothill Woodland.
Size: 3–5 feet tall.
Leaves: evergreen; 2–3 inches long, hairy, fragrant.
Flowers: April–June; white to pink, 1–2 inches long.
Soil: adaptable, well draining.
Exposure: full sun to partial shade.
Temperature: cold hardy to 0 degrees F.
Water: drought tolerant, 16 inches/year minimum.
Propagation: seeds.
Profile: This common shrub of the northern and central ranges extends south into the chaparral and foothills around Los Angeles. The evergreen leaves and rows of trumpet-shaped flowers on arching branches give the various pitcher sages instant ornamental appeal for landscapes. As chaparral plants, these tough little shrubs are adapted to hot, dry summers and suffer from excess summer irrigation, so don't plant them near other species that require summer watering. California pitcher sage complements and grows well with copper leaf, coffeeberry, snowberry, bush poppy, and flannel bush. For a hummingbird and butterfly garden, plant with California fuchsia, manzanita, salvia, and penstemons. The popular 'Rocky Point' cultivar is compact and has bluish flowers. The related fragrant pitcher sage, *Lepechinia fragrans*, offers similar landscape applications and showy bluish flowers; the 'El Tigre' cultivar has purple flowers.

Above: *Lepechinia*

Right: *Lepechinia* flower

Lycium fremontii

Fremont desert thorn

Native Distribution: desert washes, rocky, sandy slopes; Peninsular Ranges, Sonoran Desert, below 1,500 feet; Southern California: Imperial, Los Angeles, Riverside, San Bernardino, San Diego, Santa Barbara counties; east to New Mexico; Mexico.
Landscape Zone: Creosote Bush Scrub.
Size: 3–9 feet tall.
Leaves: evergreen, deciduous in drought conditions; 1–3 inches long.
Flowers: March–April; 1/2-inch bluish tubes.
Fruit: summer; 3/8-inch red, juicy berries.
Soil: adaptable, well draining.
Exposure: full sun to partial shade.
Temperature: heat tolerant, cold hardy to 0 degrees F.
Water: drought tolerant, 8 inches/year minimum.
Propagation: fresh seeds, semi-hardwood cuttings.
Profile: If you want to attract wildlife, the dense, spiny branches and small, juicy fruit of Fremont desert thorn provide great habitat for birds and small mammals. The tiny flowers, red berries, bluish green leaves, and arching limbs add a wildscape look to desert gardens or mixed plantings. Though not particularly ornamental, this thicket-forming shrub with 2- to 4-inch spines makes a good barrier or background hedge. It maintains lush foliage when given occasional water; it responds to drought by dropping its leaves. Ironwood, jojoba, palo verde, sagebrush, creosote bush, and fairy duster make good companion plants in desert gardens. Nine species of *Lycium* grow in California deserts. Anderson desert thorn, *Lycium andersonii,* is widespread below 6,000 feet, and California desert thorn, *L. californicum,* grows in Coastal Sage Scrub below 500 feet.

Lycium andersonii flower and foliage

Lycium fremontii fruit and foliage

Lycium fremontii

Mahonia fremontii (Berberis fremontii)

Fremont barberry

Mahonia haematocarpa (Berberis haematocarpa)

Red barberry

Mahonia nevinii (Berberis nevinii)

Nevin barberry

Mahonia pinnata (Berberis pinnata)

California barberry

Mahonia nevinii foliage

Native Distribution: *Mahonia fremontii:* Chaparral, Pinyon-Juniper Woodland, Joshua Tree Woodland, 2,700–5,500 feet; Southern California: San Bernardino, San Diego counties; east to Colorado, New Mexico. *Mahonia haematocarpa:* Pinyon-Juniper Woodland, 3,000–5,500 feet; Southern California: Riverside, San Bernardino counties; east to Texas. *Mahonia nevinii:* Chaparral, Foothill Woodland, Coastal Sage Scrub, below 2,000 feet; Southern California: Los Angeles, Riverside, San Bernardino, San Diego counties; endangered species. *Mahonia pinnata*: rocky slopes; Foothill Woodland, below 3,500 feet; Southern California: Los Angeles, Riverside, San Bernardino, San Diego, Santa Barbara, Ventura counties; Mexico.
Landscape Zone: widespread.
Size: 5–15 feet.
Leaves: evergreen; prickles on edges.
Flowers: February–April; clusters of small, yellow blooms.
Fruit: May–August; edible, red or purple.
Soil: adaptable, alkaline, well draining.
Exposure: full sun to partial shade.
Temperature: heat tolerant, cold hardy to –10 degrees F.
Water: drought tolerant, 12 inches/year minimum.
Propagation: fall-sown or stratified seeds.
Profile: The ornamental evergreen leaves, fragrant flowers, and colorful fruit make these barberries excellent landscape shrubs for Southern California cities. In late winter and early spring, clusters of lemon-yellow flowers accent the spiny, hollylike leaves. By May, bright red *(Mahonia haematocarpa, M. nevinii)* or purple berries create a wildlife buffet. Use these low-maintenance shrubs as specimen plants, garden accents, screens along fences, or for borders along drives. The prickly leaves and dense branching make for a good barrier hedge and cover for birds. The leaves of many selections turn mottled hues of yellow and red in the winter. Propagators have been busy with the California mahonias and have developed numerous crosses and cultivars from the native Fremont barberry (*M. fremontii*), red barberry (*M. haematocarpa*), California barberry (*M. pinnata*), and Nevin barberry (*M. nevinii*). The popular 'Golden Abundance' and 'Ken Hartman' cultivars reach 5 to 8 feet tall and wide and display purple berries. The new leaves of 'Skylark' emerge red. The tart fruit of *Mahonia* makes a tasty jelly, if you can beat the birds at picking time.

Mahonia 'Skylark'

Mahonia haematocarpa

Mahonia 'Golden Abundance'

Mahonia 'Skylark'

Malacothamnus flowers

Malacothamnus fasciculatus

Chaparral bush mallow

Native Distribution: slopes, washes; South Coast, 750–2,700 feet; Southern California: Los Angeles, Orange, Riverside, San Bernardino, San Diego, Santa Barbara, Ventura counties; northern California.

Landscape Zone: Chaparral, Coastal Sage Scrub, Foothill Woodland.
Size: 3–12 feet tall, 4–6 feet wide.
Leaves: evergreen; gray, hairy, 1–3 inches, round with lobes.
Flowers: April–June; pink, hibiscus-like, 1-inch diameter.
Soil: sandy, well draining.
Exposure: full sun to partial shade.
Temperature: heat tolerant, cold hardy to –10 degrees F.
Water: drought tolerant, 12 inches/year minimum.
Propagation: seeds.
Profile: In the spring and summer, you'll join the butterflies in admiring this mallow's extravagant miniature hibiscuslike blossoms. Hundreds of pink flowers cover the slender, arching limbs. Position this fast-growing evergreen as an accent specimen in a corner, as a background for a landscape island, or in front of a fence. The spreading limbs create a wildscape or informal appearance, and the scores of hummingbirds and butterflies flitting about the flowers add to the effect. A winter trim will produce a denser growth the following spring. Some twenty-three, often indistinct, species of bush mallows grow in California, and all but six are listed as threatened or endangered. The chaparral bush mallow grows from Mendocino to San Diego. The species and cultivars available vary in size, flower color, and frost tolerance, so pick one that matches your landscape scale and growing conditions.

Malosma laurina (Rhus laurina)

Laurel sumac

Malosma laurina

Native Distribution: slopes, canyons, stream sides; South Coast, Western Transverse Ranges, Peninsular Ranges, 3,000 feet; Southern California: Los Angeles, Orange, Riverside, San Bernardino, San Diego, Santa Barbara, Ventura counties; Baja California.

Malosma laurina foliage

Landscape Zone: Chaparral, Coastal Sage Scrub, Foothill Woodland.
Size: 6–15 feet tall and wide.
Leaves: evergreen; leathery, elliptic, 1–3 inches long.
Flowers: spring–summer; terminal clusters of tiny, white flowers.
Soil: adaptable, well draining.
Exposure: full sun.
Temperature: heat tolerant, cold hardy to 25 degrees F.
Water: drought tolerant, 12 inches/year minimum.
Propagation: seeds.
Profile: In late summer, the evergreen leaves and dense foliage of laurel sumac stand out on the dry, brown chaparral hillsides. In your yard, this large-scale shrub provides a year-round screen, fenceline hedge, or a clipped and pruned corner accent. For a dramatic all-season hedgerow, mix with toyon, sugar sumac, and lemonade berry. Use it as a backdrop in a landscape island or as a foil for smaller flowering shrubs such as sages, California fuchsia, blue witches, California sunflower, bush monkey flower, and our Lord's candle. The leaves produce volatile oils that have an applelike aroma. Birds feast on the small, white fruit and find shelter in the dense folaige. The leathery leaves are deer resistant.

Myrica californica

Wax myrtle

Native Distribution: coastal dunes and scrub, canyons, moist slopes; coastal woodlands and coniferous forests to 500 feet; Southern California: Los Angeles, Santa Barbara, Ventura counties; along coast north to Washington.
Landscape Zone: Coastal Sage Scrub.
Size: 6–30 feet tall, 15–20 feet wide.
Leaves: evergreen; narrow, dark green.
Flowers: March–May; small, white flowers on short catkins.
Fruit: July–September; 1/3-inch diameter, purple, waxy, aromatic.
Soil: adaptable, well draining.
Exposure: full sun to partial shade.
Temperature: cold hardy to 20 degrees F, wind tolerant.
Water: requires summer water, 50 inches/year minimum.
Propagation: seeds, hardwood cuttings.

Profile: If you live on the moist coast and want an attractive native hedge, plant this dense, glossy-green shrub. You can prune and shape wax myrtle as a foundation, border, screen, background, or barrier hedge. Or trim it into a specimen shrub or small, multi-trunked tree to accent your pool, patio, or entryway. The flowers are insignificant, but the purple, waxy berries add a little ornament. Both the leaves and the fruit produce a spicy, baywood scent. Once established in deep soil in coastal habitats or partial shade, this myrtle is moderately drought tolerant, but interior plantings need weekly summer watering. Avoid planting it in hot, dry exposures. Birds enjoy the seeds as a summer treat.

Above: *Myrica californica* foliage
Right: *Myrica californica*

Nolina parryi

Parry's beargrass

Native Distribution: desert mountains, rocky slopes and hills; Peninsular Ranges, Sonoran Desert, 3,000–6,000 feet; Southern California: Orange, Riverside, San Bernardino, San Diego, Santa Barbara, Ventura counties; endemic.
Landscape Zone: Chaparral, Coastal Sage Scrub, Pinyon-Juniper Woodland, and Joshua Tree Woodland.
Size: 1- to 6-foot-tall trunk.
Leaves: evergreen; wiry, grasslike, 2–4 feet long.
Flowers: May–June; large panicles of creamy white flowers on 8-foot-tall stalks.
Soil: sandy, rocky, loam, well draining.
Exposure: full sun.
Temperature: extremely heat tolerant, cold hardy to 0 degrees F.
Water: drought tolerant, 8 inches/year minimum.
Propagation: seeds, plant division.

Nolina parryi

Profile: Beargrass looks like a rounded clump of thick-bladed grass until it sends up its tall, yuccalike flower stalk. Covered with a mass of tiny, creamy flowers, the 8-foot-tall flower stalk towers above the wiry leaves, creating an eye-catching contrast in color and texture. The compact shape, symmetrical profile, and up to 200 arching, spreading leaves make beargrass an ideal focal plant for a xeriscape or cactus garden. Its stiff, grasslike leaves complement thick-bladed plants such as yuccas and agaves, silktassel, serviceberry, sacred datura, and desert thorn. You can plant beargrass on 3- to 4-foot centers for a groundcover or to stabilize rocky slopes. Beargrass is particularly attractive in a planter or along a ledge with its long leaves dangling over the edge. The similar *Nolina bigelovii* grows in Creosote Bush Scrub.

Nolina parryi in bloom

Purshia stansburiana (*Cowania mexicana* var. *stansburiana*)

Stansbury or Mexican cliffrose

Purshia stansburiana

Native Distribution: dry slopes, canyons, 3,500–8,200 feet; Southern California: Los Angeles, Riverside, San Bernardino counties; east to New Mexico, north into Idaho; Mexico.
Landscape Zone: Joshua Tree Woodland, Pinyon-Juniper Woodland.
Size: 1–6 feet.
Leaves: evergreen.
Flowers: May–July; 1 inch, creamy white.
Fruit: seeds with feathery tails.

Soil: limestone, well draining.
Exposure: full sun to partial shade.
Temperature: heat tolerant, cold hardy to –20 degrees F.
Water: drought tolerant, 12 inches/year minimum.
Propagation: stratified seeds.
Profile: From spring through summer, cliffrose is a mass of fragrant, snowy flowers. The roselike, 1-inch blooms crowd the branches and accent the dark green foliage. When the flowers go to seed, feathery plumes cover the shrub. The evergreen foliage, showy flowers, and ornamental seeds make cliffrose a year-round attraction in your landscape. Use it as a screen or in a mixed planting, or plant it alone to accent a patio, poolside, or corner of your yard. You can prune this intricately branched, densely foliated plant into formal or informal designs, but I like its natural gnarled shape best. It grows slowly and can develop into a picturesque small tree with brown shredding bark. The summer flowers and small leaves make it an attractive companion plant for three-leaf sumac, desert thorn, desert ceanothus, California buckwheat, and Apache plume.

Purshia stansburiana flowers

Rhamnus crocea

Redberry

Native Distribution: scrublands, woodlands, slopes; South Coast, Western Transverse Ranges, Peninsular Ranges, below 5,000 feet; Southern California: Los Angeles, Orange, Riverside, San Bernardino, San Diego, Santa Barbara, Ventura counties; Arizona, Baja California.

Rhamnus crocea

Landscape Zone: Coastal Sage Scrub, Chaparral, Foothill Woodland.
Size: 4–6 feet tall and wide, shrub or groundcover.
Leaves: evergreen; 1/2 inch long, toothed margins.
Flowers: spring; dense clusters of tiny, creamy flowers.
Fruit: summer–fall; 1/4-inch red drupes.
Soil: adaptable, clay, sandy, well draining.
Exposure: full sun to partial shade.
Temperature: cold hardy to 0 degrees F.
Water: drought tolerant, 16 inches/year minimum.
Propagation: seeds.

Profile: With glossy, evergreen, hollylike leaves and bright red berries throughout the fall, this small-scale shrub fills many design requirements. Plant it on 4-foot centers for groundcover, along a drive or walk as a border, as a foundatin hedge below windows, or as a foliage accent in a patio garden. It forms a dense screen and prunes well as a formal hedge or scrub. In colorscaped gardens, redberry provides year-round foliage color and a spalsh of red from summer through the winter, unless birds devour the fruit. The related hollyleaf redberry, *Rhamnus ilicifolia*, has similar landscape applications. It matures to 12 feet, but is slower growing.

Rhus ovata

Sugar sumac

Native Distribution: sunny slopes, canyons; South Coast, West Transverse Ranges, Peninsular Ranges, below 4,500 feet; Southern California: Imperial, Los Angeles, Orange, Riverside, Santa Barbara, San Bernardino, San Diego, Ventura counties; Arizona; Mexico.
Landscape Zone: Chaparral.
Size: 8–15 feet tall and wide.
Leaves: evergreen; 2–4 inches long.
Flowers: March–May; clusters of creamy flowers.
Fruit: hard, red drupes.
Soil: adaptable, well draining.
Exposure: full sun to partial shade.
Temperature: heat tolerant, cold hardy to 0 degrees F.
Water: drought tolerant, 12 inches/year minimum.
Propagation: scarified, stratified seeds, cuttings.

Rhus ovata flowers

Profile: Give this evergreen sumac a place in the sun and admire the results. In the late fall, red flower buds highlight the shiny green leaves, followed in the spring by clusters of creamy flowers. By late summer, red berries replace the flowers and attract a host of birds and small mammals. This naturally rounded shrub needs little attention other than an occasional deep watering in summer and a seasonal trim. With its broad leaves and dense foliage, sugar sumac makes a handsome speciman for patios or poolsides, or it can be sheared, shaped, and pruned into an attractive small tree. Its large scale suits it for a screen or hedgerow. As a background in a landscape garden, it provides year-round foliage texture to complement deciduous plants such as sages, fairy duster, ceanothus, bush monkey flower, and barberries. The twin species, lemonade berry (*Rhus integrifolia*), has identical landscape applications, though it is not as densely foliated. It grows on the ocean side of the coastal ranges in Chaparral and Coastal Sage Scrub below 3,000 feet, and is cold hardy to 20 degrees F.

Above: *Rhus ovata* fruit
Left: *Rhus ovata*

Rhus trilobata

Three-leaf sumac or skunkbush

Native Distribution: canyons, shrubland; South Coast, Western Transverse Ranges, Peninsular Ranges, below 3,500 feet; Southern California: Los Angeles, Orange, Riverside, San Bernardino, San Diego, Santa Barbara, Ventura counties; widespread east to Texas; north into Canada, Mexico.
Landscape Zone: Creosote Bush Scrub, Chaparral, Pinyon-Juniper Woodland, Foothill Woodland.
Size: 3–8 feet tall and wide.
Leaves: deciduous; three-lobed, red and orange fall color.
Flowers: March–April, before leaves; yellowish clusters.
Fruit: hard, 1/4-inch red drupes.
Soil: adaptable, well draining.
Exposure: full sun to partial shade.
Temperature: heat tolerant, cold hardy to –20 degrees F.
Water: drought tolerant, 12 inches/year minimum.
Propagation: scarified, stratified seeds, cuttings.
Profile: This three-season shrub delights your yard with showy flowers, colorful fruit, vibrant foliage, and fall colors. Three-leaf sumac starts spring with showy spikes of yellowish flowers that develop into clusters of red fruit, which are relished by wildlife. The dense green foliage gives a striking contrast with gray-leafed species throughout the summer, and in the autumn the three leaflets provide a showy display of red and orange. You can prune skunkbush into a moderately compact rounded form for background or specimen plantings. It grows fast and spreads by rhizomes to form thickets. It naturally grows in association with mountain mahogany, manzanita, cat-claw acacia, nolina, silktassel, junipers, and pinyon pine. Crushed leaves have a tart scent that is described as sweet by some and skunklike by others. Birds and butterfles enjoy the flowers and fruit of all sumac species.

Rhus trilobata

Rhus trilobata fruit and foliage

Rhus intergrifolia hedge

Ribes aureum flowers

Ribes aureum
Golden currant

Profile: When golden clusters of trumpet-shaped, spicy-scented flowers turn this plant into a mound of spring color, you'll know how golden currant got its name. The dense covering of small, maplelike leaves, absence of prickles or spines, colorful summer fruit, and brilliant autumn shades of burgundy, red, and yellow make this a premier plant for your pool, patio, or landscape garden. Since it spreads by rhizomes, it is well suited for mass plantings and groundcover. Prune to make it more dense, or shear to fit confined areas or containers. Several cultivars and varieties exist, so choose one that is adapted to your region. *Ribes aureum* var. *gracillimum* is adapted to mountain soils and cold winters that reach −30 degrees F. In chaparral or woodlands below 3,000 feet, select *R. aureum* var. *aureum,* or the related hillside gooseberry, *R. californicum.* At lower elevations, golden currants need regular, deep watering in the summer.

Another spectacular, though thorny, species is the fuchsia-flowered gooseberry, *Ribes speciosum,* which delights with a cascade of drooping scarlet flowers; it grows on the South Coast. The cascading blossoms of red-flowered currant, *R. sanguineum*, make a flamboyant addition to a landscape; this species is native below elevations of 7,000 feet. Another red-flowering species is the chaparral currant, *R. malvaceum*, which has a smaller flower head and grows below 5,000 feet in Chaparral. The shrubby white-flowered currant, *R. indecorum,* thrives in Chaparral and Coastal Sage Scrub landscapes. For a shade-tolerant groundcover, choose Catalina Island currant, *R. viburnifolium.* With 53 species and varieties of *Ribes* native to California, offering yellow, red, white, and violet flowers, you're sure to find one that fits your habitat and design. Butterflies and hummingbirds feed on the flowers, and birds devour the sweet fruit, which makes a fine jelly.

Native Distribution: streambanks, moist canyons, forests; South Coast, West Transverse Ranges, Peninsular Ranges, below 10,000 feet: Southern California: Imperial, Los Angeles, Orange, Riverside, San Bernardino, San Diego, Santa Barbara, Ventura counties; north to Montana, east to Texas; Canada.
Landscape Zone: Foothill Woodland.
Size: 3–6 feet tall.
Leaves: summer deciduous; three lobed, fall colors.
Flowers: April–May; clusters of 2-inch golden flowers.
Fruit: summer; 1/4-inch berries maturing yellow to red and black.
Soil: adaptable, well draining.
Exposure: full sun to partial shade.
Temperature: cold hardy to −30 degrees F.
Water: moderately drought tolerant, 16 inches/year minimum.
Propagation: stratified seeds, layering, dormant hardwood cuttings.

Ribes aureum fruit

Ribes speciosum 'Rana Creek' flowers

Ribes aureum

Ribes malvaceum flowers

Ribes sanguineum flowers

Rosa woodsii flower

Rosa minutifolia flower

Rosa californica

California rose

Native Distribution: foothills, stream sides, moist slopes; Western Transverse Ranges, Peninsular Ranges, below 6,000 feet; Southern California: Los Angeles, Orange, Riverside, San Bernardino, San Diego, Santa Barbara, Ventura counties; east to New Mexico; north into Canada.
Landscape Zone: Chaparral, Foothill Woodland, widespread.
Size: 3–6 feet tall and wide.
Leaves: deciduous; branches with sharp, straight thorns.
Flowers: spring–fall, last one day; 2 inches diameter, 5 pink petals.
Fruit: fall; deep-red rose hip.
Soil: adaptable, well draining.
Exposure: full sun to partial shade.
Temperature: high to medium heat tolerance, cold hardy to –20 degrees F.
Water: drought tolerant, 20 inches/year minimum.
Propagation: fall-sown seeds or cold stratify for 2 months.

Profile: When pruned into a rounded bush and covered with pink flowers with showy yellow stamens, California rose adds class to any garden setting. You can also let this aggressive, thicket-forming, rhizomatous bush sprawl for a wildscape look. The fragrant flowers and deep-green leaves accent poolsides and patios, landscape islands, and foundation plantings. As a midgarden show plant, it will stand out against a background of toyon, silktassel, barberries, and sumacs. For a dramatic contrast, mix it with golden currant, coffeeberry, snowberry, flannel bush, ceanothus, or bush poppy. In the spring, new canes emerge red and lined with prickles. Flowers develop on old wood. The similar Wood's rose, *Rosa woodsii* var. *ultramontane*, grows in the interior above 3,500 feet, and the early-blooming chaparral species, small-leafed rose, *R. minutifolia,* begins flowering in December.

Rosa woodsii

Salvia apiana

White sage

Salvia apiana

Native Distribution: dry slopes; South Coast, Transverse Ranges, Peninsular Ranges, deserts, below 4,500 feet; Southern California: Imperial, Los Angeles, Orange, Riverside, San Bernardino, San Diego, Santa Barbara, Ventura counties.
Landscape Zone: Coastal Sage Scrub, Chaparral.
Size: 2–4 feet tall and wide, shrubby.
Leaves: evergreen; 1–3 inches long, white, densely hairy, aromatic.
Flowers: May–August; spikelike clusters of 1-inch, tube-shaped, white flowers on 6-foot stalks.
Soil: adaptable, sandy, loam, clay, well draining.
Exposure: full sun.
Temperature: cold hardy to 20 degrees F.
Water: drought tolerant, 12 inches/year minimum.
Propagation: seeds, spring softwood tip cuttings.
Profile: If your landscape needs a diminiutive yet eye-catching evergreen to add interest to a neglected spot, white sage may fill the bill. A dense array of fuzzy white leaves covers the arching, spikelike shoots. Use this spreading subshrub as an informal groundcover, a border, or for midgarden accent. It will spread to fill a corner or surround a tree with visual interest. From spring through late summer, hundreds of creamy, pea-like flowers decorate the 4- to 6-foot-tall blooming stalks. The masses of white leaves and flowers complement other gray-foliated salvias, silktassel, buckwheats, brittle bush, and ceanothus, as well as prickly pears, nolinas, yuccas, and agaves. Numerous cutivars and compact forms exist. Butterflies and hummingbirds add a bonus to sage gardens.

Salvia clevelandii

Cleveland sage or fragrant sage

Native Distribution: dry slopes, coastal scrub; South Coast, Peninsular Ranges, below 3,000 feet; Southern California: Los Angeles, Orange, Riverside, San Diego counties; Baja California.
Landscape Zone: Chaparral, widespread.
Size: 2–5 feet tall and wide, rounded.
Leaves: evergreen; gray-green, 1–2 inches long.
Flowers: May–August; violet, fragrant, dense whorls on stems.
Soil: sandy, gravelly, loam, well draining.
Exposure: full sun.
Temperature: cold hardy to 10 degrees F.
Water: drought tolerant, 6 inches/year minimum.
Propagation: seeds.
Profile: With hundreds of flowerheads blooming all spring long, this aromatic sage will turn your yard into a purfume factory. The whorls of flowers float above the rounded bush on waving spikes. The contrast between the mass of purple flowers and the gray-green leaves makes for stunning borders, mass plantings, and accents. For colorscaping schemes, mix with California fuchsia, blue witches, buckwheats, flannel bush, bush monkey flower, and Matilija poppy. Nurseries carry numerous hybrids and cultivars that vary from bushes to groundcovers. Match the size, cold tolerance, and flower shade to your needs. 'Winfred Gilman' is compact and has deep blue flowers; it and 'Alpine' are particularly cold and drought tolerant. The 'Pozo Blue' hybrid has larger flowers and is tolerant of frost and clay soils. Deadhead and cut back salvias every winter to maintain a compact growth. Salvias make great components of butterfly and hummingbird gardens.

Salvia clevelandii

Salvia clevelandii flowers

Salvia leucophylla 'Point Sal'

Salvia leucophylla

Purple sage

Native Distribution: dry, coastal foothills; South Coast, Western Transverse Ranges, below 2,500 feet; Southern California: Los Angeles, Orange, Riverside, San Bernardino, San Diego, Santa Barbara, Ventura counties.
Landscape Zone: Coastal Sage Scrub, Chaparral.
Size: 3–6 feet tall, 4–10 feet wide.
Leaves: evergreen; gray, 1–3 inches long.
Flowers: May–July; spherical heads of small, pink to lavender flowers on stems.
Soil: adaptable, sandy, clay, well draining.
Exposure: full sun.
Temperature: cold hardy to 0 degrees F.
Water: drought tolerant, 12 inches/year minimum.
Propagation: seeds.
Profile: This mounding, spreading shrub fills its space with an abundance of lavender-pink flowers all spring and with a dense cover of gray-green foliage the rest of the year. Its rapid growth lends itself to use as a slope planting, a border along a drive, an accent around a pool or patio, or to add interest to a neglected corner. Numerous cultivars are available, including 'Bee's Bliss' and 'Point Sal', which have low, cascading growth. 'Amethyst Bluff', developed by the Santa Barbara Botanic Garden, reaches 5 feet high and wide and produces purple-pink flowers on 12-inch spikes. The spent flowers of these sages should be removed and the shrub cut back every year. For visual interest, plant gray-foliated sages with California fuchsia, bush monkey flower, ceanothus, California sunflower, and penstemons. Plant a sage and you're sure to have visits from hummingbirds and butterflies.

Shepherdia argentea

Shepherdia argentea

Silver buffaloberry

Native Distribution: moist soil near water, 3,000–6,500 feet; Southern California: Santa Barbara, Ventura counties; northern California, east to New Mexico; north to Canada.
Landscape Zone: Pinyon-Juniper Woodland.
Size: 6–10 feet tall.
Leaves: deciduous; 1–2 inches long, silver, thorny.
Fruit: summer; 1/4-inch edible, red to yellow drupes on females.
Soil: adaptable, alkaline, well draining to seasonally flooded.
Exposure: full sun to partial shade.
Temperature: cold hardy to –40 degrees F.
Water: requires regular moisture, 45 inches/year minimum.
Propagation: fresh or stratified seeds.
Profile: The ornate 2-inch silver leaves give this shrub both its name and its landscape value. Silver buffaloberry makes a beautiful background plant, and since it forms thickets in the wild, it is great for mass plantings and erosion control. You can plant silver buffaloberries close together and trim them into a hedge or a thorny barrier screen. In mixed plantings, they contrast with the green foliage of pinyons, mountain mahogany, manzanita, barbarries, and sumacs. Both male and female plants are required to get the colorful summer fruit. Wildlife enjoy the berries, which make a tart jelly. You can use *Shepherdia argentea* as a native substitute for the all-too-common Russian olive (*Elaeagnus angustifolia*).

Simmondsia chinensis

Jojoba

Native Distribution: washes, dry slopes, desert flats; Peninsular Ranges, Sonoran Desert, below 5,000 feet; Southern California: Imperial, Riverside, San Bernardino, San Diego, Santa Barbara counties; Arizona; Mexico.
Landscape Zone: Chaparral, Creosote Bush Scrub, Joshua Tree Woodland.
Size: 3–6 feet high, 10 feet wide.
Leaves: evergreen; 1-1/2 inches long, grayish green.
Fruit: summer; 1-inch acornlike nuts on females.
Soil: sandy, rocky, well draining.
Exposure: full sun.
Temperature: heat tolerant, twig damage at 20 degrees F.
Water: drought tolerant, 10 inches/year minimum.
Propagation: spring-planted seeds.
Profile: Dense, grayish green leathery leaves cover jojoba all the way to the ground, making this rounded shrub ideal for a hedge or screen. Plant them 2 feet apart for a clipped hedge that resembles boxwood or 4 feet apart for a background or screen planting. With a symmetrical shape and ornate paired leaves, jojoba provides year-round foliage as a specimen plant or a component of a mixed planting. For companion plants, combine with Apache plume, sumacs, white sage, desert thorn, creosote bush, and sagebrushes. Add cacti, California poppy, desert marigold, and buckwheat for foreground color and palo verde, mesquite, ironwood, desert olive, and Mojave yucca for background structure. You'll need both male and female plants to produce the fruit, which has become commercially important because of its high oil content. Jojoba grows slowly, but requires no maintenance or extra water. Frost kills the seedlings of this low-desert plant. The cultivar 'Vista' is a smaller, compact version.

Simmondsia chinensis foliage and fruit

Simmondsia chinensis

Trichostema lanatum

Woolly blue curls

Native Distribution: dry slopes, scrublands; South Coast, Western Transverse Ranges, Peninsular Ranges, below 2,500 feet; Southern California: Los Angeles, Orange, Riverside, San Bernardino, San Diego, Santa Barbara, Ventura counties; central coast south to Baja California.
Landscape Zone: Chaparral, Coastal Sage Scrub.
Size: 3–5 feet tall.
Leaves: evergreen; narrow, 1-1/2 to 3 inches long.
Flowers: spring–fall; 12-inch fuzzy spikes of blue, pink, or white blossoms with showy, extended stamens.
Soil: adaptable, sandy, serpentine, well draining.
Exposure: full sun.
Temperature: root hardy to 0 degrees F.
Water: drought tolerant, 14 inches/year minimum.
Propagation: cuttings.
Profile: If you make sure that the roots are kept dry, this dramatic bloomer will delight every butterfly and hummingbird on the block. As cut flowers, the spikes of velvety, royal-blue blossoms brighten up the house all summer. The vaselike, evergreen stems provide texture to a mixed planting all year long, and the plant is an eye-catching accent to a landscape garden during the long blooming period. Woolly blue curls enliven borders and patio and poolside gardens, and they provide dramatic fore- to midgarden interest. For colorscaping, plant with such compatible flowering species as white sage, California fuchsia, gooseberry, goldenrod, desert mallow, and bush monkey flower. Among the available cultivars, the popular 'Cuesta Ridge' is particularly garden hardy.

Above: *Trichostema lanatum*
Right: *Trichostema lanatum* flowers

Wildflowers

Abronia villosa

Abronia villosa flowers

Abronia villosa

Desert sand verbena

Native Distribution: sandy soils, roadsides, plains, hills; below 5,200 feet; Southern California: Imperial, Los Angeles, Orange, Riverside, San Bernardino counties; Arizona, Nevada, Utah.
Landscape Zone: Creosote Bush Scrub.
Size: 1–2 feet.
Annual.
Flowers: spring through late summer; pink, aromatic, 2-inch round clusters.

Soil: sandy, well draining.
Exposure: full sun.
Water: drought tolerant.
Propagation: fall-sown seeds; in spring, scarify seed with sandpaper or soak in water for 6 to 8 hours.
Profile: Give this flower bare ground and plenty of room to sprawl and it will cover a sandy area with dense clusters of pink flowers. You can mass plant it for a showy spring groundcover or in the foreground of a perennial garden. The abundant flowers bloom on short stalks and fill your garden with the scent of vanilla. For an interesting effect, consider a mixed planting with California poppies, blue flax, paperflower, and dogweed. *Abronia villosa* var. *aurita* has slightly larger flowers than var. *villosa*. The similar annual species *A. gracilis* grows from San Diego south into Mexico.

Achillea millefolium

Yarrow

Achillea millefolium

Achillea millefolium flowers

Native Distribution: common across California and the United States, Canada.
Landscape Zone: many plant communities.
Size: 1–2 feet.
Perennial herb.

Flowers: April–July; round clusters of white or yellow flowers.
Soil: adaptable.
Exposure: full sun to partial shade.
Temperature: cold hardy to –20 degrees F.
Water: moderately drought tolerant.

Propagation: fall-sown seeds.
Profile: The rosette of delicate, fernlike leaves of yarrow look like lace spread on the ground. In moist soil, it spreads by underground rhizomes and can form an attractive groundcover. From spring through the summer, a cluster of snowy flowers atop a slender stalk crowns the basal rosette. Crush a leaf and smell the pungent volatile oils that have made yarrow a historically important medicinal plant. You can add color to your perennial garden by choosing 'Moonshine', a yellow cultivar, or 'Island Pink', a rose-colored cultivar. For added color and visual interest, plant with penstemons, salvias, asters, and buckwheat. Yarrows planted in full sun may need extra water.

Allionia incarnata

Trailing four-o'clock

Native Distribution: Sandy hills, flats, slopes, below 6,000 feet; Southern California: Imperial, Los Angeles, Riverside, San Bernardino, San Diego counties; east to Oklahoma, Texas.
Landscape Zone: Creosote Bush Scrub.
Size: stems to 10 feet long, trailing. Herbaceous perennial.
Leaves: deciduous; oval, 1–2 inches long.
Flowers: April–September; pink, 1-inch diameter.
Soil: adaptable, well draining.
Exposure: full sun.
Temperature: cold hardy.
Water: drought tolerant.
Propagation: seeds.
Profile: Whether considered a groundcover, vine, or wildflower, this delightful little plant will beautify a bare spot for much of the year. It sprawls across rocks, between shrubs, and around posts and poles. Its trailing branches form a loose mat of fuzzy, gray-green leaves accented with an abundance of dainty, rose-magenta flowers. Plant the seeds in cracks between boulders for a dramatic cascading effect. The foliage dies back in the winter but sprouts vigorously from a woody base.

Allionia incarnata

Aquilegia formosa

Crimson columbine

Aquilegia

Native Distribution: moist soils in canyons, woodlands, and mountains; Western Transverse Ranges, Peninsular Ranges, 3,000–10,000 feet; Southern California: Los Angeles, Orange, Riverside, San Bernardino, San Diego, Santa Barbara, Ventura counties; north to Canada.
Landscape Zone: Chaparral, Pinyon-Juniper Woodland, many plant communities.
Size: 1–3 feet.
Perennial herb.
Flowers: April–September; red-orange, 2 inches long with spur.
Soil: loam, well draining.
Exposure: full to partial shade.
Temperature: cold hardy to 0 degrees F.
Water: requires regular moisture.
Propagation: fresh seeds in fall, stratified seeds in spring.
Profile: Protect this delicate plant from full sun or arid locations, and you'll marvel at the abundant crimson flowers and fine-textured foliage. The flowers waving in the breeze seem to float on a cloud of light green leaves. In rich, well-draining soil, columbines reach 3 feet high and wide with scores of blooms. They make a colorful perennial border for a woodland garden or a splash of color for an entryway. They're most dramatic when cascading over an accent boulder, wall, or fountain similar to its natural habitat of porous boulders and seeping cliffs. At low elevations and hot climates, be sure they get enough water in the summer or they will go dormant, or worse, die. However, high humidity and water-logged roots are just as deadly. Trim to the ground in early spring, then wait for the hummingbirds to discover your treasure.

Asclepias speciosa

Asclepias eriocarpa

Monarch milkweed

Native Distribution: dry areas; widespread, below 7,000 feet; Southern California: Los Angeles, Orange, Riverside, San Bernardino, San Diego, Santa Barbara, Ventura counties; northern California.
Landscape Zone: Chaparral, Foothill Woodland.
Size: 3 feet.
Perennial herb.

Leaves: deciduous; gray, hairy, 5 inches long.
Flowers: June–August; 4- to 5-inch-wide clusters of white flowers.
Fruit: 4-inch horn that releases a feathery seed mass.
Soil: adaptable, well draining.
Exposure: full sun to partial shade.
Temperature: cold hardy to –30 degrees F.

Water: drought tolerant, 12 inches/year minimum.
Propagation: fall-sown seeds.
Profile: The dense clusters of white flowers crowning the stout, hairy stalks make monarch milkweed an impressive background accent in your perennial garden. Not everyone cares for the wildscape look, but monarchs and other butterflies will thank you with their colorful displays. Southern California is on the monarch flyway, so they're looking for host milkweeds to lay their eggs. Plant a milkweed in a forgotten corner and you'll be a butterfly landlord all summer. The deep taproot allows the plant to survive drought conditions, but it needs regular water to maintain a long flowering season. The similar showy milkweed, *Asclepias speciosa,* is taller, but it is not as drought tolerant and does not range into Southern California.

Baileya multiradiata

Desert marigold

Baileya multiradiata

Baileya multiradiata flowers

Native Distribution: sandy and gravelly desert soils, 2,000–5,300 feet; Southern California: Riverside, San Bernardino, San Diego counties; east to Texas; Mexico.
Landscape Zone: Creosote Bush Scrub, Joshua Tree Woodland.
Size: 1-1/2 feet.

Short-lived perennial.
Flowers: April–October; 1 to 2 inches diameter, yellow, daisylike.
Soil: adaptable, well draining.
Exposure: full sun, radiated heat.
Temperature: damaged below 32 degrees F.
Water: drought tolerant.

Propagation: fall-sown seeds.
Profile: This wildflower of the low deserts rivals the most pampered garden variety for beauty and showmanship. Its mound of lemon-yellow flowers on 1- to 2-foot stems above the grayish green, woolly leaves presents a striking color combination, especially in a cactus garden or mixed planting. It loves radiated heat, making it perfect for an accent by a boulder, masonry wall, or rock garden. The fall-sown seeds form a small basal rosette of leaves, with the bright bouquets of flowers appearing about three months after planting and continuing until frost. For profuse blooming, water weekly if rains fail. The flowers reseed themselves readily for year-round flowers in mild winters. The only maintenance required is to remove spent flower heads.

Calochortus clavatus
Clubhair mariposa lily
Calochortus kennedyi
Desert mariposa lily
Calochortus splendens
Splendid mariposa lily

Calochortus flower

Calochortus flower

Native Distribution: rocky soils, slopes, open woodlands. *Calochortus clavatus*: below 6,000 feet; Los Angeles, San Bernardino, Santa Barbara, Ventura counties. *Calochortus kennedyi*: 2,000–7,200 feet; Los Angeles, Riverside, San Bernardino, Santa Barbara, Ventura counties. *Calochortus splendens*: below 9,000 feet; Los Angeles, Orange, Riverside, San Diego, Santa Barbara, Ventura, San Bernardino counties.
Landscape Zone: *Calochortus clavatus*: Chaparral, Foothill Woodland; *C. kennedyi*: Creosote Bush Scrub, Pinyon-Juniper Woodland, Joshua Tree Woodland; *C. splendens*: Chaparral, Foothill Woodland.
Size: 8–18 inches tall.
Perennial bulb.
Flowers: spring; 3 petals, 2–3 inches wide; *Calochortus clavatus*: yellow; *C. kennedyi*: red, lavender, or orange; *C. splendens*: pink.
Soil: adaptable, well draining.
Exposure: full sun.
Temperature: cold hardy to –10 degrees F.
Water: drought tolerant.
Propagation: fall-sown seeds; may take two years to bloom.
Profile: With such spectacular flowers, mariposa lilies stop hikers in their tracks when they come upon one in the wild. More than fifty species and varieties grow throughout the state, but these three are the most common. Many mariposa lilies are threatened or endangered in much of their range, so don't transplant them from the wild. The delicate blooms seem to burst from parched soils like jewels scattered across the countryside. Desert mariposa lily can cover the desert floor in April with rich orange-red blooms. Be sure your flower bed has perfect drainage, and then wait to be delighted when these treasures burst from the ground. They require winter moisture and summer drought while dormant. Use to soften cacti and boulder accents or at the base of a palo verde as a highlight. For a gorgeous midspring display of sunrise colors, group them with Mexican gold poppy, paintbrush, and desert marigold. The walnut-sized bulbs are readily available commercially.

Castilleja species
Indian paintbrush

Native Distribution: sandy, loam soils, desert grasslands to alpine meadows; more than seventy species and varieties in California.
Landscape Zone: widespread, depending on species.
Size: 6- to 12-inch-tall clumps.
Perennial and annual herb.
Flowers: March–September; spikes of showy, red-to-purple bracts enclosing small flowers.
Soil: adaptable, well draining.
Exposure: full sun.
Temperature: cold hardy to 0 degrees F.
Water: drought tolerant.
Propagation: fall-sown seeds, rake into loose topsoil; wet winter increases germination.
Profile: Your colorscaped garden will get rave reviews with a mixed planting of paintbrushes, lupines, poppies, and penstemons, each complementing the vertical profiles and intensifying the vivid colors of the other. The upright bouquets of blooming spikes of paintbrush make a colorful foreground for corner and courtyard gardens or border accent. Mass plant for eye-catching drama and to provide forage for hummingbirds. Some twenty-five species, including yellow and purple varieties, annuals and perennials, grow in Southern California in habitats ranging from low and high deserts to mountain meadows, so find seeds of species adapted to your habitat and climate. Seeds of woolly Indian paintbrush, *Castilleja foliolosa,* and longleaf paintbrush, *C. subinclusa,* are often sold alone and in mixes. Another consideration: Most paintbrushes are partially parasitic on grass roots, which makes them difficult to establish from seed and almost impossible to transplant from the wild. Ask your nursery for seeds of nonparasitic species, such as owl's clover paintbrush, *C. exserta.* Otherwise, purchase a seed pack that contains grama grass as a host.

Castilleja exserta

Cleome serrulata

Cleome lutea

Cleome serrulata

Rocky Mountain beeplant

Native Distribution: roadsides, open range, foothills, disturbed soils; 4,000–5,500 feet; Southern California: Los Angeles, San Bernardino, San Diego counties; west of the Mississippi River; Canada.
Landscape Zone: many plant communities.
Size: 2–5 feet tall.
Annual.
Flowers: June–September; clusters of pink to purple flowers with feathery, 2- to 3-inch-long stamens.
Fruit: copious seeds in 2- to 3-inch-long pods.
Soil: adaptable, well draining.
Exposure: full sun.
Water: drought tolerant.
Propagation: spring- or fall-sown seeds; self-sows readily.
Profile: Plant one of these aggressive annuals and next year you'll have dozens, or hundreds. Sow the seeds, or transplant the seedlings, in the background of your garden, along a fence, or as a border to a drive and enjoy dazzling, pink clouds of flowers until first frost. The spectacular airy flowers bloom upward along the stalks for a long season of color. Numerous pencil-thin pods form below, each with scores of tiny seeds, so gather and save for next year's planting. In my yard, rain washed seeds down the drive and the hardy plants sprouted in cracks of the street pavement. No wonder they blanket abandoned fields and thrive in vacant lots. Doves relish the seeds and butterflies the flowers. The yellow-flowering yellow beeplant, *Cleome lutea,* is also native to Southern California.

Coreopsis lanceolata

Coreopsis bigelovii

Bigelow coreopsis

Native Distribution: open woodlands, grasslands, slopes, deserts; Western Transverse Ranges, 1,000–5,000 feet; Southern California: Los Angles, Riverside, San Bernardino, San Diego, Santa Barbara, Ventura counties.
Landscape Zone: Creosote Bush Scrub, Joshua Tree Woodland, Pinyon-Juniper Woodland, Foothill Woodland.
Size: 1–2 feet.
Annual.
Flowers: March–May; 1-inch yellow heads with yellow centers.
Soil: adaptable, well draining.
Exposure: full sun.
Water: drought tolerant.
Propagation: seeds, reseeds readily.
Profile: Mass plant this bright flower in a naturalized area and you'll have waves of golden blooms dancing in the spring breezes. It flowers periodically after its spring burst of color, depending on the rains. Bigelow coreopsis competes well with grasses and reseeds itself, making it a popular component of meadow mixes along with paintbrush, Indian blanket, lemon mint, black-eyed Susan, and Mexican hat. It thrives in hot, dry areas and with reflected heat from drives and walls, but it might need supplemental water to sustain a long blooming season. At lower elevations, plant leafy-stemmed coreopsis, *C. calliopsidea,* which thrives from 500 to 3,000 feet. The long-lived, perennial lanceleaf coreopsis, *C. lanceolata,* is native to the Southwest and is usually available at nurseries.

Datura wrightii (Datura meteloides)

Sacred datura or jimsonweed

Native Distribution: sandy, gravelly open areas, widespread below 4,000 feet; Southern California: Imperial, Los Angeles, Orange, Riverside, San Bernardino, San Diego, Santa Barbara, Ventura; common from western U.S. to Maine; Mexico.
Landscape Zone: Coastal Sage Scrub, Joshua Tree Woodland, Pinyon-Juniper Woodland.
Size: 2–4 feet.
Perennial herb.
Flowers: April–October; 6–8 inches long, white, funnel shaped.
Soil: adaptable, deep, well draining.
Exposure: full sun to partial shade.
Temperature: cold hardy.
Water: drought tolerant.
Propagation: spring- or fall-sown seeds.

Profile: A dozen trumpet-shaped white flowers may cover this large mounding, spreading plant in the morning before the midday sun causes them to fold. The snow-white flowers contrast vividly against the dark green foliage. As with many fragrant white-flowered plants, datura flowers open at night and are pollinated by moths. Plant this vigorous grower where it has plenty of room to expand, because each year it gets bigger and bushier. With its long blooming season, you'll see flowers accompanied by the unusual fruit, a 1- to 2-inch, spine-covered capsule. The nonnative annual, *Datura stramonium,* is prized for its purple flowers. All parts of the datura plant are poisonous. Because of the plant's hallucinogenic properties, shamans have long considered the plant sacred.

Datura wrightii

Delphinium cardinale

Scarlet larkspur

Native Distribution: desert hills, scrub; South Coast, Western Transverse Ranges, Peninsular Ranges, Sonoran Desert, 1,000–5,000 feet; Southern California: Los Angeles, Orange, Riverside, San Bernardino, San Diego, Santa Barbara, Ventura counties; Arizona, Nevada, Utah; Mexico.
Landscape Zone: Coastal Sage Scrub, Chaparral, Foothill Woodland.
Size: 1–6 feet.
Perennial herb.
Flowers: February–July; spikes of pale blue, 1-inch flowers with spurs.
Soil: adaptable, well draining.
Exposure: full sun to partial shade.
Temperature: cold hardy to 0 degrees F.
Water: drought tolerant, 12 inches/year minimum.
Propagation: fall- or spring-sown seeds.

Profile: Larkspurs are an old-time garden favorite. I can remember them in my grandmother's yard, waving in the breeze. They're still a favorite, and our native species are just as attractive as the domestic garden varieties. The spurred flowers crowd the erect stalk of each plant. Since each plant has only one flowering stem, you'll need to plant them about 6 inches apart for a thick display. Sow the seeds and thin after germination. You can plant an accent patch or use them along a fence border. Larkspurs naturally go dormant in the summer, so don't try to nurse them back to life by watering. More than fifty species and subspecies grow across the state, so be sure the flower's habitat matches your yard's microclimate. You'll find these perky flowers in most meadow mixes. Another red species, canyon larkspur, *Delphinium nudicale,* and the blue-flowered desert larkspur, *D. parishii,* and western larkspur, *D. hesperium,* are often available. Hummingbirds forage on all larkspurs.

Delphinium parishii

Above: *Dodecatheon clevelandii*

Left: *Dodecatheon pulchellum*

Dodecatheon clevelandii

Padre's shooting star

Native Distribution: grassy slopes below 2,500 feet; Southern California: Imperial, Los Angeles, Orange, Riverside, Ventura, San Bernardino, San Diego, Santa Barbara, Ventura counties; north to Monterey County; Baja California.
Landscape Zone: Coastal Sage Scrub, Chaparral, Foothill Woodland.
Size: 1–2 feet.
Perennial herb.
Flowers: early spring; magenta to white, 3/4 inch long, 4 to 5 lobed petals swept back to show yellow center.
Soil: well draining.
Exposure: full sun to partial shade.
Temperature: cold hardy to 0 degrees F.
Water: drought tolerant.
Propagation: fall-sown seeds.
Profile: When the rocket-shaped flowers start blooming atop 1-foot stalks in the early spring, you'll drop to your knees for a closer look. Spread the seeds freely and a squadron of brilliant flowers will dazzle your spring garden. Mix with crimson and golden monkey flowers, columbines, spiderworts, and violets for a delightful colorscape. Shooting stars grow easily in cool, moist, humus-rich soil. Nurseries sell seeds and pots of several cultivars and similar species. For higher-elevation landscapes, dark-throated shooting star, *Dodecatheon pulchellum,* which grows above 4,000 feet, has similar landscape applications.

Epilobium canum (Zauschneria californica)

Epilobium canum

Native Distribution: dry slopes, ridges; South Coast, Transverse Ranges, Peninsula Ranges, below 10,000 feet; Southern California: Los Angeles, Orange, Riverside, San Diego, San Bernardino, Santa Barbara, Ventura counties; east to New Mexico, north to Idaho; Mexico.

Epilobium canum flowers

Landscape Zone: Chaparral, Coastal Sage Scrub.
Size: 2–3 feet tall.
Perennial herb.
Leaves: evergreen; 1–2 inches long, toothed, grayish green.
Flowers: August–October; 1–2 inches long, red or orange, trumpet shaped.
Soil: adaptable, alkaline, sandy, clay, well draining.
Exposure: full sun to partial shade.
Temperature: cold hardy to –10 degrees F.
Water: drought tolerant, 15 inches/year minimum.
Propagation: seeds.
Profile: Native California fuchsias come in all sizes and colors and grow from the desert foothills to the high Sierras. Some selections form spreading groundcovers; others grow into mounding shrubs. You'll love these perky little perennials as much as the hummingbirds. They bloom profusely through the late fall when most other landscape plants are setting seed. They are well suited as a foreground bloomer in a landscape island or xeriscape garden, as a low border plant along walkways, or as a groundcover to fill bare spaces between larger shrubs. They spread by rhizomes so will cover proficiently in loose landscape soils. More than fifty cultivars ranging from sprawling groundcovers to rounded subshrubs are available with variations in leaf and flower color, so you can choose a medley of colors for a colorscape garden. For a colorful bouquet, mix fuchsias with other fall bloomers such as globemallows, paperflower, salvias, and goldenrod. Water for the first season until established, then you and the hummingbirds will enjoy years of blooming pleasure. Fuchsias require rejuvenation, so trim back in the winter to stimulate thick spring growth and flowering.

Erigeron glaucus

Seaside daisy

Native Distribution: sandy slopes, beaches, below 100 feet; Southern California: Santa Barbara, Ventura counties; north to Oregon.
Landscape Zone: Coastal Sage Scrub.
Size: 1–2 feet high, mounding, spreading.
Perennial evergreen.
Flowers: spring–fall; 1/2 to 1-1/2 inches diameter, white to purple rays with greenish yellow disk.
Soil: adaptable, well draining.
Exposure: full sun to partial shade.
Temperature: heat tolerant, cold hardy to 0 degrees F.
Water: drought tolerant, 20 inches/year minimum.
Propagation: seeds.
Profile: Seaside daisy bursts to life in the spring and keeps blooming deep into the fall with an array of cheerful, colorful flowers. It spreads by rhizomes and forms thick mats with shiny green leaves topped with perky blooms on short stalks. Use in borders, along entry or patio walls, to surround open shrubs or landscape boulders, or in a colorscape design. The numerous cultivars vary from 2-foot to 4-foot-high mounding selections to ankle-high prostrate groundcovers, so choose the best selection for your needs. 'Bountiful' and 'Wayne Roderick' form clumps 6 inches high and 2 feet wide. 'Sea Breeze' grows 1 foot high and 2 feet wide with white to pink flowers. The diminutive 'Cape Sebastian' grows 3 to 4 inches high with a 2-foot spread and a profusion of lavender flowers. Deadhead the spent flowers, mulch, and trim gently annually and severely every other year to regenerate. Interior locations or hot exposures may need supplemental water to support a long blooming period.

Erigeron glaucus

Erigeron glaucus 'Bountiful'

Eriogonum umbellatum

Sulfur buckwheat

Native Distribution: rocky slopes, open areas; Western Transverse Ranges, Peninsular Ranges, Sonoran Desert, below 12,000 feet; Southern California: Imperial, Los Angeles, Riverside, San Bernardino, San Diego, Santa Barbara, Ventura counties; east to New Mexico, north to Washington.
Landscape Zone: Pinyon-Juniper Woodland, Foothill Woodland.
Size: 1–4 feet high and wide, mounding.
Perennial evergreen.
Flowers: April–September; yellow, 1/8 inch wide in dense terminal clusters on 4- to 6-inch-long stalks above vegetation.
Soil: adaptable, well draining.
Exposure: full sun to partial shade.
Temperature: cold hardy to –30 degrees F.
Water: drought tolerant.
Propagation: seeds, cuttings.
Profile: This mile-high member of the wide-ranging buckwheat family dazzles any garden with its display of buttery blossoms, even at low elevations. Umbrellalike clusters of yellow flowers protrude above the green vegetation on short stalks. The flowers tend to turn rusty as they age, giving a mixed planting a variety of hues. This flower looks great as a border or filler, or as a color accent to rabbitbrush, Apache plume, winterfat, or sage species. With nineteen varieties, sulfur buckwheat is perfectly adapted for both low- and high-altitude gardens and adds a soft touch to yucca, agave, and beargrass. Its long blooming period makes it a good component of a colorscape design. The popular 'Shasta Sulfur' cultivar has bright yellow flower clusters and 1- to 2-feet-tall mounds. All buckwheats are important food and host plants for butterflies and caterpillars. Another popular perennial, red-flowered buckwheat, *Eriogonum grande* var. *rubescens*, grows 1 foot high and 2 to 3 feet wide. It makes a great companion to its yellow-flowering relative.

Eriogonum umbellatum

Eschscholzia californica (Eschscholzia mexicana)

California poppy

Native Distribution: dunes, desert plains, foothills; widespread, below 6,500 feet; Southern California: Los Angeles, Orange, Riverside, San Bernardino, San Diego, Santa Barbara, Ventura counties; east to Florida, north to Utah, New Hampshire; Mexico.
Landscape Zone: Chaparral, Foothill Woodland, widespread.
Size: 6–18 inches tall.
Annual.
Flowers: February–May; 2–3 inches diameter, golden-yellow to orange.
Soil: adaptable, well draining.
Exposure: full sun.
Water: drought tolerant, 6–8 inches/year minimum.
Propagation: fall- or winter-sown seeds.
Profile: This spectacular flower blankets the California deserts with gold when winter rains have been sufficient. If you have a bright, sunny garden spot, you'll want to find a place for these gorgeous poppies. The large clumps of green foliage and vibrant flowers add an eye-catching accent to any landscape garden. They are most beautiful when planted in mass, but you can use this popular annual as a bedding plant or in mixtures. The delicate texture of the lacy foliage provides a pleasing complement for the brilliantly colored petals. Seeds for numerous color variations are available. California poppies reseed well, but for heavy cover, you may need to sow additional seeds until a good seed bank is established in the soil. For colorscaping, plant with summer blooming species such as desert bluebell, penstemons, blue flax, and desert marigold.

Clockwise, from upper left:
Eschscholzia californica
Eschscholzia californica flowers
Eschscholzia californica flowers
Eschscholzia

Eustoma exaltatum (Eustoma grandiflorum)

Prairie or tulip gentian

Native Distribution: along rivers and streams, meadows; South Coast, Peninsular Ranges, Sonoran Desert, below 2,000 feet; Southern California: Imperial, Orange, Riverside, San Bernardino, San Diego counties; east to Florida; north into Canada, Mexico.
Landscape Zone: Coastal Sage Scrub, Creosote Bush Scrub.
Size: 1–2 feet tall.
Annual or short-lived perennial.
Flowers: June–September; blue, 2–3 inches diameter.
Soil: adaptable, moist, poor or well draining.
Exposure: full sun to partial shade.
Temperature: cold hardy.
Water: moderately drought tolerant.
Propagation: fall-sown seeds on top of soil.
Profile: Many botanists still classify this spectacular flower by the species name grandiflorum. Pay special attention to any plant called grandiflorum: it means large flowers. With their gorgeous tulip-shaped blossoms, prairie gentian will be the hit of your wildflower garden from summer until frost. Use them to add color to a fenceline, as an accent group, in pots, or as long-lasting cut flowers. It's easier to buy rosettes in the spring than to try growing the tiny seeds. Prairie gentian has long been cultivated, and you can choose among pink, white, rose, lilac, and double-flowered varieties. Its summer flowers add handsomely to a colorscaped garden.

Eustoma exaltatum

Glandularia gooddingii (Verbena gooddingii)

Desert vervain

Native Distribution: roadsides, desert hills; Mojave and Sonoran deserts, 3,500–6,500 feet; Southern California: San Diego, San Bernardino counties; widespread east to Texas, north to Colorado.
Landscape Zone: Joshua Tree Woodland, Pinyon-Juniper Woodland.
Herbaceous perennial.
Size: 12–18 inches high, spreads 2–3 feet or more.
Leaves: deciduous; bright green, pubescent, deeply cut, 1-1/2 inches long and 1 inch wide.
Flowers: spring–fall; clusters of 1/2-inch-wide purple flowers in round heads.
Soil: adaptable, well draining.
Exposure: full sun.
Temperature: heat tolerant, freezes to ground.
Water: drought tolerant, 12 inches/year minimum.
Propagation: fresh seeds, self-sows readily.
Profile: With ornately lobed leaves and flamboyant heads of blue to purple flowers, this vervain proves itself from early spring through fall. As an accent, it draws attention to leafless plants such as ocotillo, yuccas, and prickly pears, or against the smooth green bark of palo verde trees. Mass planted as a seasonal groundcover, it paints your landscape in clouds of blue for much of the spring and summer, especially if given an extra drink in the heat of summer. Its color and size complement desert marigold, evening primroses, dogweed, and paperflower. Butterflies flock to the blooms. Remove the spent flower heads and cut back in the winter. Plants will live 2 or 3 years.

Glandularia gooddingii

Helianthus annuus

Common sunflower

Helianthus annuus — Inset: *Helianthus annuus*

Native Distribution: roadsides, open fields, disturbed areas; widespread below 6,500 feet; throughout California, North America.
Landscape Zone: widespread.
Size: 4–9 feet.
Annual.
Flowers: July–October; yellow, 2–3 inches diameter.
Soil: adaptable, well draining.
Exposure: full sun.
Water: drought tolerant.
Propagation: seeds.
Profile: If you have a place in your yard for a dense mass of head-high flower stalks covered with a profusion of brilliant yellow blooms, this vigorous plant is made to order. Plant common sunflower to highlight a wall or fence, to provide a background in your garden, or to accent a corner. In marginal conditions, such as shallow dry soil, these sunflowers may reach only 3 to 4 feet, but they will bloom just as profusely. Various cultivars are adapted with red petals, giant flower and seed heads, and dwarf forms. The seeds attract numerous birds.

Iris douglasiana

Douglas iris

Iris douglasiana

Native Distribution: forests, grasslands; widespread below 3,200 feet; Southern California: Santa Barbara County; north to Oregon.
Landscape Zone: widespread.
Size: 2- to 4-foot-wide clumps.
Perennial.
Leaves: evergreen; 1- to 3-foot-tall blades.
Flowers: spring–fall; purple, white, 2–3 inches diameter.
Soil: adaptable, sandy, clay, serpentine, well draining.
Exposure: full sun to partial shade.
Temperature: cold hardy to –20 degrees F.
Water: drought tolerant, 35 inches/ year minimum.
Propagation: seeds, bulbs, rhizomes.
Profile: From ruby red to canary yellow, white, and the standard shades of blues and purples, this versatile iris comes in a dozen Technicolor cultivars. It adds long-seasonal color to borders, bare spots under shrubs, and as an accent for boulders, fences, and lamp posts. Irises grow well in shady gardens under trees, and their rhizomes compete well with species that have aggressive roots. For colorscapes, mix with seaside daisy, columbine, and penstemons. This clumping, spreading flower also blends well with groundcovers such as hummingbird sage, creeping barberry, and snowberry. In the summer, water twice a month in hot, sunny locations.

Layia platyglossa
Tidy tips

Layia platyglossa

Native Distribution: meadows, grasslands, hillsides; widespread below 4,000 feet; Southern California: Los Angeles, Orange, Riverside, San Bernardino, San Diego, Santa Barbara, Ventura counties; north to Oregon, Arizona, Utah.
Landscape Zone: widespread.
Size: 6- to 12-inch-tall stems.
Annual.
Flowers: March–June; yellow rays edged with white, 2–3 inches diameter.
Soil: adaptable, clay, loam, well draining.
Exposure: full sun to partial shade.
Temperature: cold hardy to 0 degrees F.
Water: drought tolerant, 15 inches/year minimum.
Propagation: fall-sown seeds.
Profile: You know spring has arrived when the tidy tips burst into buttery bloom. The yellow rays highlighted with white tips make these flowers a dramatic color accent when planted in drifts or in a mixed bed. Enjoy the beauty of a Technicolor palette of blue lupines and baby blue eyes, red poppies, and the two-toned hues of tidy tips. Use tidy tips in open spaces, around trees, in landscape islands, and enjoy the vibrant colors until the heat of summer burns them back. Provide supplemental winter water if rains fail. Tidy tips reseed, but summer watering will cause the seeds, as with most spring-blooming California annuals, to rot.

Linum lewisii
Blue flax

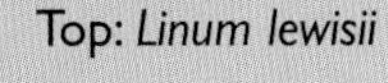
Top: *Linum lewisii*

Right: *Linum lewisii* flower

Native Distribution: roadsides, grasslands, hills, mountains; widespread, 1,300–12,000 feet; Southern California: Los Angeles, Orange, Riverside, San Bernardino, San Diego, Santa Barbara, Ventura counties; widespread west of the Mississippi River; Canada, Mexico.
Landscape Zone: Pinyon-Juniper Woodland, Foothill Woodland.
Size: 1–2 feet tall.
Short-lived perennial.
Flowers: April–September; blue, 1–2 inches diameter.
Soil: adaptable, well draining.
Exposure: full sun to partial shade.
Temperature: cold hardy to -40 degrees F.
Water: drought tolerant.
Propagation: fall-sown seeds.
Profile: A profusion of sky-blue flowers covers the slender stems of this airy, erect plant. Each wandlike stem branches near the top and displays a bouquet of blooms and buds. The dainty blossoms fade and drop by afternoon, but new ones replace them the next morning. The petals can vary from light to dark blue to almost white, with darker lines (nectar guides for insects) leading to the contrasting yellow centers. Flax lives for one or two years and reseeds itself readily. Most seed mixtures contain blue flax. Trim it back and give it extra water in the summer to encourage fall blooming. In addition to this and other blue-flowered species, numerous yellow species of flax grow throughout the west.

Lobelia cardinalis

Lobelia cardinalis
Cardinal flower

Native Distribution: moist meadows, stream sides, wetlands; Peninsular Ranges, 1,500–5,300 feet; Southern California: Los Angeles, Orange, Riverside, San Bernardino, San Diego counties; throughout U.S., Canada, Mexico.
Landscape Zone: Chaparral, Coastal Sage Scrub.
Size: 2–5 feet tall.
Perennial.
Flowers: August–October; spikes of 2-inch red flowers.
Soil: moist, poor to well draining.
Exposure: partial shade, morning sun.
Temperature: cold hardy to –20 degrees F.
Water: requires regular moisture.
Propagation: fall-sown seeds, cuttings, layering, division.
Profile: This tall plant with crimson flowers thrives in moist, rich soil and partly sunny locations, such as pond sides. However, it does surprisingly well in a filtered shade setting if kept moist during the blooming season. The tall leafy stems with brilliant scarlet flowers make an eye-catching, long-blooming accent plant. Space the plants 8 to 12 inches apart and add peat moss to the soil mixture. Mulch well to keep the soil cool and moist. The first year, the plant forms a rosette, then blooms the second and succeeding years. If you bend down a stem and cover it with soil, it will root at the leaf nodes. Transplant the new plant in the spring. The moisture-loving monkey flowers, columbines, and shooting stars make ideal companion plants. Plant cardinal flowers and you'll get a bonus: hummingbirds.

Lupinus sparsiflorus

Lupinus sparsiflorus
Coulter's lupine
Lupinus succulentus
Arroyo lupine

Native Distribution: sandy, rocky soils; widespread, below 4,300 feet; Southern California: Imperial, Los Angeles, Orange, Riverside, San Bernardino, San Diego, Santa Barbara, Ventura counties.
Landscape Zone: Chaparral, Coastal Sage Scrub, Creosote Bush Scrub, Foothill Woodland, widespread.
Size: 1–2 feet tall.
Annual.
Flowers: spring; spikes of blue flowers.
Soil: rocky, sandy, well draining.
Exposure: full sun.
Temperature: winter rosettes cold hardy to 0 degrees F.
Water: drought tolerant, 10 inches/year minimum.
Propagation: scarify and soak fall-sown seeds.
Profile: In the spring, lupines blanket roadsides, desert flats, mountain slopes, and meadows. The erect spikes of fragrant, pea-like flowers thrive in sunny, well-draining locations and make dramatic naturalized mass plantings or accent patches in your yard or garden. More than 130 species and varieties, both annuals and perennials, herbs and shrubs, grow in California from the parched deserts to mountain meadows. Nurseries carry seeds and seedlings from dozens of species, so check the habitat requirements to ensure they match your conditions. All lupines have a tough seed coat adapted to harsh and unpredictable growing conditions, which allows the seeds to germinate periodically over a several-year period. Propagators spin the rock-hard seeds in a tumbler for 12 hours, then soak to ensure that they germinate immediately. Dusting the wet seeds with the bacterial inoculant Rhizobium may produce hardier plants. Plant in the fall 1/4 to 1/2 inch deep in lightly tilled soil. Twelve seeds per square foot will give a dense display. The seeds overwinter as a small rosette, so water them if fall rains fail. In the spring, don't mow until the seeds have matured and dispersed and you'll have a colorful show every spring.

Mimulus cardinalis
Crimson monkey flower
Mimulus guttatus
Golden monkey flower

Native Distribution: along flowing water, seeping springs, below 8,500 feet in many plant communities; Southern California: Los Angeles, Orange, Riverside, San Bernardino, San Diego, Santa Barbara, Ventura; east to New Mexico, north to Canada.
Landscape Zone: Foothill Woodland, Chaparral, many plant communities.
Size: 1/2 to 3 feet tall, spreading clumps.
Perennial.
Flowers: March–August; tubular, 2 inches long, 1 inch wide. *Mimulus cardinalis*, red; *M. guttatus*, yellow.
Soil: adaptable, moist.
Exposure: afternoon shade.
Temperature: cold hardy to –20 degrees F.
Water: requires regular moisture, 40 inches/year minimum.
Propagation: seeds or potted nursery stock.
Profile: If you have a corner in your garden protected from afternoon sun and reflected heat, you may be a candidate for a monkey flower. These summer-blooming, water/humidity-loving natives produce a mass of tubular flowers with lobed petals. The brilliant scarlet or golden flowers stand out in sharp contrast to the large, dark-green leaves. Plant one and every hummingbird on the block will thank you. Given the proper microhabitat, monkey flowers grow well from the low desert to mountain forests; just don't let them dry out. They make good neighbors to other humid-loving flowers, such as columbine, skyrocket, and cardinal flower.

Above: *Mimulus cardinalis*

Right: *Mimulus cardinalis* flowers

Below: *Mimulus guttatus*

Mirabilis multiflora

Mirabilis multiflora flower

Mirabilis multiflora

Mirabilis multiflora

Giant four-o'clock

Native Distribution: sandy, rocky hills, grasslands; Mojave and Sonoran deserts, below 8,000 feet; Southern California: Imperial, Los Angeles, Orange, Riverside, San Bernardino, San Diego, Santa Barbara, Ventura counties; east to Texas, Colorado, Nevada; Mexico.
Landscape Zone: Coastal Sage Scrub, Creosote Bush Scrub, Pinyon-Juniper Woodland.
Size: 2 feet tall, 4 feet wide.
Perennial.
Flowers: April–September; 2-inch-long trumpet, purplish red, 1 inch across.
Soil: adaptable, well draining.
Exposure: full sun to partial shade.
Temperature: cold hardy to 10 degrees F.
Water: drought tolerant, 12 inches/year minimum.
Propagation: fall-sown seeds; in spring scarify seeds, stratify one month; soft cuttings.
Profile: The mass of vivid, tubular flowers nestled against the bright green heart-shaped leaves of giant four-o'clock creates a spectacular accent in your yard. With dense foliage and a rounded profile, this robust plant presents a commanding appearance when used as a mounding groundcover, border plant, or to surround a pole or tree. An extensive tubular root system helps this plant stabilize slopes and prevent erosion, but it also enables it to crowd out less vigorously growing plants. So give it plenty of room. Each cluster of the majestic flowers has three to six blooms, which close by afternoon, hence the common name. The plant dies back in freezing winters. Hummingbirds and hawk moths sip from the flowers and birds feed on the seeds.

Nama hispidum

Rough nama or purple mat

Native Distribution: sunny, sandy roadsides, desert hills, washes; widespread, below 2,000 feet; Southern California: Imperial, Los Angeles, Riverside, San Diego, San Bernardino counties; east to Texas, Oklahoma to Nevada; Mexico.
Landscape Zone: many plant communities.
Size: 4–20 inches high, upright to sprawling.
Annual.
Leaves: 1/2 to 1-1/4 inches long, narrow, covered in rough hairs.
Flowers: March–November; pink to purple, bell shaped, yellow center, 5/16 to 5/8 inches diameter.
Soil: sandy, gravelly, well draining.
Exposure: full sun.
Temperature: extremely heat tolerant.
Water: drought tolerant.
Propagation: spring-sown seeds; readily reseeds itself.

Nama hispidum

Nama demissum

Profile: Trying to grow this sprawling flower will bring you to your knees . . . to get a closer look at the array of purple flowers set in a thick mat of gray leaves. The densely booming clumps of flowers brighten bare patches in cactus or xeriscape gardens throughout the summer, especially if given an extra drink now and then. The stems sometime grow as tall as 4 to 20 inches but usually are prostrate. Sow the seeds in the spring and enjoy the pink to purple blooms throughout the summer. Though an annual, nama reseeds itself for next year's display. The mounds of gray-green, narrow leaves and dime-sized flowers complement hedgehog and barrel cacti and clumping wildflowers such as paperflower and desert marigold. Seventeen species and varieties of nama grow in California. The similar purple mat, *Nama demissum,* grows in Creosote Bush Scrub and Pinyon-Juniper Woodland.

Nemophila menziesii

Baby blue eyes

Native Distribution: meadows, woodlands, roadsides, grasslands, canyons; widespread, below 6,000 feet; Southern California: Imperial, Los Angeles, Orange, Riverside, San Bernardino, Santa Barbara, Ventura counties.
Landscape Zone: Chaparral, Coastal Sage Scrub, Creosote Bush Scrub, Joshua Tree Woodland, Foothill Woodland.
Size: 2- to 4-inch stem.
Annual.
Leaves: 1/2 to 2 inches long.
Flowers: March–April; 1 to 1-1/2 inches round, bright blue with white center.
Soil: sandy, gravelly, well draining.
Exposure: full sun.
Temperature: cold hardy to 10 degrees F.
Water: drought tolerant, 20 inches/year minimum.
Propagation: fall-sown seeds.

Above: *Nemophila menziesii*

Right: *Nemophila menziesii* flower

Profile: Following nature's admonition that no ground should go uncovered, this delightful little annual adds an early spring burst of blue to bare spots in pool and patio gardens, between shrubs, or around a tree or mailbox. The soft blue flowers make a perfect component for a colorscape garden or mass planting with poppies, flax, primroses, larkspurs, and tidy tips. Seeds are often available for other showy blue eyes. Look for meadow nemophila, *Nemophila pedunculata,* and five spot, *N. maculata,* each with bright blue dots on the tips of their petals.

Oenothera caespitosa

Tufted evening primrose

Oenothera caespitosa

Oenothera caespitosa flower

Native Distribution: rocky slopes, hillsides, deserts, below 10,000 feet; Southern California: Imperial, Los Angeles, Riverside, San Bernardino, San Diego counties; east to Texas; north to Canada.
Landscape Zone: Pinyon-Juniper Woodland.
Size: 6–12 inches tall, 1–2 feet wide.
Perennial herb.
Flowers: April–September; white, 3–4 inches across.
Soil: adaptable, rocky, well draining.
Exposure: full sun.
Temperature: cold hardy.
Water: drought tolerant.
Propagation: fall-sown seeds.
Profile: The tissuelike, snow-white flowers and slender dark green leaves create a cheerful color combination for your landscape decor. This low-sprawling plant makes a delightful accent for rock gardens. The stems may spread out over 2 feet, so give the plant enough room to show off. The blooms open in the evening and close during the heat of the next day. Nurseries carry seeds for the numerous species of evening primroses that grow in California. You can choose among yellow and white flowers, tall and prostrate, annuals and perennials. Another white-flowered perennial, California evening primrose, *Oenothera californica*, forms clumps to 10 feet in diameter. For a vertical accent, Hooker's evening primrose, *O. elata,* a perennial, bears bright yellow flowers profusely on 2- to 6-foot stalks. It favors wet habitats. The pink Mexican evening primrose, *O. speciosa,* a native of the Southwest, is naturalized over much of Southern California.

Penstemon species

Beardtongues

Native Distribution: varies with species from low deserts to mountain meadows.
Landscape Zone: see species descriptions.
Size: 1–6 feet.
Perennial herb.
Flowers: spring–summer.
Soil: adaptable, well draining.
Exposure: full sun to partial shade.
Water: drought tolerant.
Propagation: fall-sown seeds, potted nursery stock.
Profile: With stately spikes of tubular flowers, penstemons are truly one of the aristocrats of the garden, and we have scores of species in California to choose from. The ninety-one species and varieties of penstemons in the state grow from the low deserts to alpine meadows, from shaded canyons to sandy, arid hillsides, so you can choose species suited for your growing conditions no matter where you live. Some grow 6 feet tall, some 1 foot short, and they come in a rainbow of reds, pinks, oranges, blues, purples, and whites. Use shorter species as border plants and the taller ones as desert garden accents against a tall cactus or boulder. Mass plant them for a stunning effect, especially if you like hummingbirds. To ensure next year's bloom, remove the spent flower stalk. Penstemons have an attractive basal rosette of leaves year-round. Listed here are just a few of the various species and colors available by seed and seedling. Many cultivars and crosses are available. When buying, look at the scientific name since common names vary widely. Protect penstemons from rabbits and deer, which enjoy nibbling the plants.

Penstemon eatoni

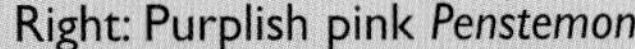

Right: Purplish pink *Penstemon*

Penstemon pseudospectabilis

Penstemon palmeri

Right: Blue *Penstemon*

Red-to-Pink Penstemons

Penstemon centranthifolius, Scarlet bugler: Chaparral, Pinyon-Juniper Woodland, below 6,000 feet. Drought tolerant, full sun, April–July, 2–4 feet tall.

Penstemon eatoni, Eaton's penstemon or firecracker penstemon: Pinyon-Juniper Woodland, Creosote Bush Scrub, 5,000–9,000 feet. Drought tolerant, full sun, February–June, 2 feet tall.

Penstemon pseudospectabilis,. Desert penstemon: Creosote Bush Scrub, below 4,600 feet. Drought tolerant, full sun, April–July, 2–4 feet tall.

Blue-to-Pink Penstemons

Penstemon incertus, Mojave penstemon: Joshua Tree Woodland, Pinyon-Juniper Woodland, 3,000–6,000 feet. Drought tolerant, full sun, May–June, 2–3 feet tall.

Penstemon heterophyllus and cultivars, Foothill penstemon: Chaparral, Foothill Woodland, below 5,300 feet. Drought tolerant, full sun, April–August, 3 feet tall.

Penstemon spectabilis and cultivars, Showy penstemon: Chaparral, Coastal Sage Scrub, below 8,000 feet. Drought tolerant, full sun, April–June, 3–6 feet tall.

White-to-Pink Penstemons

Penstemon clevelandii and cultivars, Cleveland penstemon: Creosote Bush Scrub, Pinion-Juniper Woodland, Chaparal, below 4,800 feet. Drought tolerant, full sun to partial shade, spring, 2–3 feet tall.

Penstemon palmeri, Palmer's penstemon: Joshua Tree Woodland, Pinyon-Juniper Woodland, 3,500–7,500 feet. Drought tolerant, full sun, May–September, 3–5 feet tall.

Penstemon X *parishii (Penstemon centranthifolius* X *P. spectabilis),* Parish penstemon: Chaparral, Foothill Woodland. Drought tolerant, full sun, June–July, 3 feet tall.

Phacelia campanularia

Desert bluebell

Native Distribution: sandy plains, hillsides; deserts, below 5,300 feet; Southern California: Los Angeles, Riverside, San Bernardino, San Diego, Santa Barbara counties; Arizona.
Landscape Zone: Creosote Bush Scrub.
Size: 1–2 feet tall.
Annual herb.
Flowers: March–April; 1-inch diameter, bell shaped, bright blue.
Soil: adaptable, well draining.
Exposure: full sun.
Temperature: heat tolerant.
Water: drought tolerant, 6 inches/year minimum.
Propagation: seeds.
Profile: Annual wildflowers deserve a prominent place in any landscape design. Their seasonal flair perks up xeriscape and perennial gardens and adds dramatic shades and hues to an otherwise foliage-centered design. Instead of buying all those pansies and petunias from the big-box garden center, save a place in your yard for some of nature's treasures. The rich blue of desert bluebells complements desert marigold, California poppy, evening primroses, penstemons . . . you get the idea. Go wild with your seed packs and enjoy the colorful pageant that unfolds in your yard. Nurseries sell many species of bluebells. If you live in the Chaparral and Coastal Sage Scrub plant communities, look for giant-flowered bluebell, *Phacelia grandiflora*.

Phacelia campanularia

Psilostrophe cooperi

Paperflower or Cooper's paper-daisy

Native Distribution: desert plains, hillsides; deserts, below 5,000 feet; Southern California: Imperial, Riverside, San Bernardino counties; Arizona, New Mexico, Utah, Nevada; Mexico.
Landscape Zone: Creosote Bush Scrub, Joshua Tree Woodland.

Size: 1–2 feet tall, 3 feet wide.
Short-lived perennial.
Flowers: April–June, October–December; 1 inch diameter, yellow
Soil: adaptable, well draining.
Exposure: full sun.
Temperature:
Water: drought tolerant.
Propagation: spring- or fall-sown seeds.
Profile: This densely branching perennial forms a rounded mass of bright butter-colored flowers so thick you won't be able to see the grayish green foliage. The mounding shape of paperflower makes it an attractive border or accent plant in a xeriscape garden and matches well with rough nama, desert marigold, California poppy, and evening primroses. When the vibrant flowers fade with age and become papery, you can use them in dried-flower arrangements.

Psilostrophe

Romneya coulteri

Romneya coulteri

Matilija poppy

Native Distribution: desert washes, canyons; South Coast, Peninsular Ranges, below 3,500 feet; Southern California: Los Angeles, Orange, Riverside, San Diego, San Bernardino, Santa Barbara, Ventura counties; central and coastal California.
Landscape Zone: Chaparral, Coastal Sage Scrub.
Size: 6–8 feet tall and wide.
Leaves: summer deciduous; 2–8 inches long, 3 to 5 lobes.
Flowers: May–July; 6–12 inches diameter, white with a yellow center.
Fruit: bristly, oblong pods, 1–2 inches wide.
Soil: adaptable, well draining.
Exposure: full sun to partial shade.
Temperature: heat tolerant, cold hardy to –10 degrees F.
Water: drought tolerant, 25 inches/year minimum.
Propagation: seeds, rhizomes.
Profile: When the large, white, tissue-paper flowers with buttery stamens cover this perennial shrub, you won't have to invite your friends over to see the show. But before you fall head over heels in love with California's largest wildflower, be careful that this aggressive beauty doesn't move in and take over. In sandy or well-draining soil, the rhizomes easily invade its corner of the yard. In a mixed planting, it adds seasonal color as a background drift or fence line screen. Confined as a corner accent, it adds zest to patios, pools, and entry gardens. Trim back in the winter to keep a compact shape. The cultivar Romneya 'White Cloud' is more compact and produces extra-large flowers. The look-alike species, hairy matilija poppy, *Romneya trichocalyx,* grows in similar settings. Both of these species occur in only a few locations in the wild and are classified as uncommon on the watch list of plants that need regular monitoring.

Sisyrinchium bellum

Blue-eyed grass

Sisyinchium bellum

Sisyrinchium bellum flowers

Native Distribution: slopes, foothills, woodlands, below 6,000 feet; South Coast, Western Transverse Ranges, Peninsular Ranges; Southern California: Los Angeles, Orange, Riverside, San Bernardino, San Diego, Santa Barbara, Ventura counties.
Landscape Zone: Chaparral, Foothill Woodland, Coastal Sage Scrub.
Size: 1-foot-long, irislike leaves.
Perennial.
Flowers: January–June; 1-inch diameter, blue.
Soil: adaptable, sandy to clay.
Exposure: full sun to partial shade.
Temperature: cold hardy to 0 degrees F.
Water: drought tolerant, 12 inches/year minimum.
Propagation: seeds.
Profile: For a splash of color to accent a boulder or wall, or as a delicate balance to the bold colors of California poppy, seaside daisy, or evening primrose, look no further. Blue-eyed grass adds its understated pizzazz from the first warmth of spring until the heat of summer burns it back. Its dense clump of grass- or irislike leaves provides a color accent to nooks and bare areas and forms an attractive border planting or a natural touch to perennial flower gardens. This little jewel easily seeds itself and comes back stronger year after year. Several cultivars are available including white-flowering varieties, and the yellow-flowering species, golden-eyed grass, *Sisyrinchium californicum.*

Solanum parishii
Solanum umbelliferum
Solanum xanti

Blue witches, purple nightshade

Native Distribution: slopes, foothills, woodlands, below 6,000 feet; South Coast, Western Transverse Ranges, Peninsular Ranges; Southern California: Los Angeles, Orange, Riverside, San Bernardino, San Diego, Santa Barbara, Ventura counties.
Landscape Zone: Chaparral, Foothill Woodland, Coastal Sage Scrub.
Size: 2–3 feet tall, erect.
Perennial, semi-evergreen, subshrub.
Flowers: spring–fall; 1-inch diameter, blue to lavender, white.
Fruit: 1/2 inch, round, tomato-like.
Soil: adaptable, well draining.
Exposure: full sun to partial shade.
Temperature: cold hardy to 0 degrees F.
Water: drought tolerant, 12 inches/ year minimum.
Propagation: seeds.
Profile: These three look-alike species form small, densely branching subshrubs with delicate blue flowers that bloom throughout the year. They hybridize in the wild and have the same landscape applications. Best used as filler accents and container plants, place them around your pool or patio to add extra interest and a splash of color. Cultivars are available with variations in flower and foliage colors. For a dramatic combination, mix with plants compatible in size and foliage, such as California fuchsia, bush monkey flower, buckwheats, and wood rose. All parts of blue witches, as with most members of the Nightshade family, are poisonous, so remove the fruit if children are nearby.

Solanum

Solidago californica

California goldenrod

Solidago canadensis

Canada goldenrod

Solidago confines

Southern goldenrod

Solidago spathulata

Coast goldenrod

Native Distribution: throughout California.
Landscape Zone: widespread.
Size: 1–6 feet.
Herbaceous perennial.
Flowers: July–October; dense spikes of small yellow flowers.
Soil: adaptable, poor to well draining.
Exposure: full sun to partial shade.
Temperature: cold hardy.
Water: some species drought tolerant.
Propagation: fresh seeds, root division when dormant.
Profile: From deserts to mountains and marshes to prairies, you'll find ten species of goldenrod native to California. The large flowering spike crowning a waving stalk makes it among the most conspicuous late-summer and fall wildflowers. Because of the diversity in size and aggressiveness within the genus, choose your species and where you plant carefully. *Solidago canadensis* grows to 5 feet tall while *S. californica* and *S. confines* reach 2 to 4 feet, and the smallest, coast goldenrod, *S. spathulata,* reaches 4 to 20 inches. The taller species make a colorful complement for meadows and naturalized areas, but beware: they spread by rhizomes and tend to overtake garden settings, so take care before planting in rich garden soil unless you want a groundcover. Use as a garden background, border, or an accent along a fence or wall. Mass plant goldenrods to get extended color, since each plant has a short blooming period, and enjoy the hordes of butterflies attracted to the flowers. Contrary to popular belief, goldenrods, which are insect pollinated, seldom cause hay fever. (Wind-pollinated ragweed, which blooms concurrently, is the major culprit.)

Solidago canadensis

Solidago with monarch butterfly

Sphaeralcea ambigua

Sphaeralcea ambigua

Desert globemallow

Native Distribution: sandy, rocky soils, deserts and hills; Mojave and Sonoran deserts, below 8,200 feet; Southern California: Imperial, Orange, Riverside, San Bernardino, San Diego, Santa Barbara, Ventura; throughout the West; Mexico.
Landscape Zone: Creosote Bush Scrub, Joshua Tree Woodland, Pinyon-Juniper Woodland.
Size: 1–6 feet tall.
Perennial.
Flowers: throughout year; 1-1/2 inches diameter, red, pink, to lavender.
Soil: adaptable, well draining.
Exposure: full sun.
Water: drought tolerant.
Propagation: fall-sown seeds.
Profile: If you like hollyhocks, you'll want these miniature versions in your xeriscape garden. The cuplike flowers bloom all along the upper portion of the stalk with shades of orange, pink, peach, red, and lavender. These vigorous growers send up numerous stems from a single root. Plant the graceful perennials as a silhouette along a wall or fence line. As a background accent in a cactus garden, the airy, spreading profile complements agaves, beargrass, ocotillo, and yuccas. The long blooming season fills a colorscape design and accents the sunset hues of desert marigold, California poppy, and goldenrod. In the fall, cut back to 6 inches to produce thick, new growth. Several cultivars are available with large pink, white, or red flowers. The 'La Luna' cultivar blooms with snow-white flowers and 'Louis Hamilton' has rich apricot-red flowers. Most seed packs contain a variety of shades. If you can't find globemallows at a nursery, don't despair. Pick a few seed heads from the wild and you'll have your own specimens in a few months. About a dozen species grow in California from low deserts to mountain slopes.

Sphaeralcea ambigua 'Louis Hamilton' flowers

Stanleya pinnata

Stanleya pinnata

Prince's plume

Native Distribution: open areas, hillsides, canyons; South Coast, Western Transverse Ranges, Peninsular Ranges, Mojave Desert, below 5,500 feet; Southern California: Imperial, Los Angeles, Orange, Riverside, San Bernardino, San Diego, Santa Barbara, Ventura counties; western U.S.
Landscape Zone: Creosote Bush Scrub, Joshua Tree Woodland, Pinyon-Juniper Woodland.
Size: 1–5 feet.
Perennial herb.
Flowers: July–October; dense spikes of small yellow flowers at end of 3-foot stem.
Soil: adaptable, well draining.
Exposure: full sun.
Temperature: root hardy to –20 degrees F.
Water: drought tolerant, 10 inches/year minimum.
Propagation: seeds.
Profile: Nature loves to confound gardeners with flowers that grow in the most forsaken places, yet prove difficult to establish in our pampered yards. The gorgeous spikes of yellow flowers of prince's plume decorate gravelly washes, mountain ridges, and desert canyons—they require a more unforgiving habitat than we like to have around our homes. But don't be bashful; give it a try and enjoy the rewards. Plant against a sunny wall, along a drive, or in a corner xeriscape garden. The mound of coarse foliage and tall bloom stems complement a wildscape design with giant rye grass, beargrass, fairy duster, desert thorn, desert broom, and sagebrush.

Thymophylla pentachaeta (Dyssodia pentachaeta)

Dogweed or five-needle pricklyleaf

Native Distribution: dry, rocky soils; Mojave Desert, 3,000–6,000 feet; Southern California: Riverside, San Bernardino, San Diego counties; east to Texas; Mexico.
Landscape Zone: Creosote Bush Scrub, Joshua Tree Woodland.
Size: 4–10 inches tall, 1–3 feet diameter.
Short-lived perennial.
Flowers: March–September; 1/2 inch diameter, yellow.
Soil: adaptable, well draining.
Exposure: full sun.
Water: drought tolerant.
Propagation: fall-sown seeds.

Profile: What a delightful little plant dogweed is. Numerous dime-sized flowers on 1- to 4-inch stems cover mounds of dark green, fine-textured leaves. The petite clumps, which may range from the size of a dinner plate to 3 feet in diameter, make perfect border or accent plants for your cactus or patio garden—or plant one in a rocky crevice. As a groundcover or garden filler, it makes a colorful bouquet with paperflower, owl's clover, and desert marigold. You can count on a dogweed's delicate beauty year after year because it reseeds itself readily.

Thymophylla pentachaeta

Viguiera laciniata

California sunflower

Native Distribution: wooded slopes, canyons; Western Transverse Ranges, Peninsular Ranges, below 2,200 feet; Southern California: Los Angeles, Orange, Riverside, San Diego, Ventura counties; Arizona through central Texas.
Landscape Zone: Coastal Sage Scrub.
Size: 3–6 feet.
Perennial subshrub.
Flowers: February–June, September–October; 2 inches diameter, yellow.
Soil: adaptable, well draining.
Exposure: full sun to partial shade.
Temperature: cold hardy to 8 degrees F.
Water: drought tolerant.
Propagation: fall- or spring-sown seeds.

Profile: Golden flowers blanket this low-growing, rounded subshrub in the summer and even more profusely in the fall. The mass of lemon-yellow blooms on 8-inch stems provide a surprising contrast with the bright-green foliage. This bushy, long-flowering plant makes a colorful addition to informal wildscape gardens and slope plantings for much of the year. This vigorous grower needs elbow room or it will run over its neighbors, but let it spread and it's spectacular. It is compatible in size with the sugar sumac, shrubby salvias, brittle bush, rabbitbrush, joint fir, and small yuccas and agaves. To keep it compact and neat in appearance, remove the flower stalks after flowering and trim it back. Don't despair if it freezes to the ground—it is root hardy. The similar species, desert sunflower, *Viguiera parishii,* grows in the Creosote Bush Scrub zone in the Mojave and Sonoran deserts.

Above: *Viguiera laciniata*

Left: *Viguiera laciniata* flowers

Native Plant Profiles

Vines

Aristolochia californica

California pipevine

Aristolochia californica flower

Native Distribution: stream sides, forests, below 1,500 feet; Southern California: Los Angeles County and north, endemic.
Landscape Zone: Chaparral, Foothill Woodland.
Growth Habit: moderate climber from woody base; twining.
Woody deciduous.
Leaves: deciduous; 2–6 inches long, heart shaped.
Flowers: March–April; 1- to 2-inch, J-shaped tube, greenish brown with purple stripes.
Fruit: winged capsule.
Soil: adaptable, well draining.
Exposure: full to partial shade.
Temperature: cold hardy to 10 degrees F.
Water: moderately drought tolerant, 25 inches/year minimum.
Propagation: seeds.
Profile: The flower of the pipevine is bizarre enough by itself to convince you to find a place in your yard for the plant. In early spring, pipe-shaped flowers with red throats cover the vine profusely. By summer, the flowers turn into winged capsules that look like miniature lanterns dangling on the vine. This fast grower will twine its way up trees, around poles, and along fences, so give it room to show its ornate beauty. Use it as a seasonal accent to add interest to rock walls, trellises, and lamp posts, but avoid letting it climb on wooden structures. The plant hosts the larva of pipevine swallowtail butterfly.

Calystegia macrostegia flower

Calystegia macrostegia

Island morning glory

Native Distribution: coastal, rocky areas, below 3,000 feet; Southern California: Los Angeles, Orange, Riverside, San Bernardino, San Diego, Santa Barbara, Ventura counties; central coast, Channel islands.
Landscape Zone: Coastal Sage Scrub, Chaparral, Foothill Woodland.
Growth Habit: weakly climbing; twining.
Herbaceous perennial.
Leaves: deciduous.
Flowers: winter–spring; 1–3 inches diameter, white to pink.
Soil: adaptable, well draining.
Exposure: full sun, afternoon shade.
Temperature: root hardy to 0 degrees F.
Water: moderately drought tolerant, 12 inches/year minimum.
Propagation: seeds.
Profile: Morning glories do two things well: they bloom profusely and spread like weeds. Their pizzazz comes from the abundance of showy flowers that dramatically accent a trellis, mailbox, or lamp pole throughout most of the year. The morning dew glistening on a fresh flower is worth getting up early to see. The flower color varies from creamy white to pinkish and even yellow, and some have reddish veins. Morning glories tend to get out of hand and pop up where you least want a vine to take over a plant, so be careful with their use in rich, garden settings.

Clematis ligusticifolia

Western virgin's bower

Clematis ligusticifolia

Native Distribution: moist soils, roadsides, thickets, streambanks, below 7,000 feet; Southern California: Los Angeles, Orange, Riverside, San Bernardino, San Diego, Santa Barbara, Ventura counties; east to New Mexico; north to Canada.
Landscape Zone: Chaparral, Foothill Woodland.
Growth Habit: climbing to 20 feet; twining leaf stalk.
Herbaceous perennial.
Flowers: May–September; clusters of 1/2-inch white flowers; feathery seed heads on female plants.
Soil: adaptable, well draining.
Exposure: full sun to partial shade.
Temperature: root hardy to –20 degrees F.
Water: drought tolerant, 7 inches/year minimum.
Propagation: fresh seeds, semi-softwood cuttings.
Profile: This vigorously growing vine quickly covers a lattice shading your porch or patio or will sprawl across an open slope. Plant it on a fence or trellis to shade your windows or air conditioning unit in the summer. The dense flower clusters attract an abundance of bees and other insects, and the female plants have showy feathery seed heads. Although western virgin's bower dies back in the winter, it is hard to eradicate once established. The vine prefers moist soil, but a deep taproot allows it to survive drought conditions. One wild specimen at the Grand Canyon covered 30 square feet with luxuriant foliage even though it hadn't rained for six months. Another showy species, chaparral clematis, *Clematis lasiantha*, has showy white to yellow flowers and grows in chaparral and pine forests.

Lonicera subspicata

Southern honeysuckle

Lonicera flowers

Native Distribution: slopes, forests, thickets; South Coast, Transverse Ranges, Peninsular Ranges, below 6,000 feet; Southern California: Imperial, Los Angeles, Orange, Riverside, San Diego, San Bernardino, Santa Barbara, Ventura counties; northern California, endemic.
Landscape Zone: Chaparral.
Growth Habit: low climbing or trailing woody vine to 8 feet; twining.
Woody perennial.
Leaves: evergreen; 2 inches long.
Flowers: summer; spikes of 1/2-inch trumpet-shaped yellow flowers.
Fruit: fall; red or yellow berries, 2/5-inch diameter.
Soil: adaptable, well draining.
Exposure: full sun to partial shade.
Temperature: cold hardy to –10 degrees F.
Water: moderately drought tolerant, 20 inches/year minimum.
Propagation: fresh seeds, softwood or semi-hardwood cuttings.
Profile: California is blessed with a variety of native honeysuckle plants. Unlike the invasive Japanese species, native honeysuckles are well mannered and never trespass. Their woody pencil-thin branches sprawl across the ground, or give them some support and they form a dense, low-climbing shrubby bush. The clusters of yellow flowers contrast with the round evergreen leaves throughout most of the year, making them an all-season complement to your yard. Plant them along a fence at 4- to 6-foot intervals for a background, or let them sprawl over an open area as a groundcover. I used a similar species to surround a utility pole and in two years it was a rounded mass about 5 feet high. Other related species suitable for Southern California landscapes include chaparral honeysuckle, *Lonicera interrupta* (yellow flowers); California honeysuckle, *L. hispidula* (red flowers); and the shrubby twinberry, *L. involucrata* (red flowers).

Maurandya antirrhiniflora

Maurandya antirrhiniflora

Snapdragon Vine

Native Distribution: sandy soils, desert flats, washes, below 8,500 feet; Southern California: San Bernardino County; east to Texas; Mexico.
Landscape Zone: Creosote Bush Scrub, Joshua Tree Woodland.
Growth Habit: low climbing; twining.
Herbaceous perennial.
Leaves: evergreen in frost-free conditions.
Flowers: February–October; 1 inch, purple to pink.
Soil: adaptable, well draining.
Exposure: full sun to partial shade.
Temperature: freezes to ground.
Water: drought tolerant.
Propagation: seeds.
Profile: This prostrate to low-climbing vine has a jumble of slender, tangled stems, small leaves, and a few flowers blooming all the time, nothing glamorous, but definitely interesting, especially the unusual flowers. Each petite bloom has two brightly colored lips and a creamy yellow throat. To best show off the subtle beauty of this vine, plant it on a trellis or post wrapped in wire. For an accent, you can let it dangle over a rock border, out of a crevice, or spread on a slope beneath a shrub. It reseeds itself readily, even in cold climates where it grows as an annual.

Parthenocissus vitacea (Parthenocissus inserta)

Thicket creeper or woodbine

Parthenocissus vitacea

Parthenocissus vitacea fall color and fruit

Native Distribution: moist canyons, woodlands, roadsides; South Coast, Transverse Ranges, Peninsular Ranges, below 3,500 feet; Southern California: Los Angeles, Riverside, San Bernardino counties; east to Texas, northeast to Maine; Canada, Mexico.
Landscape Zone: Foothill Woodland.
Growth Habit: high climbing; tendrils.
Woody perennial.
Leaves: deciduous; 5 lobes, brilliant red and orange fall colors.
Fruit: fall; blue berries, poisonous.
Soil: adaptable, well draining.
Exposure: full sun to full shade.
Temperature: cold hardy.
Water: moderately drought tolerant.
Propagation: fresh seeds, cuttings.
Profile: Plant a robust creeper vine where it can climb unchallenged. It has dense foliage with five leaflets and will rapidly cover masonry, a fence, or a trellis with a luxuriant growth. The thick layer of leaves provides an insulating dead-air space against a building and in the fall paints it with brilliant shades of red, orange, and burgundy. You also can use these vigorous growers as groundcovers, if you keep them trimmed off trees and shrubs. Don't let the vine become established on wooden structures that need periodic painting.

Vitis californica

California wild grape

Native Distribution: stream sides, moist canyons, woodlands, below 5,500 feet; Southern California: San Bernardino County; north to Oregon.
Landscape Zone: Foothill Woodland, widespread.
Growth Habit: high climbing; tendrils.
Woody perennial.
Leaves: deciduous; heart-shaped, brilliant reds and burgundies in fall.
Fruit: summer; purple, 1/4-inch diameter in dense bundles.
Soil: adaptable, well draining.
Exposure: full sun to full shade.
Temperature: cold hardy to 0 degrees F.
Water: moderately drought tolerant, 50 inches/year minimum.
Propagation: seeds, cuttings.
Profile: For three-season interest, wild grape brings dense foliage, ornate fruit, and brilliant fall colors that turn your yard into a calendar scene. This aggressive, fast-spreading vine will cover a patio arbor by summer with dense foliage and provide welcome shade for outdoor activities. Plant one to accent a wall or rail fence, but since they develop into heavy, robust vines, be careful about letting it overtake a structure that it might damage. A weekly summer watering may be necessary in dry exposures. Numerous cultivars exist: be sure the plant you buy suits your application. The closely related desert wild grape, *Vitis girdiana*, grows in Chaparral and Coastal Sage Scrub communities and is a better selection for arid landscapes. Birds enjoy the tasty fruit of wild grapes.

Vitis californica fall color

Vitis californica

Groundcovers

Adiantum capillus-veneris

Maidenhair fern

Adiantum capillus-veneris

Native Distribution: Moist canyons, streambanks, springs, below 4,000 feet; Southern California: Los Angeles, Riverside, San Diego, San Bernardino, Santa Barbara, Ventura counties; north to Alaska, throughout U.S.; Canada.
Landscape Zone: Chaparral, Foothill Woodland, widespread.
Size: 1–3 feet tall.
Leaves: deciduous; 10–20 inches long, sprouting from base, deeply lobed with wiry, black midrib and petiole.
Soil: adaptable, clay, well draining.
Exposure: full to partial shade.
Temperature: root hardy to 10 degrees F.
Water: requires regular moisture.
Propagation: dormant root division.
Profile: Give this lacy-looking specialty plant regular moisture and protection from drying afternoon heat and it will add an idyllic woodland touch to a landscape garden. Tuck it into a rock crevice to soften boulders in rock gardens or retaining walls. The black-veined fronds add delicate texture to a garden surrounding a tree or post. If allowed to dry out, maidenhair goes summer dormant. Though it looks like the perfect deer salad, browsers tend to ignore it. The look-alike species, California maidenhair fern, *Adiantum jordanii*, and the closely related, five-fingered fern, *A. aleuticum*, with long, tapering fronds, grow in the same habitat and have similar landscape applications.

Artemisia californica cultivars

California sagebrush

Native Distribution: coastal hills, sunny slopes, below 2,600 feet; Southern California: Los Angeles, Riverside, San Bernardino, San Diego, Santa Barbara, Ventura counties; north to Mendocino County; Mexico.
Landscape Zone: Coastal Sage Scrub, Chaparral.
Size: 1–2 feet tall, 4 feet wide.
Leaves: evergreen; gray, threadlike, 1–4 inches long.
Flowers: summer–fall; insignificant, releases allergenic pollen.
Soil: adaptable, well draining.
Exposure: full sun to partial shade.
Temperature: heat tolerant, cold hardy to 0 degrees F.
Water: drought tolerant, 12 inches/year minimum.
Propagation: seeds.
Profile: Though California sagebrush normally grows as a 3- to 6-foot-tall shrub, several mat-forming cultivars exist that make dramatic groundcovers. The silver, evergreen foliage, and spreading, prostrate stance make 'Canyon Gray' an adaptable, large-scale groundcover that can spread to 10 feet wide. The smaller 'Montara' mounds to 2 feet high and 3 to 5 feet wide. Plant the cultivars as a border along a walk, curb, a midgarden accent, or sprawling over a boulder. Trim plants back during the summer dormancy and remove upright limbs to keep them thick and densely foliated. For contrasting leaf color, mix with coffeeberry, manzanitas, ceanothus, and coyote brush. For colorscaping, add goldenrod, California fuchsia, blue witches, or bush monkey flower. Two related mugworts, *Artemisia ludoviciana* and *A. douglasiana*, grow 1 to 3 feet tall and spread aggressively by rhizomes, so be careful about planting them in rich soil. Artemisias produce a pungent odor, copious seedlings, and are wind-pollinated, so beware if you suffer from hay fever. Also see page 88.

Artemisia ludoviciana

Baccharis pilularis

Prostrate coyote brush

Native Distribution: coastal bluffs, canyons, woodlands; South Coast Ranges, South Coast, Transverse Ranges, Peninsular Ranges, below 2,000 feet; Southern California: Los Angeles, Orange, Riverside, San Bernardino, San Diego, Santa Barbara, Ventura; Oregon; Mexico.
Landscape Zone: Coastal Sage Scrub, Chaparral, Foothill Woodland.
Size: 1–3 feet tall.
Leaves: evergreen.
Flowers: fall–winter; 1- to 2-inch heads with small white petals.
Soil: adaptable, well draining.
Exposure: full sun to partial shade.
Temperature: heat tolerant, cold hardy to 0 degrees F.
Water: drought tolerant.
Propagation: seeds.
Profile: Coyote brush comes naturally in two styles, a dwarf and an upright form with various grades in between. Be sure to choose the growth habit that matches your habitat. The dwarf develops into a mound 1 to 2 feet high and 8 to 12 feet wide. Plant on 6-foot centers for complete coverage of bare areas. For a change of pace, plant it in the corner island of your lot instead of the junipers everybody else on the block uses. The white, tuffy flowers aren't much in themselves, but in the fall they cover the branches like snow. For most of the year the deep green foliage benefits from a little color from companion plants. For visual variety in a mass planting, mix in a few mounding, flowering shrubs such as ceanothus, sages, manzanitas, or chuparosa. The cultivar 'Twin Peaks' is cold hardy to 35 degrees F, while 'Pigeon Point' can tolerate 15 degrees.

Baccharis pilularis 'Twin Peaks'

Dudleya caespitosa

Coast dudleya

Native Distribution: dry slopes, coastal bluffs; South Coast, Channel Islands, below 350 feet; Southern California: Los Angeles, Orange, Santa Barbara, Ventura counties.
Landscape Zone: Coastal Sage Scrub.
Size: 4- to 6-inch-wide clumps.
Leaves: gray, succulent, narrow, 2–3 inches long.
Flowers: spring, summer; yellow clusters on 1- to 2-foot-tall bloom stalks.
Soil: adaptable, sandy, well draining.
Exposure: full sun to partial shade.
Temperature: cold hardy.
Water: moderately drought tolerant, 16 inches/year minimum.
Propagation: seeds, division.
Profile: Dudleya species are essential additions to any Southern California succulent garden and perform the double duty of groundcover and dramatic garden accent. Use coast dudleya as a fill along a border or to surround a boulder, to cover a gentle garden slope, or as a container accent. The succulent leaves form a dense rosette, then in the spring each plant sends up several spectacular bloom stalks. Brilliant red leaves cover stems crowned with bundles of gold flowers. For another interesting garden addition, mix with clumps of fingertips, *Dudleya edulis*. The pencil-thin leaves grow in tight clumps that send up bloom stalks with white flowers. Plant dudleyas in rapid-draining soil and withhold summer water. Try to purchase plants of this wide-ranging genus native to your immediate area.

Top: *Dudleya caespitosa*

Left: *Dudleya edulis*

Frangula californica cultivars (*Rhamnus californica*)

California coffeeberry

Native Distribution: coastal foothills, shaded canyons, scrublands, forests; South Coast, Western Transverse Ranges, Peninsular Ranges, Desert Mountains, below 7,500 feet; Southern California: Imperial, Los Angeles, Orange, Riverside, San Bernardino, San Diego, Santa Barbara, Ventura counties; north to Oregon, Arizona; Mexico.
Landscape Zone: Coastal Sage Scrub, Chaparral, Creosote Bush Scrub, Pinyon-Juniper Woodland, Joshua Tree Woodland, Foothill Woodland.
Size: 4–6 feet, shrub.
Leaves: evergreen; shiny green.
Fruit: July–November; red maturing to black, 1/4- to 1/2-inch diameter.
Soil: adaptable, well draining.
Exposure: full sun to partial shade.
Temperature: cold hardy to 0 degrees F.
Water: moderately drought tolerant, 32 inches/year minimum.
Propagation: cuttings, fresh seeds in fall, stratified seeds in spring.
Profile: This ornate evergreen naturally forms a dense, 6- to 12-foot-high and -wide shrub covered with colorful drupes in the late summer and fall (see profile under "Shrubs and Small Trees")—but this versatile shrub has more to offer than a thick hedge. Propagators have cloned specimens that naturally have a low, prostrate growth habit. The 'Little Star' and 'Mound San Bruno' cultivars produce a low, bushy growth that is ideal for borders, slopes, or back corners that need a cover. For contrasting texture, mix in some bracken fern, or create a wildlife-friendly island with mahonias, sumacs, snowberries, and manzanitas. The closely related redberry, *Rhamnus crocea* (see "Shrubs and Small Trees"), also has a dwarf cultivar that is suitable as a groundcover. Deer, bears, and many species of birds relish the berries.

Frangula californica fruit and foliage

Frangula californica

Leymus condensatus 'Canyon Prince' (*Elymus condensatus*)

Giant rye grass

Native Distribution: dry slopes, open woodlands, below 5,000 feet; Southern California: Los Angeles, Orange, Riverside, San Diego, San Bernardino, Santa Barbara, Ventura counties; Mexico.
Landscape Zone: Coastal Sage Scrub, Chaparral, Foothill Woodland, Joshua Tree Woodland.
Size: 3- to 8-foot-tall clumps.
Leaves: gray, 1 inch wide.
Fruit: June–August; seed head 4–17 inches long.
Soil: adaptable, sandy, clay, well draining.
Exposure: full sun to partial shade.
Temperature: root hardy to –35 degrees F.
Water: moderately drought tolerant, 14 inches/year minimum.
Propagation: seeds, root division.
Profile: Unlike its green-leaved parent species, the 'Canyon Prince' cultivar of *Leymus condensatus* sports a distinctive silver-greenish foliage. This multitasking, large, clumping grass species grows in a variety of habitats from sun to shade, moist to dry—just be sure not to overwater. The gray-green leaf blades complement a covering of California sage and buckwheats and provide a visual contrast the deep green of coyote brush. The tall leaf blades and summer seed plumes add a vertical interest to a landscape island, fence, or a mass planting of wildflowers. Trim back the bushy clump when the grass goes dormant. Giant rye, which spreads by rhizomes, needs 18 inches of soil, and can become aggressive in a deep, rich garden setting. The related creeping wild rye, *L. triticoides*, is a finer-textured, spreading meadow grass.

Leymus condensatus

Mahonia aquifolium (Berberis aquifolium)
Mahonia repens (Berberis repens)

Creeping barberry

Native Distribution: streambanks, shaded slopes, below 7,000-foot elevations; Southern California: Los Angeles, Riverside, San Bernardino, San Diego, Santa Barbara, Ventura counties; northern California to Canada, east to Texas.
Landscape Zone: Chaparral, conifer forests.
Size: 4–12 inches.
Leaves: evergreen; red in winter.
Flowers: spring; clusters of small yellow blooms.
Fruit: summer, fall; blue-black berries.
Soil: adaptable, well draining.
Exposure: full to partial shade.
Temperature: not heat tolerant, cold hardy to –40 degrees F.
Water: moderately drought tolerant.
Propagation: fresh, triple-stratified, or scarified seeds, semi-softwood cuttings, suckers.

Profile: With hollylike evergreen leaves, colorful flowers, ornate fruit, and a naturally low growth habit, these two look-alike mahonias are almost the perfect groundcover. Almost, because they just can't tolerate desert heat. Sometimes lumped together as the same species, they like the cool summers of higher elevations. If you live in an arid climate, mulch around this beautiful groundcover to keep the soil cool and moist and plant it in the shade. These plants grow moderately slowly but the stems root where they touch the ground and new sprouts grow from underground rhizomes to form a dense mat. The Santa Barbara Botanic Garden developed the tough, easy-to-grow cultivar 'Mission Canyon'. Set plants 10 to 12 inches apart for immediate cover.

Mahonia repens

Mahonia aquifolium

Muhlenbergia rigens

Deer grass

Native Distribution: sandy, gravelly soils, grasslands, canyons, slopes, below 7,000 feet; Southern California: Los Angeles, Orange, Riverside, San Diego, San Bernardino, Santa Barbara, Ventura counties; northern California, east to Texas.
Landscape Zone: Chaparral, Foothill Woodland.
Size: clumps to 4 feet high and wide.
Leaves: slender, gray-green, brown in cold winters.
Fruit: fall; fluffy seed plumes on 2-foot stalks.
Soil: adaptable, well draining.
Exposure: full sun to filtered shade.
Temperature: root hardy to -20 degrees F.
Water: drought tolerant, 15 inches/year minimum.
Propagation: clump division, seeds.
Profile: You'll love the picturesque effect of this tall bunch grass either as a lone accent, in a landscape mix, or grouped as a groundcover or slope planting. You can use it to droop over a wall or as a focal plant to balance a corner garden. It's a perfect match for rockwork or to soften rock gardens. The erect seed heads decorate the plant in the fall, and the graceful, arching, pale-green blades contribute color until the plant goes dormant in late winter. Even then its artistic shape and grayish brown hues continue to complement your yard. Cut the clumps back to the ground in late winter for rigorous spring growth. It grows fast and, despite its name, is deer resistant.

Top: *Muhlenbergia rigens*

Right: *Muhlenbergia rigens*

Nassella species

Needlegrass

Native Distribution: rocky slopes, dry open woods and grasslands; Western Transverse Ranges, Peninsular Ranges, below 4,500 feet; Southern California: Los Angeles, Orange, Riverside, San Bernardo, San Diego, Santa Barbara, Ventura counties.

Landscape Zone: Coastal Sage Scrub, Chaparral, Foothill Woodland.
Size: 6- to 12-inch-long flowering stalks, clumps to 18–24 inches tall and wide.
Leaves: 6–14 inches long, slender gray-green, turn brown in summer.

Fruit: early fall; fluffy seed plumes on stalk ends.
Soil: adaptable, well draining.
Exposure: full sun to partial shade.
Temperature: root hardy to 10 degrees F.
Water: drought tolerant.
Propagation: seeds, self-seeding, plant division.
Profile: California has three species of these fine-textured grasses, including the state grass, purple needlegrass, *Nassella pulchra.* This and several introduced species and cultivars grow in dense fountainlike clumps with slender, wiry, threadlike leaves and a 3-foot-tall, feathery seed stalk. The airy leaves sway gracefully in breezes and the back-lighted seed stalks glow brilliantly in the afternoon sun. The flower clusters develop in the spring and last well into the fall as they ripen to golden brown. The leaves stay green in winter; needlegrass naturalizes easily and stabilizes sunny slopes. Planted alone, the fluffy seed heads and leaves add a soft accent to a bare spot, corner, median, or fence. In a mixed planting, the size, green color, and vertical profile complement ground-hugging groundcovers such as manzanitas and coffeeberry. For a burst of spring color, fill bare spaces between plants with a brilliant display of annual wildflowers. The grass self-seeds, so remove the seed heads before they ripen if you want to contain it. A similar-looking species, purple three-awn, *Aristida purpurea* var. *purpurea,* has the same landscape applications.

Top: *Nassella tenuissima*

Left: *Nassella tenuissima*

Polystichum munitum

Western sword fern

Native Distribution: Shady slopes, streambanks, moist canyons, below 7,000 feet; Southern California: Los Angeles, Orange, Riverside, San Diego, San Bernardino, Santa Barbara, Ventura counties; north to Alaska.
Landscape Zone: Chaparral, widespread.
Size: 2–4 feet tall, erect to arching fronds.
Leaves: drought deciduous; sprouting from base.
Soil: adaptable, well draining, clay.
Exposure: full shade.
Temperature: root hardy to 0 degrees F.
Water: requires regular moisture, 45 inches/year minimum.
Propagation: dormant root division.
Profile: More than any other plant, ferns can turn a barren, shady corner into a lush, eye-catching attraction. A cluster of arching, delicate fronds brings an airy freshness to an entryway or courtyard, or the neglected side of a garage. When the new fiddleheads develop in the spring, you'll be on your knees to watch them unfold. Sword fern naturally grows in shady zones under trees and shrubs that strike fear in the hearts of most plants. In warm Southern California gardens, give it shade and deep soil to spread its rhizomes and it will turn a bare spot into a lush woodland vignette. Plant it under oaks, maples, or, for a multitextured combination, mix in other woodland species such as monkey flowers, cardinal flower, columbine, snowberry, and coffeeberry and salvia groundcovers. Add mulch if necessary to keep the soil from drying out.

Polystichum munitum

Pteridium aquilinum var. *pubescens*

Bracken fern

Native Distribution: meadows, hillsides, woodlands, below 10,000 feet; throughout California and North America.
Landscape Zone: Coastal Sage Scrub, Chaparral, Foothill Woodland.
Size: 1–3 feet tall.
Leaves: deciduous.
Soil: deep, loose, well draining.
Exposure: sun, full shade.
Temperature: root hardy, freezes to ground.
Water: moderate summer water.
Propagation: dormant root division.
Profile: Nothing creates that idyllic forest atmosphere like a stand of bracken fern underneath a canopy of trees. If you don't have your own private woodland, use these dramatic ferns to surround a mature oak or other tree with a tall trunk and shade-producing crown. Avoid planting in shallow, rocky soils. Bracken fern needs loose, rich soil to allow its rhizomes to spread and develop a thick colony, but it can become invasive in a garden habitat. Keep transplants moist until the rhizomes become established. As with other native ferns available from nurseries, the species with broad, luxuriant foliage generally require moist soil, semi-shade, and moderately humid conditions. Another dramatic fern, giant chain fern, *Woodwardia fimbriata,* has similar landscape requirements and applications.

Pteridium aquilinum var. *pubescens*

Pteridium aquilinum var. *pubescens*

Salvia spathacea

Hummingbird sage

Native Distribution: coastal slopes and open habitats, below 2,500 feet; Southern California: Los Angeles, Orange, San Diego, Santa Barbara, Ventura counties.
Landscape Zone: Chaparral, Foothill Woodland.
Size: 1–2 feet tall.
Flowers: spring–fall; red, 1- to 2-inch tube in whorls on 1- to 2-foot spikes.
Soil: adaptable, well draining.
Exposure: full sun to full shade.
Temperature: heat tolerant, cold hardy to 0 degrees F.
Water: drought tolerant, 20 inches/year minimum.
Propagation: seeds, root division.
Profile: When this little evergreen begins to bloom, you and every hummingbird in the area will take notice. Numerous bundles of scarlet, trumpet-shaped flowers encircle the blooming stalk like multiple hummingbird buffet tables. The low-growing forms (some varieties reach for the sky) crowd together to create an attractive groundcover that forms dense colonies by rhizomes. Nurseries often propagate forms they discover that exhibit superior characteristics. The 'Las Pilitas' variety, grown by Las Pilitas Nursery, forms a 1-foot-high mat that bursts with flowers in the spring. It thrives in the shade or in full sun. Santa Barbara Botanic Garden developed two premier groundcovers, 'Dara's Choice', that forms a dense, 3-foot-tall mat with purple flowers, and 'Avis Keedy' with white flowers.

Salvia spathacea flowers

Salvia spathacea

Symphoricarpos albus

Common snowberry

Native Distribution: streambanks, canyons, open woods, below 4,000 feet; Southern California: Los Angeles, Orange, Riverside, San Diego, San Bernardino, Santa Barbara; north to Alaska.
Landscape Zone: Foothill Woodland.
Size: 2–5 feet tall and wide.
Leaves: deciduous; gray-green, 1 inch long.
Flowers: pink, bell-shaped.
Fruit: fall; white, 1/3- to 1/2-inch diameter.
Soil: adaptable, well draining.
Exposure: full to partial shade.
Temperature: cold hardy to 0 degrees F.
Water: drought tolerant, 25 inches/year minimum.
Propagation: rooting branch nodes.
Profile: This mounding, thicket-forming bush may be the perfect plant to fill in a neglected area beneath a shady tree or the north side of a house. Common snowberry flourishes where other plants gasp for lack of light. Some slender branches arch upward while others sprawl and root to form a dense shrub. In the spring, tiny reddish flowers attract hummingbirds and by fall the ornate, white fruit provides forage for birds. Mix with currants, honeysuckles, coffeeberry, manzanitas, and sumacs for a border or island that adds texture to difficult areas. The desert snowberry, *Symphoricarpos longiflorus,* with 1/2-inch trumpet-shaped flowers and similar landscape applications, occurs in pinyon-juniper woodlands from 4,500 to 5,500 feet. Trailing snowberry, *S. mollis,* thrives in coastal areas and oak woodlands.

Symphoricarpos albus

Symphoricarpos albus fruit

Cacti and Succulents

Blue- and green-foliage *Agave* plants

Agave shawii

Native Distribution: sandy, gravelly hills, slopes, desert flats; Southern California: *Agave deserti,* Imperial, San Bernardo, Riverside, San Diego; *A. shawii,* San Diego; *A. utahensis,* San Bernardino County; Southwest U.S.; Mexico.
Landscape Zone: *Agave deserti:* Creosote Bush Scrub; *A. shawii:* Coastal Sage Scrub; *A. utahensis:* Creosote Bush Scrub, Joshua Tree Woodland, Pinyon-Juniper Woodland.
Size: 2–6 feet diameter.
Leaves: evergreen; swordlike, 18 inches long, vicious thorns.

Agave deserti
Desert agave
Agave shawii
Shaw's agave
Agave utahensis
Utah agave

Flowers: May–July; yellow clusters on 6- to 15-foot stalks.
Soil: adaptable, well draining.
Exposure: full sun.
Temperature: extremely heat tolerant, cold hardy to 10 degrees F.
Water: drought tolerant, 8 inches/year minimum.
Propagation: fresh seeds, root suckers.
Profile: As the classic desert plant, agaves add a distinctive accent to your xeriscape landscape. These three species form medium-sized plants with 2-foot leaves. The perfectly symmetrical rosette of grayish green leaves creates a natural focal point for cactus gardens, a commanding accent for a corner planting, or an unusual container plant. The stiff, viciously armed leaves have needlelike thorns at the tips and catclaw teeth along the edges. For this reason, avoid planting along walks or entryways where human contact, especially by children, is probable. Agaves grow rapidly for eight to twenty-five years and then send up a tall flowering stalk and die, but by then they're surrounded by offshoots. *Agave utahensis,* a high-desert, freeze-tolerant species, sends up a bottle-brush flower stalk instead of the typical candelabra.

With dozens of Western and Mexican species and numerous cultivars available in nurseries, agaves (or century plants) come in all sizes, so be sure to choose one compatible with your habitat and landscape design. *Agave americana,* native to the Southwest but not California, is the largest, with leaves up to 6 feet long. Many horticultural varieties of *A. Americana* exist, including ones with yellow and white striped leaves. *Agave* 'Blue Flame', a cross between *A. shawii* and *A. attenuata* from Mexico, has 3-foot leaves and a tall, bottle-brush bloom stalk. Several Mexican species used in landscaping have leaves without catclaws on the edges, but all are thorn tipped. The terminal thorns can be clipped, but that diminishes the ornamental appeal. Mexican species tend to be frost sensitive.

Agave shawii

Agave 'Blue Flame'

Cylindropuntia acanthocarpa var. *coloradensis* (*Opuntia acanthocarpa*)

Buckhorn cholla

Native Distribution: deserts, below 4,300 feet; Southern California: Imperial, Riverside, San Diego, San Bernardino counties; Nevada, Arizona.
Landscape Zone: Creosote Bush Scrub, Joshua Tree Woodland.
Size: 5–12 feet tall, treelike.
Flowers: May–June; yellow with purple-red filaments, 1-1/2 inches diameter at end of jointed stems.
Fruit: yellowish, 3/4-inch knobby oval.
Spines: yellow to reddish, 1–2 inches long, covered with sheath.
Exposure: full sun.
Temperature: cold hardy.
Propagation: scarified seeds, stem division.

Profile: You'll probably never find a very large cholla in a nursery; they're just too thorny to handle. To grow one, simply stick a stem joint in the ground and stand back. The intricately branching stems look like braided ropes, with each section ready to break off and hang onto any unfortunate passerby, then it roots where it drops. In the spring, showy red, burgundy, or yellow flowers crown the tips of the canelike stems. The size of this cactus makes it a good focal plant for your rock garden and a favorite nesting site for cactus wrens. Numerous other species of cholla with similar landscape applications are available.

Cylindropuntia acanthocarpa

Cylindropuntia acanthocarpa flowers

Cylindropuntia bigelovii (*Opuntia bigelovii*)

Teddy bear cholla

Native Distribution: deserts, south-facing hillsides, below 3,300 feet; Southern California: Imperial, Riverside, San Bernardino, San Diego counties; Arizona, Nevada; Mexico.
Landscape Zone: Creosote Bush Scrub.
Size: 5–8 feet tall, shrubby.
Flowers: February–May; greenish, 1-1/2 inches across at end of jointed stems.
Fruit: yellowish, 3/4-inch knobby oval.
Spines: silver to golden, 1 inch long, covered with sheath.
Exposure: full sun.
Temperature: cold hardy.
Propagation: scarified seeds, stem division.
Profile: The dense covering of golden spines gives this dramatic cholla a fuzzy appearance, but look closer and the thorny stems resemble a porcupine more than a teddy bear. Unlike other chollas with vivid red flowers, this species blooms with waxy, pale-green, almost translucent flowers highlighted with a dense cluster of yellow stamens. Chollas make spectacular focal plants for cactus gardens, but plant them far away from any possible human contact. The brittle, spiny joints seem to jump onto pant legs and shoes. This hitchhiking design makes growing chollas a snap, just plant one of the easily rooting joints in a sunny, well-draining spot and you'll have your own teddy bear. Cane cholla, *Cylindropuntia californica,* grows in the Chaparral and also makes a good landscape accent, but lacks the ornate thorns.

Cylindropuntia bigelovii

Cylindropuntia bigelovii at Anza-Borrego Desert State Park

Dudleya pulverulenta

Chalk dudleya

Native Distribution: rocky soils, coastal flats, hills; South Coast, Transverse Ranges, Peninsular Ranges, desert mountains, below 5,000 feet; Southern California: Imperial, Los Angeles, Orange, Riverside, San Bernardino, San Diego, Santa Barbara, Ventura counties; Arizona, Nevada, Utah; Mexico.
Landscape Zone: Chaparral, Coastal Sage Scrub.
Size: 2 feet diameter, basal rosette.
Perennial herb.
Flowers: May–July; red flowers on 2- to 3-foot stems.
Soil: adaptable, well draining.
Exposure: full sun to partial shade.
Temperature: cold hardy to 10 degrees F.
Water: drought tolerant, 12 inches/year minimum.
Propagation: seeds.
Profile: With a basal rosette of broad leaves covered with a chalky powder or wax, this unusual plant makes a handsome focal point for any cactus or xeriscape garden, accent for a rock wall or ledge, or a container plant. In the spring, the bizarre plant puts on a fireworks show with arching 2- to 3-foot flower stalks covered with red-tinged leaves. The profusion of small, cone-shaped red flowers attracts oohs and ahhs, as well as butterflies and hummingbirds. The symmetrical, compact size of chalk dudleya complements barrel and hedgehog cacti, Parry agave, and wild rye grass; its white color contrasts well with penstemons, paintbrushes, desert marigold, and California poppy. The popular Britton dudleya, *Dudleya brittonii,* from Baja California is similar to chalk dudleya but not freeze tolerant. Keep all dudleyas dry on a slope, in a well-draining garden spot, or container, avoid summer moisture, and enjoy the year-round beauty. About forty-five diverse species of *Dudleya* grow in California and several cultivars are available, so be sure to include one in your xeriscape design.

Dudleya brittonii

Echinocereus triglochidiatus

Hedgehog or Mohave mound cactus

Echinocereus triglochidiatus

Echinocereus triglochidiatus flowers

Native Distribution: rocky hillsides and mountains, 500–9,000 feet; Southern California: Los Angeles, Riverside, San Bernardino, San Diego counties; east to central Texas, Colorado; Mexico.
Landscape Zone: Creosote Bush Scrub, Joshua Tree Woodland, Pinyon-Juniper Woodland.
Size: 1-foot stems forming a mound 1–4 feet in diameter.
Flowers: April–June; 1–2 inch diameter, scarlet.
Fruit: spiny, red.
Spines: 5 to 7 radials to 1 inch long, 1 to 4 centrals to 1-3/4 inches long.
Soil: sandy, igneous, rich in humus, well draining.
Exposure: full sun.
Temperature: cold hardy.
Water: drought tolerant.
Propagation: seeds.
Profile: This wide-ranging and highly variable species has confused botanists since it was first named in 1848. Experts can't decide whether this is one species with numerous varieties or multiple species. But they do agree that the waxy, long-lasting flowers are spectacular. With age, this cactus forms rounded mounds, a picturesque addition to your desert garden, especially when covered with scarlet blooms. Since some varieties are adapted to desert chaparral while others thrive in montane forests, try to buy one propagated from a locally indigenous plant. They normally grow in humus-rich soil, so plant them in a well-draining soil mix with leaf mold. The related *Echinocereus engelmannii* has similar habitat requirements and landscape applications.

Ferocactus cylindraceus

California barrel cactus

Native Distribution: sandy, rocky soils, deserts and grasslands, below 5,000 feet; Southern California: Imperial, Los Angeles, Orange, San Bernardino, San Diego, Riverside counties; east into Texas; Mexico.
Landscape Zone: Creosote Bush Scrub, Joshua Tree Woodland.
Size: unbranched cylindrical stems 4–10 feet tall, 2 feet in diameter; usually grows 2–3 feet tall in landscape settings.
Flowers: spring, summer; yellow to orange, 1–3 inches round.
Fruit: yellow, 1–2 inches long.
Spines: 12 to 20 or more bristlelike radials to 1–2 inches long, 4 stout centrals to 3 inches long.
Soil: gravelly, sandy, well draining.
Exposure: full sun.
Temperature: cold hardy.
Propagation: seeds.
Profile: Barrel cactus provides a medium-height accent between the taller chollas and prickly pears and the smaller hedgehogs and pincushions. A half dozen or more of the yellow flowers bloom at once in a circle around the tip of the stem, followed by yellow, barrel-shaped fruit. Heavy, sometimes hooked, spines cover the stem to protect its succulent flesh from thirsty predators. The dense cover of spines of the red-spined variety gives the cactus a distinctive reddish color. The popular golden barrel cactus, *Echinocactus grusonii,* from Mexico where it is endangered from over-collecting, is widely available in the trade. The basketball-sized specimens make a dramatic statement when mass planted on a sunny slope or rock garden. It is frost hardy to 14 degrees F for brief periods, but requires an average minimum temperature above 55 degrees F to thrive. The California barrel cactus, as are most native cacti, is also threatened by over-collecting, so always purchase seed-grown stock.

Ferocactus cylindraceus

Ferocactus cylindraceus flowers

Ferocactus cylindraceus

Mammillaria tetrancistra

Fishhook cactus or strawberry cactus

Native Distribution: desert washes, valleys, hillsides, below 5,000 feet; Southern California: Imperial, Riverside, San Diego, San Bernardino, Los Angeles counties; Utah, Arizona; Mexico.
Landscape Zone: Creosote Bush Scrub.
Size: 1–3 inches in diameter.
Flowers: April; pink to lavender, 1–2 inches across, in circle around top.
Fruit: 1/2 to 1-1/4 inches, oval, fleshy, green.
Spines: 30 to 60 radials to 1/2 to 1 inch long, 3 to 4 centrals 3/4 to 1 inch long, hooked at the tip.
Soil: gravelly, sandy, well draining.
Exposure: full sun.
Temperature: cold hardy.
Propagation: seeds.
Profile: This fishhook cactus may be small, but it's armed with vicious hooked spines. The gorgeous flowers burst from the stem tip like fireworks, as many as a dozen open at the same time. A layer of fruit often surrounds the new blooms, adding bright red to green colors to the arrangement. Mammillarias, many from Central and South America, are some of the most popular cacti in the nursery trade. Some are golf-ball-sized pincushions while others grow to almost a foot in diameter and are armed with vicious fishhook spines. Flower colors vary from creamy to purple. The name *Mammillaria* comes from the nipple-shaped tubercles that cover the stem. If you like the idea of your rock garden representing native species, buy a *Mammillaria* propagated from species indigenous to your area. Another native fishhook, *M. dioica,* blooms with white to yellow flowers.

Mammillaria tetrancistra

Opuntia basilaris

Beavertail prickly pear

Opuntia basilaris

Opuntia basilaris flowers

Native Distribution: sandy desert soils, canyons, dry mountain slopes, below 7,200 feet; Southern California: Imperial, Los Angeles, Orange, Riverside, San Bernardino, San Diego counties; Nevada, Utah, Arizona; Mexico.
Landscape Zone: Coastal Sage Scrub, Chaparral, Creosote Bush Scrub, Pinyon-Juniper Woodland, Joshua Tree Woodland, Foothill Woodland.
Size: 2–4 feet high, 6 feet diameter, low growing, spreading.
Flowers: March–June; pink to magenta, 3 inches across.
Fruit: 3-inch oval, purple.
Spines: absent or few along top of pad
Soil: sandy, well draining.
Exposure: full sun.
Temperature: cold hardy to –10 degrees F.
Propagation: scarified seeds, stem division.
Profile: Unlike the most prickly pears that produce yellow flowers, beavertail blooms with an abundance of brilliant red to pink blossoms. And as a bonus, the pads lack the vicious long spines of most opuntias. But if you think the pads are naked and harmless, think again. Clusters of tiny brown barbs (glochids) grow in rows all over the stems and fruit of all *Opuntia*, so hands off. The spineless pads provide a textural contrast to other thorn-covered cacti, while the pastel flowers add zip to a xeriscape design. Nurseries carry cultivars with blue-gray to green pads and pink to magenta flowers. For winter color in your landscape garden, choose the similar *Opuntia santa-rita* with pads that turn red in the winter.

Opuntia santa-rita

Opuntia littoralis

Coastal or western prickly pear

Native Distribution: arid washes, ridges, and hillsides, below 1,500 feet: Southern California: Los Angeles, Orange, Riverside, San Bernardino, San Diego, Santa Barbara, Ventura counties; Channel Islands; Mexico.
Landscape Zone: Coastal Sage Scrub, Chaparral.
Size: upright to sprawling clumps to 3 feet tall, 15 feet diameter.
Flowers: spring; yellow to red, 1-1/2 inches across at end of jointed stems.
Fruit: 1- to 2-inch oval, dark red-purple, juicy.
Spines: 1–2 inches long, straight in clusters of 4 to 11.
Exposure: full sun.
Temperature: cold hardy to 10 degrees F.
Propagation: scarified seeds, stem division.
Profile: This widespread prickly pear will be right at home in your xeriscape garden, as long as it has plenty of room to develop through the years. The bristle-covered pads, flowers, and red fruit add color and texture year-round, and its mature size provides a strong vertical accent as a background plant or companion to other large-scale desert specimens such as yucca, cholla, and palo verde. Caution: All *Opuntia* have tiny, hairlike glochid thorns in clusters on the pads and fruit. The barbed glochids cause extreme discomfort and must be meticulously removed with tweezers.

Opuntia littoralis

Opuntia phaeacantha (*Opuntia mojavensis*)

Brown-spined or Mojave prickly pear

Native Distribution: coastal ranges, desert mountains and flats, below 7,500 feet; Southern California: Riverside, San Diego, Santa Barbara counties; east to Texas, Kansas to Nevada, South Dakota.
Landscape Zone: Joshua Tree Woodland, Pinyon-Juniper Woodland.
Size: 3–7 feet tall, 10–15 feet in diameter.
Flowers: April–June; 3–4 inches, yellow to orange.
Fruit: summer, fall; 2–3 inches long, purple to red, edible.
Spines: white, to 3 inches long.
Soil: sandy, well draining.
Exposure: full sun.
Temperature: cold hardy.
Propagation: scarified seeds, stem division.
Profile: This large-proportioned prickly pear will grow to fill the space of a large shrub, but with the multileveled texture of dozens of prickly stems and pads. Start by rooting a single pad and enjoy the evolving shape of the plant for years. Maintaining the size to match the scale of your site is easy: just snap off a stem and start another plant. The profusion of yellow flowers and red fruit along the edges of the pads make prickly pears the highlight of any xeriscape. Combine with chollas, yuccas, palo verde, and desert willow for a spectacular desert exhibition garden. The most widespread species in the West, Engelmann prickly pear, *Opuntia engelmannii,* is usually available at nurseries. The variety *O. engelmannii* var. *linguiformis* grows with ornate, elongated pads. Caution: All *Opuntia* have tiny, hairlike glochid thorns in clusters on the pads and fruit. The barbed glochids cause extreme discomfort and must be meticulously removed with tweezers.

Opuntia phaeacantha

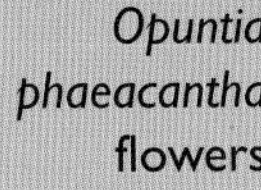

Opuntia phaeacantha flowers

Right: *Opuntia engelmannii* flowers

Opuntia polyacantha var. *erinacea* (*Opuntia erinacea*)

Old-man prickly pear or Mojave prickly pear

Native Distribution: desert mountains and flats, 2,500–10,000 feet; Mojave Desert, Peninsular Ranges; Southern California: Imperial, Los Angeles, Riverside, San Diego, Santa Barbara counties; north to Washington, east to New Mexico.
Landscape Zone: Creosote Bush Scrub, Chaparral, Pinyon-Juniper Woodland, Joshua Tree Woodland.
Size: 1–2 feet tall, segments to 7 inches in diameter.
Flowers: April–June; 1 inch diameter, yellow to pink.
Fruit: summer, fall; 2–3 inches long, red, edible.
Spines: white, to 5 inches long.
Soil: sandy, well draining.
Exposure: full sun.
Temperature: cold hardy.
Propagation: scarified seeds, stem division.
Profile: This dense-clumping cactus earns one of its common names from the thick covering of spines that cover the slender segments like an old man's grizzled beard. Plant old-man prickly pear when you need a small-proportioned but distinctive addition to your xeriscape garden. The stems multiply to form a bristly mat several yards in diameter. In the spring, waxlike flowers seem to float on a cloud of white, fuzzy thorns. The red fruit adds to the ornamental accent. Caution: All *Opuntia* have tiny, hairlike glochid thorns in clusters on the pads and fruit. The barbed glochids cause extreme discomfort and must be meticulously removed with tweezers.

Opuntia polyacantha var. *erinacea*

Opuntia polyacantha var. *erinacea*

Yucca baccata
Banana yucca
Yucca whipplei
Our Lord's candle or chaparral yucca

Native Distribution: sunny slopes, coastal and desert scrub; *Yucca baccata:* 2,500–4,000 feet, Riverside, San Bernardino, San Diego counties; *Y. whipplei:* below 4,000 feet, Los Angeles, Orange, Riverside, San Bernardino, San Diego, Santa Barbara, Ventura counties.
Landscape Zone: *Yucca baccata*: Chaparral, Joshua Tree Woodland; *Y. whipplei:* Coastal Sage Scrub, Creosote Bush Scrub, Chaparral, Pinyon-Juniper Woodland, Joshua Tree Woodland.
Size: 1–3 feet tall and wide.
Leaves: evergreen; swordlike, spine tipped.
Flowers: spring–summer; large clusters of white flowers on stalks.
Fruit: leathery capsules 2–6 inches long.
Soil: variable, well draining.
Exposure: full sun.
Temperature: extremely heat tolerant, cold hardy to –10 degrees F.
Water: drought tolerant, 8 inches/year minimum.
Propagation: fresh seeds.
Profile: Trunkless yuccas give your landscape a distinctive desert flavor. Their knee-high height suits them to midgarden placement and side-yard or corner plantings. The bladelike leaves add vertical structure to a cactus or xeriscape garden. Small yuccas make ideal accent plants and when they bloom become the center of attention. The flowering stalk of banana yucca nestles inside or just above the stiff, 3-foot-long leaves. Our Lord's candle sends up a spectacular 10- to 15-foot stalk above a dense clump of narrow, gray-green, 3-foot-long leaves. Besides cactus gardens, these yuccas complement mixed plantings with sages, silktassel, three-leaf sumac, chamise, coyote brush, and coffeeberry. Like their larger counterparts, these yuccas have needle-tipped leaves, so don't plant them near play or walk areas.

Yucca baccata

Yucca baccata in flower

Yucca whipplei

Yucca brevifolia

Joshua tree

Yucca schidigera

Mohave yucca

Yucca brevifolia at Joshua Tree National Park

Native Distribution: sunny slopes, deserts; *Yucca brevifolia:* Los Angeles, Riverside, San Bernardino counties, 1,600–6,500 feet; *Y. schidigera:* Los Angeles, San Bernardino, Riverside, San Diego, Imperial counties, below 8,000 feet.
Landscape Zone: *Yucca brevifolia:* Joshua Tree Woodland; *Y. schidigera:* Chaparral, Creosote Bush Scrub.
Size: 3–20 feet tall.
Leaves: evergreen; swordlike, 1–5 feet long.
Flowers: spring–summer; large clusters of white flowers on tall stalks.
Fruit: leathery capsules 1–4 inches long.
Soil: variable, well draining.
Exposure: full sun.
Temperature: cold hardy to 5 degrees F.
Water: drought tolerant.
Propagation: fresh seeds.

Profile: With their large, multiple branches and tall flower stalks, tree yuccas gracefully dominate almost any landscape design. If you plant one in your xeriscape garden, make it the center of interest. Several planted together create a dramatic setting. Mohave yucca reaches 9 to 15 feet tall with multiple arms and grows from low deserts to 8,000 feet. The large-scale Joshua tree grows 30 feet tall and 3 feet in diameter with multiple branches and is suitable primarily for park, boulevard, and campus landscaping. The popular blue yucca, *Yucca rigida,* a native of northern Mexico, has a single trunk crowned with a compact rosette of stiff, 3-foot-long, bluish leaves. Tree yuccas grow slow and may take decades to develop their characteristic trunk. Large specimens are dug from the wild, which unfortunately has decimated some native populations.

Yucca schidigera

Yucca brevifolia foliage and flowers

Yucca schidigera

Glossary of Terms

Bract: Usually small and leaflike structures located below the petals of a flower. In some plants, the bracts are as colorful and showy as the petals.

Budding (propagation): A twig axis with a dormant bud is removed and inserted into an actively growing limb by making a T-shaped cut, peeling back the bark and inserting the bud section.

California Floristic Province: Portions of California, Oregon, and Baja California, excluding the desert regions, that have plants associated with a Mediterranean climate.

Chlorosis: Iron deficiency usually caused by soil with a pH greater than 7.5. The high calcium content inhibits iron utilization by the plant. The abiotic disease causes yellow leaves, slow growth, and branch dieback.

Cold hardy: Can survive hard winter freezes.

Corm: An underground structure similar to a bulb but without scales.

Cultivar: Abbreviated form of "cultivated variety." A plant with particularly ornamental qualities usually cloned by cuttings. A cultivar's unique name is enclosed in single quotation marks.

Cuttings, hardwood: Cuttings taken from the current season's growth after the wood matures in the fall or dormant season. Take a section from just above a leaf node, about 12 to 16 inches long and up to 1/2 inch in diameter. Store the cuttings in moist sand until spring. To root, dust with a rooting powder and place in moist sand, vermiculite, or peat. Cover with polyethylene, which is permeable to oxygen but holds in water vapor.

Cuttings, semi-hardwood: Cuttings taken soon after seasonal growth stops but before the wood hardens, usually in the summer.

Cuttings, softwood: Cuttings taken from actively growing wood, usually in the spring.

Deadheading: To prune dead flower heads after the bloom fades but before they set seeds to encourage further flowering.

Deciduous: Seasonal loss of leaves in response to drought or winter as the plant goes dormant to conserve energy.

Dieback: The gradual dying of plant shoots, beginning from the growing tips.

Division (propagation): Separating a plant and its roots into two or more sections for replanting.

Drought deciduous: Plants that cope with the hot summer drought by shedding their leaves to conserve energy until the rainy winter season.

Drought tolerant: Requiring no supplemental water to survive extended periods of drought, but may need periodic deep watering to maintain maximum flowering, foliage, and growth.

Endemic: A species of plant or animal restricted to a particular geographic region and nowhere else in the world.

Fire-follower: A plant that colonizes recently burned areas and grows abundantly for several years in the ash-fertilized soil.

Grafting (propagation): A delicate procedure that removes a twig with a leaf and leaf bud and inserts it into a growing limb.

Holdfast: A rootlike structure that a vine uses to attach to a surface.

Layering (propagation): Bending a growing limb and covering it with soil, leaving 6 to 12 inches of the end exposed. The buried portion will grow roots and can be cut from the parent plant.

Mediterranean climate: A subtropical climate with hot, dry summers and mild, rainy winters that occurs in five regions in the world outside the Mediterranean basin: California, excluding the desert regions; the western Cape in South Africa; central Chile; and western and southern Australia.

Microhabitat: A combination of physical and biological conditions that is different from the surrounding conditions. For example, a flower bed located in the southwest corner of a house receives more sun and reflected heat than one in a shady entryway.

Plant community: An association of plants in a particular region dominated by a particular species. Plant communities are not uniform and they often intergrade with no sharp division.

Rhizome: An underground stem that grows under the surface and sprouts to produce new plants vegetatively.

Rosette: A plant with a small cluster of leaves with radical symmetry, common in wildflowers that germinate in the fall and overwinter, then bloom in the spring.

Scarifying seed: Mechanically pricking, filing, or wearing down tough seed coat so it will absorb water and germinate.

Shade, full: No direct sun; heavily filtered sun okay.

Shade, partial: Less than six hours of full or filtered sun per day.

Shrub: A woody plant that usually has multiple trunks or stems and a mature height of less than 15 feet.

Stolon: An underground stem that roots at nodes to form new plants.

Stratification: Placing seeds in moist sand or other medium, sealing in polyethylene bags, and storing in the refrigerator for a designated time, typically three months at 40 degrees F.

Subshrub: An herbaceous perennial larger than a wildflower but smaller than a shrub, usually 2 to 3 feet tall and wide, with a woody stem that usually dies back in the winter.

Sun, full: At least six hours of direct or reflected sun per day.

Tree: A woody plant that usually has a single trunk and a mature height of more than 15 feet.

Tubercle: A knoblike protrusion on the surface of a plant. Found most notably on *Mammillaria* cactus plants.

Vegetation types: A group of plant species that occur together in a specific type of habitat.

Vegetative propagation: Seedless reproduction, such as bulbs, softwood cuttings, layering, and root shoots.

Xeriscape: A landscape that uses plants that require little supplemental water, even during droughts.

Appendix 1

Colorscaping with Flowering Trees, Shrubs, Vines, and Groundcovers

Note: Dates refer to the range of flowering or fruiting times of the species through a variety of conditions; bloom times for individual plants may vary.

Trees

Acacia farnesiana, huisache, February–May

Acacia greggii, catclaw acacia, April–June

Aesculus californica, California buckeye, April–September

Arbutus menziesii, Pacific madrone, February–March

Cercis orbiculata, western redbud, February–April

Chilopsis linearis, desert willow, May–September

Lyonothamnus floribundus, Catalina ironwood, spring, summer

Olneya tesota, desert ironwood, April–May

Parkinsonia florida, blue palo verde, March–May

Parkinsonia microphylla, foothills palo verde, April–May

Prosopis glandulosa, honey mesquite, April–August

Prosopis velutina, velvet mesquite, April–August

Prunus virginiana var. *demissa*, western chokecherry, May–June

Robinia neomexicana, desert locust, April–August

Sambucus nigra ssp. canadensis, Mexican elderberry, March–September

Shrubs

Abutilon palmeri, Indian mallow, April–May

Acalypha californica, copper leaf, April–May

Adenostoma fasciculatum, chamise, May–June

Agave, agaves, June–August

Amelanchier utahensis, Utah serviceberry, April–May.

Amorpha fruticosa, false indigo, May–June

Arctostaphylos densiflora, Vine Hill manzanita, March–May

Arctostaphylos emundsonii, Little Sur manzanita, March–May

Arctostaphylos glauca, big-berry manzanita, December, March

Baccharis sarothroides, desert broom, August–September

Caesalpinia gilliesii, desert bird of paradise, April–September

Calliandra conferta, fairy duster, March–April

Ceanothus arboreus, island ceanothus, February–May

Ceanothus cyaneus, San Diego mountain lilac, March–June

Ceanothus greggii, desert ceanothus, March–June

Ceanothus griseus, Carmel ceanothus, spring–fall

Ceanothus thyrsiflorus, blue blossom, May–June

Comarostaphylis diversifolia, summer holly, spring

Cornus sericea, redosier dogwood, May–July

Dendromecon harfordii, island bush poppy, spring–fall

Diplacus aurantiacus, bush monkey flower, spring–fall

Encelia californica, California sunflower, spring–fall after rain

Ericameria laricifolia, larchleaf goldenbush, September–October

Ericameria nauseosa, rabbitbrush, July–October

Eriogonum fasciculatum, California buckwheat, March–November

Eriogonum giganteum, Saint Catherine's lace, May–December

Fallugia paradoxa, Apache plume, April–October

Fouquieria splendens, ocotillo, March–June

Fremontodendron californicum, California flannel bush, spring

Garrya elliptica, coast silktassel, January–February

Heteromeles arbutifolia, toyon, flowers June–July; fruits October–January

Justicia californica, chuparosa, spring–summer after rain

Krascheninnikovia lanata, winterfat, seedheads in fall–winter

Larrea tridentata, creosote bush, spring–winter

Lavatera assurgentiflora, island mallow, spring–fall

Lepechinia calycina, white pitcher plant, April–June

Lupinus albifrons, silver bush lupine, spring

Lycium fremontii, Fremont desert thorn, March–April

Mahonia fremontii, Fremont barberry, February–April

Mahonia haemetocarpa, red barberry, February–April

Shrubs *(continued)*

Malacothamnus fasciculatus, chaparral bush mallow, April–June

Malosma laurina, laurel sumac, spring–summer

Nolina, beargrass, May–June

Psorothamnus fremontii, indigo bush, April–May

Purshia stansburiana, Stansbury cliffrose, May–July

Rhamnus crocea, redberry, spring

Rhus ovata, sugar sumac, March–May

Rhus trilobata, three-leaf sumac, April–May

Ribes aureum, golden currant, April–May

Romneya coulteri, matilija poppy, May–July

Rosa californica, California rose, spring–fall

Salvia apiana, white sage, May–August

Salvia clevelandii, Cleveland sage, May–August

Salvia leucophylla, purple sage, May–July

Solanum parishi, blue witches, spring–fall

Solanum umbelliferum, blue witches, spring–fall

Solanum xantii, blue witches, spring–fall

Trichostema lanatum, woolly blue curls, spring–fall

Yucca specues, March–June

Vines and Groundcovers

Aristolochia californica, California pipevine, March–May

Calystegia macrostegia, island morning glory, winter–spring

Dudleya caespitosa, coast dudleya, spring–summer

Clematis ligusticifolia, western virgin's bower, May–September

Lonicera subspicata, southern honeysuckle, summer

Mahonia repens, creeping barberry, spring

Maurandya antirrhiniflora, snapdragon vine, February–October

Parthenocissus vitacea, thicket creeper, fall leaf color

Salvia spathacea, hummingbird sage, spring–fall

Symphoricarpos albus var. *laevigatus*, common snowberry, white fruit, fall, winter

Vitis californica, California wild grape, fall leaf color

Appendix II
Landscape Palettes Zone by Zone

Each of the six plant communities, or landscape zones, featured in this book contains plants that are specialized to the unique combination of soil, climate, exposure, and companion plants in their association. Besides the specialists, additional species overlap into or form a transition between adjacent plant communities. Like an artist with a spectrum of paints, the plants in each landscape zone can be combined to create a variety of color, texture, size, and composition. These lists are by no means exclusive; see the Native Plant Profiles for more exact growing requirements and related species with similar landscape applications. See the chapter on landscape zones earlier in the book for detailed descriptions of the zones.

Coastal Sage Scrub

Landscapes from Los Angeles to San Diego and inland from Riverside to Escondido fall in this semi-arid habitat characterized by warm, wet winters and dry summers. Many plants exhibit summer dormancy, with the primary bloom season extending from fall through spring. For year-round color and texture, include evergreen and evergray shrubs as hedges and foliage plants. The gardens should have well-draining soils and sunny exposures. A weekly light sprinkle in the drought season will keep plants perky, but soaking is detrimental.

Trees

Aesculus californica, California buckeye
Platanus racemosa, California sycamore
Populus fremontii, western cottonwood
Prunus ilicifolia, hollyleaf cherry

Shrubs

Adenostoma fasciculatum, chamise
Amorpha fruticosa, desert indigo
Arctostaphylos species and cultivars, manzanitas
Artemisia californica, California sagebrush
Artemisia tridentate, Great Basin sagebrush
Baccharis pilularis, coyote brush
Ceanothus species and cultivars, ceanothus
Dendromecon harfordii, island bush poppy
Diplacus aurantiacus, bush monkey flower
Encelia californica, California sunflower
Encelia farinosa, white brittle bush
Epilobium canum, California fuchsia
Eriogonum fasciculatum, California buckwheat
Eriogonum giganteum, St. Catherine's lace
Forestiera pubescens, desert olive
Frangula californica, coffeeberry
Lupinus sparsiflorus, Coulter's lupine
Lupinus succulentus, arroyo lupine
Lycium species, desert thorns
Mahonia species, barberries
Malosma laurina, laurel sumac
Quercus berberidifolia, scrub oak
Rhus species, sumacs
Ribes species, gooseberries
Rosa species, wild roses
Salvia species, sages
Solanum umbelliferum, blue witches
Solidago species, goldenrods

Wildflowers

Abronia villosa, desert sand verbena
Achillea millefolium, yarrow
Calochortus species, mariposa lilies
Castilleja exserta, owl's clover paintbrush
Datura wrightii, sacred datura
Delphinium cardinale, scarlet larkspur
Dodecatheon clevelandii, padre's shooting star
Erigeron glaucus, seaside daisy
Eriogonum grande, red-flowered buckwheat
Eschscholzia californica, California poppy
Penstemon species, beardtongues
Sphaeralcea species, globemallows
Viguiera laciniata, California sunflower

Groundcovers and Vines

Calystegia macrostegia, island morning glory
Leymus condensatus 'Canyon Prince', giant rye grass
Muhlenbergia species, deer grass
Nassella species, needlegrass

Cacti and Succulents

Agave shawii, Shaw's agave
Dudleya species
Ferocactus cylindraceus, barrel cactus
Mammillaria species, fishhook cacti
Opuntia species, chollas
Opuntia littoralis, coast prickly pear

Chaparral

Landscapes designed with representatives from this plant community may combine a diverse palette of evergreen shrubs, groundcovers, and perennials, but few trees. You can colorscape with rainbow hues of flowers, fruit, and foliage that brighten your yard throughout the year. These plants thrive on sunny exposures and shallow, rocky soil, so be sure your garden is well draining. Most set deep taproots to acquire year-round moisture to support their evergreen foliage. An occasional summer drink will keep them in peak condition.

Trees

Acacia farnesiana, huische
Arbutus menziesii, madrone
Lyonothamnus floribundus, Catalina ironwood
Prunus ilicifolia, hollyleaf cherry
Prunus virginiana, chokecherry
Quercus agrifolia, coast live oak
Quercus engelmannii, Engelmann oak

Shrubs

Adenostoma fasciculatum, chamise
Amelanchier utahensis, Utah serviceberry
Amorpha fruticosa, desert indigo
Arctostaphylos species and cultivars, manzanitas
Ceanothus species and cultivars, ceanothus
Dendromecon harfordii, island bush poppy
Diplacus aurantiacus, bush monkey flower
Eriogonum species, buckwheats
Forestiera pubescens, desert olive
Frangula californica, coffeeberry
Fremontodendron californicum, flannel bush
Garrya elliptica, silk tassel
Heteromeles arbutifolia, toyon
Lupinus albifrons, silver bush lupine
Lycium andersonii, Anderson desert thorn
Mahonia species and cultivars, barberries
Quercus berberidifolia, inland scrub oak
Rhus species, sumacs
Ribes speciosum, fuchsia-flowered gooseberry
Romneya coulteri, matilija poppy
Rosa species, wild roses
Salvia species, sages
Solanum xantii, blue witches
Trichostema lanatum, woolly blue curls

Wildflowers

Abronia villosa, desert sand verbena
Achillea millefolium, yarrow
Aquilegia formosa, crimson columbine
Asclepias eriocarpa, monarch milkweed
Calochortus species, mariposa lilies
Delphinium cardinale, scarlet larkspur
Epilobium californica, California fuchsia
Lupinus sparsiflorus, Coulter's lupine
Oenothera species, evening primroses
Penstemon species, beardtongues

Groundcovers and Vines

Aristolochia californica, California pipevine
Artemisia californica 'Canyon Gray', California sagebrush
Artemisia ludoviciana, mugwort
Arctostaphylos species and cultivars, manzanitas
Baccharis pilularis, dwarf coyote brush
Calystegia macrostegia, island morning glory
Ceanothus griseus, Carmel ceanothus
Clematis ligusticifolia, western virgin's bower
Leymus condensatus 'Canyon Prince', giant rye grass
Lonicera interrupta, chaparral honeysuckle
Muhlenbergia rigens, deer grass
Salvia spathacea, hummingbird sage
Symphoricarpos albus, snowberry

Cacti and Succulents

Dudeya species
Opuntia littoralis, coastal prickly pear
Yucca species

Foothill Woodland

The oaks of California occur in foothills and canyons that have enough soil to support a deep root system. The woodland habitats include both closed-canopy evergreen forests and deciduous oaks interspersed with grasses, shrubs, and herbaceous plants. Landscapes compatible with oaks consist of shade-tolerant and partially shade-tolerant understory plants. Oaks require well-draining soil, natural leaf litter, and no extra fertilizers. Mature trees and established saplings require no supplemental water, so pick compatible plants that will flourish without drip or frequent irrigation.

Trees

Acer macrophyllum, big-leaf maple
Aesculus californica, California buckeye
Alnus rhombifolia, white alder
Arbutus menziesii, Pacific madrone
Fraxinus velutina, Arizona ash
Platanus racemosa, California sycamore
Populus fremontii, western cottonwood
Quercus agrifolia, coast live oak
Quercus engelmannii, Engelmann oak
Quercus lobata, valley oak
Sambucus nigra subsp. *canadensis*, Mexican elderberry
Umbellularia californica, California bay

Shrubs

Arctostaphylos species and cultivars, manzanitas
Ceanothus species and cultivars, ceanothus
Cornus species, dogwoods
Dendromecon harfordii, bush poppy
Diplacus aurantiacus, bush monkey flower
Ericameria nauseosa, rabbitbrush
Eriogonum fasciculatum, California buckwheat
Fremontodendron californicum, flannel bush
Garrya species, silktassels
Heteromeles arbutifolia, toyon
Mahonia species and cultivars, barberries
Malosma laurina, laurel sumac
Rhamnus crocea, redberry
Rhus ovata, sugar sumac
Ribes aureum, golden currant
Ribes speciosum, fuchsia-flowered gooseberry
Solanum xantii, blue witches

Wildflowers

Achillea millefolium, yarrow
Calochortus species, mariposa lilies
Delphinium species, larkspur
Eschscholzia californica, California poppy
Iris douglasiana, Douglas iris
Mimulus cardinalis, scarlet monkey flower
Oenothera species, evening primroses
Penstemon species, beardtongues

Groundcovers and Vines

Adiantum capillus-veneris, maidenhair fern
Arctostaphylos species and cultivars, manzanitas
Baccharis pilularis, prostrate coyote brush
Calystegia macrostegia, island morning glory
Clematis ligusticifolia, western virgin's bower
Ceanothus species and cultivars, ceanothus
Leymus condensatus 'Canyon Prince', giant rye grass
Lonicera species, honeysuckle
Mahonia repens, creeping barberry
Muhlenbergia rigens, deer grass
Parthenocissus vitacea, thicket creeper
Salvia spathacea, hummingbird sage
Symphoricarpos mollis, snowberry
Vitis californica, wild grape

Cacti and Succulents

Opuntia basilaris, beavertail prickly pear
Dudleya species, dudleya

Creosote Bush Scrub

Landscapes in this plant community should be designed exclusively with drought-tolerant species. In areas with winters that drop below freezing (Mojave Desert), choose plants that can tolerate freezing air and soil temperatures. In warm-winter areas (Sonoran, or Colorado, Desert), you can add freeze-intolerant plants to your palette. Refer to the Plant Profiles for temperature tolerances. Choose from the classic desert species of cactus, yucca, small-leaved evergreen shrubs, and small trees that typically grow along washes. Compose gardens in well-draining, sandy-loam soil and sunny exposures, on open ground without mulch, and with total weed control. Since these desert plants absorb water through a network of surface roots, avoid tilling or disturbing the soil. Water primarily in the summer, the thunderstorm season in the desert.

Trees

Acacia farnesiana, huisache
Acacia greggii, catclaw acacia
Celtis reticulata, hackberry
Chilopsis linearis, desert willow
Olneya tesota, desert ironwood
Parkinsonia species and hybrids, palo verde
Prosopis glandulosa, honey mesquite

Shrubs

Baccharis sarothroides, desert broom
Baileya multiradiata, desert marigold
Caesalpina gilliesii, desert bird of paradise
Calliandra eriophylla, fairy duster
Encelia farinosa, white brittle bush
Ephedra species, joint firs
Ericameria nauseosus, rabbitbrush
Eriogonum fasciculatum, California buckwheat
Fallugia paradoxa, Apache plume
Forestiera pubescens, desert olive
Fouquieria splendens, ocotillo
Frangula californica, coffeeberry
Justicia californica, chuparosa
Krascheninnikovia lanata, winterfat
Larrea tridentata, creosote
Lycium species, desert thorn
Psorothamnus fremontii, indigo bush
Rhus triilobata, three-leaf sumac
Rosa woodsii, wild rose
Simmondsia chinensis, jojoba

Wildflowers

Abronia villosa, desert sand verbena
Allionia incarnata, trailing four-o'clock
Baileya multiradiata, desert marigold
Calochortus species, mariposa lilies
Castilleja exserta, owl's clover paintbrush
Coreopsis bigelovii, Bigelow coreopsis
Delphinium parishii, desert larkspur
Eriogonum umbellatum, sulfur buckwheat
Eschscholzia californica, California poppy
Mirabilis multiflora, giant four-o'clock
Nama species, purple mat
Penstemon species, beardtongues
Phacelia campanularia, desert bluebell
Psilostrophe cooperi, paperflower
Stanleya pinnata, prince's plume
Sphaeralcea ambigua, desert globemallow
Viguiera parishii, desert sunflower

Groundcovers and Vines

Leymus condensatus 'Canyon Prince', giant rye grass
Nolina species, beargrass
Vitis girdiana, desert grape

Cacti and Succulents

Agave species
Dudleya species
Echinocereus triglochidiatus, hedgehog cactus
Ferocactus cylindraceus, barrel cactus
Mammillaria species, fishhook cactus
Oenothera caespitosa, tufted evening primrose
Opuntia basilaris, beavertail prickly pear
Opuntia bigelovii, teddy bear cholla
Yucca species

Joshua Tree Woodland

Landscapes in this high-desert habitat must use plants adapted to extreme xeriscape conditions, torrid summer heat, extended drought, and winter temperatures that can plunge into the teens. Compose with well-draining sandy loam, and the more sunlight the better. Small-scale trees can provide vertical structure for a variety of low-profile, densely foliated shrubs. Choose accent plants that burst into flower after summer thunderstorms and keep blooming as long as water is available. Your plants will appreciate an occasional drink, but overwatering is the kiss of death.

Trees

Celtis reticulata, hackberry
Chilopsis linearis, desert willow
Juniperus californica, California juniper
Parkinsonia species, palo verde
Prosopis glandulosa, honey mesquite
Washingtonia filifera, California fan palm
Yucca brevifolia, Joshua tree

Shrubs

Ceanothus greggii, desert ceanothus
Diplacus aurantiacus, bush monkey flower
Ephedra species, joint firs
Ericameria nauseosa, rabbitbrush
Eriogonum fasciculatum, California buckwheat
Fallugia paradoxa, Apache plume
Frangula californica, coffeeberry
Fremontodendron californicum, California flannel bush
Isomeris arborea, bladderpod
Larrea tridentata, creosote bush
Psorothamnus fremontii, indigo bush
Purshia stansburiana, Stansbury cliffrose
Quercus turbinella, shrub oak
Rosa woodsii, wild rose
Simmondsia chinensis, jojoba

Wildflowers

Baileya multiradiata, desert marigold
Calochortus species, mariposa lilies
Castilleja exserta, owl's clover paintbrush
Coreopsis bigelovii, Bigelow coreopsis
Datura wrightii, sacred datura
Eriogonum fasciculatum, California buckwheat
Eschscholzia californica, California poppy
Penstemon species, beardtongues
Psilostrophe cooperi, paperflower
Sphaeralcea ambigua, desert globemallow
Stanleya pinnata, prince's plume

Groundcovers and Vines

Leymus condensatus 'Canyon Prince', giant rye grass
Nolina species, beargrass
Maurandya antirrhiniflora, snapdragon vine
Vitis girdiana, desert grape

Cacti and Succulents

Agave utahensis, Utah agave
Dudleya species
Echinocereus triglochidiatus, hedgehog
Ferocactus cylindraceus, barrel cactus
Mammillaria species, fishhook cactus
Oenothera caespitosa, tufted evening primrose
Opuntia species, chollas and prickly pears
Yucca species

Pinyon-Juniper Woodland

Landscapers in this mid-elevation habitat can work with a palette of small-scale trees and evergreen shrubs, plus a few species with dramatic blooms. The trees, shrubs, yuccas, and cacti favor wildscape concepts, rather than formal sheared and shaped hedges or tidy, symmetrical garden layouts. Design with accent rocks, rock walls and borders, and grasses. Mix colorful flowering species with foliage plants for seasonal drama. Blanket bare areas with annuals that burst into luxuriant bloom when they get sufficient water. The species in this zone are drought tolerant, so supplemental water isn't necessary once young plants are established.

Trees

Acacia greggii, catclaw acacia
Celtis reticulata, hackberry
Chilopsis linearis, desert willow
Juniperus species, junipers
Pinus edulis, pinyon pine

Shrubs

Adenostoma sparsifolium, red shanks
Arctostaphylos species and cultivars, manzanita
Artemisia tridentata, Great Basin sagebrush
Ceanothus species and cultivars, ceanothus
Cercocarpus montanus, mountain mahogany
Ericameria linearifolia, larchleaf goldenbush
Ericameria nauseosa, rabbitbrush
Ephedra species, joint firs
Eriogonum fasciculatum, California buckwheat
Fallugia paradoxa, Apache plume
Frangula californica, coffeeberry
Fremontodendron californicum, California flannel bush
Garrya flavescens, silktassel
Krascheninnikovia lanata, winterfat
Mahonia fremontii, Fremont barberry
Psorothamnus fremontii, indigo bush
Purshia stansburiana, Stansbury cliffrose
Quercus turbinella, shrub live oak
Rosa woodsii, Wood's rose
Shepherdia argentea, silver buffaloberry
Simmondsia chinensis, jojoba

Wildflowers

Achillea millefolium, yarrow
Aquilegia species, columbine
Baileya multiradiata, desert marigold
Calochortus species, mariposa lily
Coreopsis bigelovii, Bigelow coreopsis
Datura wrightii, sacred datura
Delphinium parishii, desert larkspur
Epilobium canum, California fuchsia
Eriogonum umbellatum, sulfur buckwheat
Eschscholzia californica, California poppy
Delphinium parishii, desert larkspur
Linum lewisii, blue flax
Mimulus species, monkey flowers
Nama demissum, purple mat
Oenothera caespitosa, tuffed evening primrose
Penstemon species, beardtongues
Psilostrophe cooperi, paperflower
Sphaeralcea ambigua, desert globemallow
Stanleya pinnata, prince's plume

Groundcovers and Vines

Leymus condensatus 'Canyon Prince', giant rye grass
Nolina parryi, Parry's beargrass
Symphoricarpos species, snowberries
Vitis girdiana, desert grape

Cacti and Succulents

Agave utahensis, Utah agave
Dudleya pulverulenta, chalk dudleya
Ferocactus cylindraceus, barrel cactus
Opuntia acanthocarpa, buckhorn cholla
Opuntia basilaris, beavertail prickly pear
Opuntia phaeacantha, Mojave prickly per
Yucca bacatta, banana yucca
Yucca whipplei, our Lord's candle

Useful Organizations and Demonstration Gardens

California has a number of public gardens, arboretums, parks, native plant associations, and special-interest groups that offer information on landscaping and conserving native plants. To learn more about local organizations, visit one of the arboretums, nature and botanical centers, or public gardens in your area to see examples of how beautiful native plant landscaping can be. Other sources for information are county water districts, agricultural extension services, and the university departments of agriculture; printed materials on landscaping with native plants are often available.

Demonstration Gardens

Cuyamaca College Water Conservation Garden
12122 Cuyamaca
College Drive West
El Cajon, CA 92019
www.thegarden.org
Xericsape gardens include native species

Fullerton Arboretum
1900 Associated Road
Fullerton CA 92831
714-278-3579; Horticultural Helpline: 714-278-4005
farboretum@fullerton.edu
www.arboretum.fullerton.edu

Huntington Botanical Gardens
1151 Oxford Road
San Marino, CA 91108
626-405-2100
publicinformation@huntington.org
www.huntington.org

Living Desert Zoo and Botanical Gardens
47-900 Portola Avenue
Palm Desert, CA 92260
760-346-5694
zooinfo@livingdesert.org
www.livingdesert.org

The Old Mill Foundation
1120 Old Mill Road
San Marino, CA 91108
626-449-5458
oldmill@sbcglobal.net

Quail Botanical Gardens
230 Quail Gardens Drive
Encinitas, CA 92023
760-436-3036; fax: 760-632-0917
info@qbgardens.org
www.qbgardens.org

Rancho Santa Ana Botanic Garden
1500 North College Avenue
Claremont, CA 91711
909-625-8767;
Native Plant Garden Hotline: 909-624-0838
rsabg.hortinfo@cgu.edu
www.rsabg.org

Ridgehaven Demonstration Project
9601 Ridgehaven Court
San Diego, CA 92123
858-694-7000
www.sandiego.gov/environmental-services/geninfo/ridgehaven/garden.shtml

San Diego Zoo Wild Animal Park
Nativescapes Garden
15500 San Pasqual Valley Road
Escondido, CA 92027
760-747-8702
www.sandiegozoo.org

Santa Barbara Botanic Garden
1212 Mission Canyon Road
Santa Barbara, CA 93105
805-682-4726
www.sbbg.org

Susanna Bixby Bryant Museum and Botanic Garden
5700 Susanna Bryant Drive
Yorba Linda, CA 92887
714-694-0235
www.ylpl.lib.ca.us/sbb.php

Theodore Payne Foundation
10459 Tuxford Street
Sun Valley, CA 91352
818-768-1802;
Wildflower hotline (March–May): 818-768-3533
info@theodorepayne.org
www.theodorepayne.org

Tilden Botanic Garden
East Bay Regional Parks
Wildcat Canyon Road
Berkeley, CA 94708
510-841-8732
info@nativeplants.org
www.ebparks.org/parks/bot.htm
www.nativeplants.org
Includes Southern California gardens

University of California Riverside Botanic Gardens
Riverside, CA 92521
951-784-6962
ucrbg@ucr.edu
www.gardens.ucr.edu

University of California Botanical Garden
200 Centennial Drive #5045
Berkeley, CA 94720
510-643-2755
Garden@uclink4.Berkeley.edu
http://botanicalgarden.berkeley.edu

Organizations

California Native Plant Society
www.cnps.org
Chapters around the state host meetings, workshops, outings, and plant sales.

Lady Bird Johnson Wildflower Center
4801 La Crosse Avenue
Austin, TX 78739
512-292-4100
www.wildflower.org
The Lady Bird Johnson Wildflower Center is a nationwide clearinghouse and information source for all aspects of native plants. The center offers information sheets on growing different species of plants, recommended species for each state, how-to plant guides, guidelines for collecting seeds, a data file of regional organizations offering information and activities about native plants, and lists of nurseries and seed sources for each state. Individual membership includes a quarterly magazine.

Useful Websites

Calflora
www.calflora.org

California Native Plant Exchange
www.cnplx.info/index.html

eFloras.org
www.efloras.org

Jepson Floral Project Horticultural Database
http://ucjeps.berkeley.edu/interchange/hort_form.html

Las Pilitas Nursery native plants manual
www.laspilitas.com/cat1.htm

A Manual of California Vegetation
http://endeavor.des.ucdavis.edu/cnps/index.html

Natural Resources Conservation Service
http://plants.nrcs.usda.gov

Plant Profiler for Greater Los Angeles
www.lasgrwc.org/LandscapeEthic/plantprofilerlist.htm

Plants of San Diego County
www.sci.sdsu.edu/plants/sdpls/index.html

Bibliography

Atlas of the Biodiveristy of California. Sacramento: State of California Resources Agency, Department of Fish and Game, 2003.

Bakker, Elna. *An Island Called California: An Ecological Introduction to Its Natural Communities.* 2nd ed. Berkeley, Calif.: University of California Press, 1985.

Baldwin, Bruce G., et al., eds. *The Jepson Desert Manual: Vascular Plants of Southeastern California.* Berkeley, Calif.: University of California Press, 2002.

Benson, Lyman, and Robert Darrow. *Trees and Shrubs of the Southwest Deserts.* Tucson: The University of Arizona Press, 1981.

Bornstein, Carol, David Fross, and Bart O'Brien. *California Native Plants for the Garden.* Los Olivos, Calif.: Cachuma Press, 2005.

Bossard, Carla C., John M. Randall, and Marc C. Hoshovsky, eds. *Invasive Plants of California's Wildlands.* Berkeley, Calif.: University of California Press, 2000.

Bowers, Janice Emily. *100 Desert Wildflowers of the Southwest.* Globe, Arizona: Southwest Parks and Monuments Association, 1989.

Bowers, Janice Emily. *100 Roadside Wildflowers of the Southwest.* Globe, Arizona: Southwest Parks and Monuments Association, 1987.

Carter, Jack, et al. *Common Southwestern Native Plants.* Silver City, Nevada: Mimbres Publishers, 2003.

Connelly, K. *Gardener's Guide to California Wildflowers.* Sun Valley, Calif.: Theodore Payne Foundation, 1991.

Dole, J. W., and B. B. Rose. *Shrubs and Trees of the Southern California Deserts.* Big Bear Lake, Calif.: Foot-Loose Press, 1996.

Donahue Brown, Brian V. and Julian P. *Butterfly Gardening in Southern California.* Los Angeles: Natural History Museum of Los Angeles County, 1999.

Duffield, Mary Rose, and Warren D. Jones. *Plants for Dry Climates.* Tucson: HP Books, 2001.

Emmel, Thomas C., and John F. *The Butterflies of Southern California.* Natural History Museum of Los Angeles County, Science Series No. 26 (1973).

Faber, Phyllis M., ed. *California's Wild Gardens: A Guide to Favorite Botanical Sites.* Berkeley, Calif.: University of California Press, 2005.

Fuller, Thomas C., and Elizabeth McClintock. *Poisonous Plants of California.* California Natural History Guides 53. Berkeley, Calif.: University of California Press, 1986.

Grant, Karen, and Verne Grant. *Hummingbirds and Their Flowers.* New York: Columbia University Press, 1968.

Hickman, James C., ed. *The Jepson Manual: Higher Plants of California.* Berkeley, Calif.: University of California Press, 1993.

Holmes, Roger. *Home Landscaping: California Region.* Upper Saddle River, N.J.: The Creative Homeowner, 2001.

Johnson, Eric, and David Harbison. *Landscaping to Save Water in the Desert.* Rancho Mirage, California: E&P Products, 1985.

Keator, G. *The Complete Garden Guide to Native Perennials of California.* San Francisco, Calif.: Chronicle Books, 1990.

Keator, G. *The Complete Garden Guide to Native Shrubs of California.* San Francisco, Calif.: Chronicle Books, 1994.

Kruckeberg, Arthur R. *Introduction to California Soils and Plants: Serpentine, Vernal Pools, and Other Geobotanical Wonders.* California Natural History Guides, 86. Berkeley, Calif.: University of California Press, 2006.

Larson, Peggy, and Lane Larson. *The Deserts of the Southwest: A Sierra Club Naturalist's Guide.* 2nd ed. Berkeley, Calif.: University of California Press, 2000.

Lenz, L., and J. L. Dourley. *California Native Trees and Shrubs for Garden and Environmental Use in Southern California.* Claremont, Calif.: Ranch Santa Anna Botanic Garden, 1981.

Lowry, Judith. L. *Gardening with a Wild Heart: Restoring California's Native Landscape at Home.* Berkeley: University of California Press, 1999.

Martino, Steve, and Vernon Swaback. *Desert Excellence: A Guide to Natural Landscapes.* Phoenix: Bellamah Community Development, 1986.

Mielke, Judy. *Native Plants for Southwestern Landscapes.* Austin: The University of Texas Press, 1993.

Miller, George O. *Landscaping with Native Plants of the Southwest.* St. Paul, Minn.: Voyageur Press, 2007.

Miller, George O. *Landscaping with Native Plants of Texas.* St. Paul, Minn.: Voyageur Press, 2006.

Moffat, Ann, and Mark Schiler. *Landscape Design That Saves Energy.* New York: William Morrow and Co., 1981.

Morhardt, Sia, and Emil Morhardt. *California Desert Flowers: An Introduction to Families, Genera, and Species.* Berkeley, Calif.: University of California Press, 2004.

Munz, Philip A. *Introduction to California Desert Wildflowers.* rev. ed. Berkeley, Calif.: University of California Press, 2004.

Munz, Philip A. *Introduction to California Spring Wildflowers of the Foothills, Valleys, and Coast.* rev. ed. Berkeley, Calif.: University of California Press, 2004.

Munz, Philip A. *Introduction to California Mountain Wildflowers.* rev. ed. Berkeley, Calif.: University of California Press, 2003.

Munz, Philip A. *Introduction to Shore Wildflowers of California, Oregon, and Washington.* rev. ed. Berkeley, Calif.: University of California Press, 2003.

O'Brien, Bart, Lorrae C. Fuentes, and Lydia F. Newcomb, eds. *Out of the Wild and into the Garden I.* California's Horticulturally Significant Plants. Rancho Santa Ana Botanic Garden Occasionally Publications Number 1. Claremont, Calif. (1997).

O'Brien, Bart, Lorrae C. Fuentes, and Lydia F. Newcomb, eds. *Out of the Wild and into the Garden II.* California's Horticulturally Significant Plants. Rancho Santa Ana Botanic Garden Occasionally Publications Number 1. Claremont, Calif. (1997).

O'Brien, Bart, Lorrae C. Fuentes, and Lydia F. Newcomb, eds. *Out of the Wild and into the Garden III.* California's Horticulturally Significant Plants. Rancho Santa Ana Botanic Garden Occasionally Publications Number 1. Claremont, Calif. (1997).

O'Brien, Bart, Betsey Landis, and Ellen Mackey. *Care & Maintenance of Southern California Native Plant Gardens.* Los Angeles: Metropolitan Water District of Southern California, 2006.

Ornduff, Robert, Phyllis M. Faber, and Todd Keeler-Wolf. *Introduction to California Plant Life.* rev. ed. Berkeley, Calif.: University of California Press, 2003.

Nokes, Jill. *How to Grow Native Plants of Texas and the Southwest.* Austin: Texas Monthly Press, 1986.

Pavlik, B. M. *Oaks of California.* Los Olivos, Calif.: California Oak Foundation, 1995.

Peterson, P., Victor Whitmore, and Rita Whitmore. *Native Trees of Southern California.* Natural History Guides: 14. Berkeley, Calif.: University of California Press, 1966.

Phillips, Judith. *Southwestern Landscaping with Native Plants.* Santa Fe: Museum of New Mexico Press, 1987.

Phillips, Steven J., ed. *A Natural History of the Sonoran Desert.* Tucson: Arizona-Sonora Desert Museum, 1999.

Roberts, Fred M. *Illustrated Guide to the Oaks of the Southern Californian Floristic Province: The Oaks of Coastal Southern California and Northwestern Baja California.* California: F. M. Publishing, 1995.

Rundel, Philip W., and Robert Gustafson, eds. *Introduction to the Plant Life of Southern California: Coast to Foothills.* California Natural History Guides, 85. Berkeley, Calif.: University of California Press, 2005.

Shuler, Carol. *Low-Water-Use Plants for California & the Southwest.* Cambridge, Mass.: Fisher Books, 1993.

Stokes, Donald, Lillian Stokes, and Ernest Williams. *Stokes Butterfly Book: The Complete Guide to Butterfly Gardening, Identification, and Behavior.* New York: Little, Brown and Company, 1991.

Stuart, John D., and John O. Sawyer. *Trees and Shrubs of California.* Berkeley, Calif.: University of California Press, 2001.

Sunset Book Editors. *Sunset Western Garden Book.* Menlo Park, California: Lane Publishing Co., 1988.

Wasowski, Sally, and Andy Wasowski. *Native Landscaping From El Paso to L. A.* New York: McGraw Hill, Contemporary Books, 2000.

Welsh, Pat. *Pat Welsh's Southern California Gardening: A Month-by-Month Guide.* San Francisco: Chronicle Books, 2000.

Index